INDONESIA

Number 116   October 2023

Published by Southeast Asia Program Publications • Cornell University Press

Submissions: Submit manuscript as double-spaced document in MS word or similar. Please format citation and footnotes according to the style guidelines in *The Chicago Manual of Style*, 17th edition.

Address: Please address all correspondence and manuscripts to the managing editor at sg265@cornell.edu. We prefer electronic submissions.

Reprints: Contributors will receive one complimentary copy of the issue in which their articles appear.

Abstracts: Abstracts of articles published in *Indonesia* appear in *Excerpta Indonesica*, which is published semiannually by the Royal Institute of Linguistics and Anthropology, Leiden. Articles appearing in this journal are also abstracted and indexed in *Historical Abstracts* and *America: History and Life.*

Subscription information: Contact subscriptions@dukeupress.edu for more information. Digital subscriptions for individuals and institutions are handled by Project Muse (muse@jhu.press.edu)

INDONESIA online: All *Indonesia* articles published at least five years prior to the date of the current issue are accessible to our readers on the internet free of charge. For more information concerning annual print and online subscriptions, pay-per-view access to recent articles, and access to our archives, please see: seap.einaudi.cornell.edu/ indonesia_journal or http://ecommons.cornell.edu

Managing Editor   Sarah E. M. Grossman

Cover credit: AP Wire, Horst Faas, photographer. Communist prisoners march to a river near Jogjakarta, Indonesia.

ISBN 978-1-5017-7568-0
ISSN 0019-7289
©2023 Cornell University

Table of Contents 116

Book Reviews

Prefatory Note

Siddarth Chandra and Mark Winward

The papers in this special issue of *Indonesia* were originally presented at the inaugural American Institute for Indonesian Studies—Michigan State University (AIFIS—MSU) Conference on Indonesian Studies in 2021. The aim of the conference was to leverage a virtual format to bring scholars from all over the world together to share their research on Indonesia regardless of their physical location or economic circumstances. This virtual format minimized the costs of attendance, enabling over five hundred scholars from over 20 countries and from a variety of circumstances to exchange their ideas. Many of these ideas were new and refreshing to attendees, and stimulated engagements long after the conference had concluded. In addition, the usual imbalances in the composition of the attendee pool that financial, location, and time constraints impose on in-person conferences were eliminated—approximately half of the attendees were from Indonesia (many of them early-career academics), and the other half came from the twenty or so other countries that were represented at the conference.

This diversity and inclusiveness was reflected in the mix of authors who contributed over twenty papers on the violence of 1965–66 that were presented in five interrelated panels at the conference. The articles in this volume represent a selection of those papers, again reflecting a balance of scholars from Indonesia and other countries, and at various stages of their careers.

We would also like to thank the editors of *Indonesia* and the editorial team at Cornell University Press for their interest in publishing this collection of papers. We hope that the reader will find in this volume a rich and stimulating array of perspectives on the violence of 1965–66 and be inspired to contribute to our knowledge of these events by building on and around this body of work.

New Directions in the Historiography of Indonesia's Mass Killings, 1965–66

Robert Cribb

Over the course of about six months from October 1965, some half a million members and supporters of the Indonesian Communist Party (PKI, Partai Komunis Indonesia) were murdered in what we now recognize as the twentieth century's largest white terror.[1] The killings, which destroyed the PKI as a political force, were a significant part of the process by which Indonesia's first President, Sukarno, was displaced from power and replaced by the anti-communist General Suharto in March 1966. Killing continued on a smaller scale after that time, but it shaded into the general repression of the developmentalist New Order, which survived until Suharto's authority was finally undone by the Asian Financial Crisis in 1998.

In the decades immediately after 1965, the killings received remarkably little scholarly attention. For the most part they were discussed obliquely, as if they were not a major event in Indonesian history requiring investigation and explanation.[2] Some observers

---

[1] The only considered attempt to assess the likely number of deaths on the basis of evidence is Robert Cribb, "How Many Deaths? Problems in the Statistics of Massacre in Indonesia (1965–1966) and East Timor (1975–1980)," in *Violence in Indonesia*, ed. Ingrid Wessel and Georgia Wimhöfer (Hamburg: Abera, 2001), 82–98. This analysis, however, is more than two decades old and the issue is ripe for reassessment. Chandra has laid the groundwork for such a reassessment in several articles on the killings that employ sophisticated demographic analysis, including Siddharth Chandra, "Glimpses of Indonesia's 1965 Massacre through the Lens of the Census: The Role of Trucks and Roads in 'Crushing' the Indonesian Communist Party in East Java," *Indonesia* 108 (2019): 1–21; "New Findings on the Indonesian Killings of 1965–66," *Journal of Asian Studies* 76, no. 4 (2017): 1059–86, https://doi.org/10.1017/S002191181700081X

[2] Robert Cribb, "Problems in the Historiography of the Killings in Indonesia," in *The Indonesian Killings 1965–1966: Studies from Java and Bali*, ed. Robert Cribb (Clayton: Monash University of Southeast Asian Studies, 1990), 1–2.

offered what amounted to a culture-based explanation, implying that Indonesians were naturally inclined to intense violence. More commonly, observers saw the killings as an uncomplicated manifestation of the high stakes and bitter antagonisms of the Cold War. The New Order presented the destruction of the PKI as an appropriate response to what was portrayed as the party's grab for power. This narrative of a communist attempt to seize power was based partly on the PKI's alleged direct involvement in a coup in Jakarta on October 1, 1965, conventionally known as G30S, in which junior soldiers affiliated with the left kidnapped and murdered several senior anti-communist generals and replaced the Sukarno government with a Revolutionary Council. It was also based on the perception of a global struggle between communism and its enemies in which countries like Indonesia were prizes to be fought over. Within this discourse, the killings were simply the harsh measures—"kill or be killed"—that were needed to keep Indonesia out of the global communist camp.

In the 1990s, researchers began to confront the enormity of the mass killings and to treat them as a phenomenon requiring special explanation.[3] These researchers started from two assumptions. First, they understood the killings as having not just mass victims but also mass perpetrators. In other words, they understood the pogroms as the work of Indonesian society as a whole. Second, they held that the killings were an exceptional event in Indonesian history and that the roots of the slaughter needed to be sought in the extraordinary political circumstances of the time. The regime of Indonesia's first president, Sukarno, known as Guided Democracy, was simultaneously authoritarian and ramshackle, divisive and unifying, opaque and polarized. These researchers rejected the crude culturalist explanations offered by the earliest observers of the killings. Instead, anticipating broader insights from the rise of the history of emotions, they stressed the acute sense of uncertainty that beset all sides of Indonesian politics, portraying the killings as a consequence of intense but transient circumstances, as a storm created by unformed nature of the Indonesian nation, the desperate uncertainty of late Guided Democracy politics, and the sense that everything was at stake.[4] Although scholars in this 'circumstantialist' school rejected the New Order assertion that the killings were justifiable retaliation against the PKI, they suggested that the PKI's vigorous political activism—including sharply worded campaigns against the so-called "Seven Village Devils" and "capitalist bureaucrats"—had contributed to the intensely strained atmosphere that underpinned the killings.

During the final decade of the 20th century, scholarly misgivings with the circumstantialist approach began to accumulate. Scholars examining the killings became increasingly aware of the pervasive role played in the massacre by the Suharto group within the Indonesian army. Whereas the circumstantialist scholars had recognized the role of the military in authorizing violence by civilian militias, the new wave of scholarship noted that army units had not only carried out many massacres but had also assembled, trained, and armed those militias, rather than simply condoning their independent activity. Scholars also noted that a very large proportion of the victims had been in military detention immediately before they were killed. They also characterized

---

[3] For an account typifying the approach of this period, see Robert Cribb, "Genocide in Indonesia, 1965–1966," *Journal of Genocide Research*, 3 no 2 (2001): 219–39, https://doi.org/10.1080/713677655.

[4] For an evocation of the uncertainty that attended the conflict, see Pipit Rochijat, "Am I PKI or Non-PKI?," *Indonesia* 40 (1985): 37–52.

the PKI as a "normal" leftist party that had pursued social justice across a wide range of issues and that had done little to warrant the fear and loathing expressed by its opponents. The image of fearful, vengeful anti-communist villagers waylaying their local enemies in the street or in their houses gave way to one in which leftists had naively reported to the military after the coup, only to be detained in harsh conditions before being taken out in batches and killed. Garin Nugroho's film *A Poet*, while focussing on the experience of the victims, graphically depicted the callous and unemotional mood of the killers.[5]

Misgivings with the circumstantialist argument were catalyzed by the publication of Jess Melvin's study of the role of the Indonesian army in the killings in Aceh.[6] Using a cache of military documents obtained from government archives, Melvin demonstrated that, in Aceh at least, the Indonesian army had been planning anti-communist operations even before the trigger provided by the G30S coup and that it closely monitored and coordinated the killings as they proceeded. Melvin's work marked the emergence of a new "intentionalist" argument that explained the killings as a planned and deliberate mass murder carried out by the Indonesian military.[7]

Intellectually, the new argument was primarily a rebuttal of the older circumstantialist argument, but it also rested on earlier work that had discredited the New Order version of events. That earlier scholarship had already demolished key elements in the New Order contention that the PKI was a party whose savage intent justified its destruction. In particular, the widely circulated stories that the generals who were murdered on October 1, 1965 had been tortured and sexually mutilated by communist women were shown to be a deliberate fabrication to demonize the PKI.[8] John Roosa, moreover, showed that although the party leader, D. N. Aidit, had played a significant role in planning the kidnapping of the generals in the G30S incident, only a handful of party members were involved in the plot and that the vast majority of Indonesian communists were as surprised by the events in Jakarta as their political opponents were.[9] Roosa also breathed new life into the hypothesis, first suggested by W. F. Wertheim, that the kidnapping of the generals had been a black operation intended to provide a pretext for harsh action against the PKI.[10]

---

[5] *Puisi Tak Terkuburkan* (released in English as *A Poet: Unconcealed Poetry*), dir. Garin Nugroho, 2000.

[6] Jess Melvin, *The Army and the Indonesian Genocide: Mechanics of Mass Murder* (Milton: Taylor and Francis, 2018).

[7] Aside from the Melvin monograph, key works in this reassessment are Douglas Kammen and Katharine McGregor eds., *The Contours of Mass Violence in Indonesia, 1965–68* (Singapore: NUS Press, 2012); Katharine McGregor, Jess Melvin, and Annie Pohlman, eds., *The Indonesian Genocide of 1965: Causes, Dynamics and Legacies* (Cham, Switzerland: Palgrave Macmillan, 2018); and John Roosa, *Buried Histories: The Anticommunist Massacres of 1965–1966 in Indonesia* (Madison: University of Wisconsin Press, 2020). For a general history of the killings written from the intentionalist perspective, see Geoffrey B. Robinson, *The Killing Season: A History of the Indonesian Massacres, 1965–66* (Princeton NJ: Princeton University Press, 2018), https://doi.org /10.2307/j.ctvc774sg.

[8] Ben Anderson, "How Did the Generals Die?," *Indonesia* 43 (1987): 109–34, https://hdl.handle.net/1813 /53860; Saskia Wieringa and Nursyahbani Katjasungkana, *Propaganda and the Genocide in Indonesia: Imagined Evil* (Abingdon: Routledge, 2019).

[9] John Roosa, *Pretext for Mass Murder: the September 30th Movement and Suharto's Coup d'état in Indonesia* (Madison: University of Wisconsin Press, 2006).

[10] W.F. Wertheim, "Suharto and the Untung Coup—The Missing Link," *Journal of Contemporary Asia* 1, no. 2 (1970): 50–57, https://doi.org/10.1080/00472337085390151. See also Benedict R. O'G. Anderson, "Petrus Dadi Ratu," *Indonesia* 70 (2000): 1–7.

The moral and emotional force of the intentionalist argument was bolstered by a growing range of studies that provided new details of the experiences of those persecuted by the Suharto regime, both in the course of the killings and afterwards.[11] This research revealed the deliberate cruelty of the repression far more vividly than did bald statistics. New insights included the widespread use of torture intended to destroy the humanity of the victims and the deliberate sexual humiliation of women victims.[12]

This research established, which the circumstantialist argument had not done, that killings were criminal according to the emerging standards of international law, thereby raising the question of reckoning. The fall of Suharto in 1998 had already given rise to hopes that the injustices of the past might somehow be addressed, whether by some form of compensation and restitution for the victims, some kind of punishment or rebuke for the perpetrators, or simply by public acknowledgment of the crime. Scholars devoted much attention to efforts to memorialize the killings and to the obduracy of Indonesian authorities and some civil society groups, even in the post-Suharto *reformasi* era, in refusing to admit past wrongs. Although Indonesian authorities sometimes offered vague hopes that there might be some form of official accounting for the killings, the vagueness of that prospect led scholarly activists to convene an unofficial International People's Tribunal for 1965 in The Hague in November 2015, on the fiftieth anniversary of the start of the killings, to hear a wide range of testimony against the Suharto regime. The tribunal found the Indonesian state "responsible for and guilty of crimes against humanity" as well as for genocide.[13]

Although the IPT 1965 indictment implicated the Indonesian state as a whole, the intentionalist analysis on which it was based greatly narrowed responsibility for the killings. According to this analysis, Suharto and a group of officers who shared his views were the primary perpetrators. The non-military groups that assisted the killing were stooges or useful idiots, either intimidated into collaborating with the military or deceived by the clever propaganda of the Suharto group. The intentionalist analysis, however, did not convincingly explore the origins of Suharto's anti-communist agenda. Research on Suharto's background has so far failed to find evidence of an acute and deeply seated anti-communism that would suggest that he seized power in order to destroy the PKI.[14] Some intentionalist analysis implies that Suharto and his circle were merely the pawns of Western powers that were indeed pathologically anti-communist. Those external powers allegedly provided Suharto with practical and moral support so

---

[11] John Roosa, Ayu Ratih, and Hilmar Farid, eds., *Tahun Yang Tak Pernah Berakhir: Memahami Pengalaman Korban 65: Esai-Esai Sejarah Lisan* (Jakarta: Lembaga Studi dan Advokasi Masyarakat, 2004); Vannessa Hearman, *Unmarked Graves: Death and Survival in the Anti-Communist Violence in East Java, Indonesia* (Singapore: Asian Studies Association of Australia in association with NUS Press, 2018).

[12] Annie Pohlman, "Torture Camps in Indonesia, 1965–1970," in *Detention Camps in Asia: The Conditions of Confinement in Modern Asian History*, ed. Robert Cribb, Christina Twomey, and Sandra Wilson (Leiden: Brill, 2022), 137–55, https://doi.org/10.1163/9789004512573_009; *Women, Sexual Violence and the Indonesian Killings of 1965–66* (New York: Routledge, 2015).

[13] IPT 1965 Foundation, "Final Report of the IPT 1965" (The Hague; Jakarta: IPT 1965 Foundation, 2016); Saskia Wieringa, Jess Melvin, and Annie Pohlman, eds., *The International People's Tribunal for 1965 and the Indonesian Genocide* (Abingdon: Routledge, 2019).

[14] David Jenkins, *Young Soeharto: The Making of a Soldier, 1921–1945* (Singapore: ISEAS-Yusof Ishak Institute, 2021).

that he would carry out their intentions.[15] This externalization of the intent to destroy Indonesian communism, however, is hard to reconcile with the complex and competing political agendas that characterized Indonesian politics well into 1966.

The small but accumulating body of preserved testimony from victims and witnesses of the 1965–66 killings contains sporadic but repeated claims that individuals were victimized for reasons other than their political affiliation. Stories tell of victims who were sometimes of the left but who had played no activist role in PKI campaigns. They were targeted by members of their own communities, the stories claim, for more personal reasons—sometimes old enmities, sometimes current disputes or jealousies over land, or position, or women. For the circumstantialists, these stories were suspect because they contradicted the narrative of pogroms driven by an existential antagonism between communism and anti-communism. For the intentionalists, such stories were evidence only of the army's determination to eradicate the PKI *sampai akarnya* (down to its roots) by targeting even those only marginally on the left.

Taken together, however, these stories suggest an account of the killings in which initiative lay significantly at the lower levels of society. According to this emerging account, the political chaos after October 1965 did not simply offer individuals and groups in Indonesian society the opportunity to settle old scores in the manner of premodern vendettas.[16] More important was the sudden opportunity to seek personal advantage in volatile circumstances. Both identifying oneself as anti-communist and portraying others as communist were tactics to seek social and material advantage, including the removal of potential rivals and appropriation of their property.[17] Whereas the intentionalist scholars portrayed local participants in the killings as the dupes of a ferociously anti-communist army, this alternative account reverses the lines of manipulation: the poorly informed army blundered into complex local politics and were used by canny local forces to settle local disputes in a brutal way that would not have been possible in normal times.[18] Close studies of the Indonesian military in this era have confirmed that it was far from being the omnipotent and omniscient perpetrator implied in the intentionalist argument.[19] The evidence underpinning this "social opportunist" argument helps to account for the deep sense of betrayal which leftists felt as a consequence of their victimization: they were in many cases not the victims of an impersonal ideological conflict but instead of former friends and neighbours.

---

[15] See Bradley R. Simpson, *Economists with Guns: Authoritarian Development and U.S.-Indonesian Relations, 1960–1968* (Stanford: Stanford University Press, 2008).

[16] Adrian Vickers, "Reopening Old Wounds: Bali and the Indonesian Killings—A Review Article," *Journal of Asian Studies* 57, no. 3 (1998): 774–785, https://doi.org/10.2307/2658741.

[17] In 2005, an article on this topic by Hilmar Farid prompted a brief debate on this topic. See Hilmar Farid, "Indonesia's Original Sin: Mass Killings and Capitalist Expansion, 1965–66," *Inter-Asia Cultural Studies* 6, no. 1 (2005): 3–16, https://doi.org/10.1080/1462394042000326879; and responses to his article in the same issue of the journal.

[18] Mathias Hammer, "The Organisation of the Killings and the Interaction between State and Society in Central Java, 1965," *Journal of Current Southeast Asian Affairs* 32, no. 3 (2013): 37–62; Grace Leksana, "Collaboration in Mass Violence: The Case of the Indonesian Anti-Leftist Mass Killings in 1965–66 in East Java," *Journal of Genocide Research* 23, no. 1 (2021): 58–80, https://doi.org/10.1177/186810341303200.

[19] Mark Winward, "Capture from Below: Civil–Military Relations during Indonesia's Anticommunist Violence, 1965–66," *Indonesia* 106 (2018): 111–36; "Intelligence Capacity and Mass Violence: Evidence from Indonesia," *Comparative Political Studies* 54, no. 3–4 (2021): 553–84, https://doi.org/10.1177/0010414020938072.

The emergence of analysis stressing the role of civil society and of elite competition in generating the mass killing of 1965–66 brings the Indonesian debate into consonance with continuing debate over the Holocaust, that is, Nazi Germany's attempted extermination of the Jews of Europe. That debate has been characterized as having two camps.[20] On one side are the intentionalists, who contend that Hitler's hegemonic power within German politics enabled him to implement a long-standing personal plan to destroy the Jews and that Germans collectively were so anti-Semitic that they acted as "Hitler's willing executioners" in implementing the Holocaust.[21] On the other side are the so-called "functionalists," who note that the Holocaust was not implemented in its full force as soon as the Nazis had the power to do so. Instead, in a process they call "cumulative radicalization," the initial suite of anti-Jewish policies became progressively harsher as a consequence of elite competition, peer pressure, institutional imperatives, and the changing circumstances of the Second World War in Europe.[22] In the Indonesian context, the emerging social opportunist school of analysis echoes the old circumstantialist argument in stressing the roots of the killings in the social and political circumstances of late Guided Democracy, but crucially it follows the intentionalist school in placing state institutions at the center of the extermination program. It differs from the intentionalists, however, in arguing that state institutions were fragmented: they lacked any singular purpose and were routinely captured by sectional interests that pursued their own agendas. The mass killing, thus, had many motives, some of which took shape opportunistically only after October 1965. In some respects, the immediate roots of the violence were extraordinarily shallow.

In Holocaust studies, the initially polarized debate between intentionalists and functionalists has given way for the most part to a more hybrid approach that recognizes the strengths in both arguments. It is likely that our understanding of the mass killings in Indonesia will follow a similar trajectory, but much more research is needed before our conclusions can start to become firm.

The articles in this special issue make important contributions to that process. Siddharth Chandra continues his meticulous demographic research into correlations between the pattern of killings and other social phenomena, in this case the location of pesantren in East Java. Robert W. Hefner, who conducted some of the earliest detailed research on the killings in upland East Java, revisits his former research and confirms the complexity of local agency in the killings.[23] Mark Winward explores the interplay between military and local agency in Gunung Kidul in the Yogyakarta region of Central Java.

Vannessa Hearman explores the relationship between Balinese landscape and memory of the killings in the artistic work of Leyla Stevens. Arif Subekti and Hervina

---

[20] The controversy was articulated early on in Tim Mason, "Intention and Explanation: A Current Controversy About the Interpretation of National Socialism," in *Der Führerstaat: Mythos und Realität*, ed. Gerhard Hirschfeld and Lothar Kettenacker (Stuttgart: Klett-Cotta, 1981), 21–40.

[21] Among the major intentionalist works are Lucy Dawidowicz, *The Holocaust and the Historians* (Cambridge, MA: Harvard University Press, 1981); and Daniel Jonah Goldhagen, *Hitler's Willing Executioners: Ordinary Germans and the Holocaust* (New York: Knopf, 1996).

[22] Raul Hilberg, *The Destruction of the European Jews* (Chicago: Quadrangle Books, 1961); Christopher R. Browning, *Ordinary Men: Reserve Police Battalion 101 and the Final Solution in Poland* (New York: Aaron Asher, 1992).

[23] Robert W. Hefner, *The Political Economy of Mountain Java: An Interpretive History* (Berkeley, CA: University of California Press, 1990).

Nurullita explore the ways in which songs have become a vehicle for the preservation of memories of the time of violence. Kar-Yen Leong explores the vexed moral issues surrounding the quasi-documentary films of Joshua Oppenheimer, *The Act of Killing* (2012) and *The Look of Silence* (2014), that explore the present-day mentality of a small number of perpetrators of the 1965 killings. Stephen Pratama examines the psychological challenges that contemporary Indonesian teachers face in presenting their classes with accounts of the killings that diverge from the official narrative, while Sri Lestari Wahyuningroem examines official constraints on more truthful history-telling. These articles do not directly address the challenges of explaining the killings but vividly illustrate the enduring importance of that time for the ways in which contemporary Indonesia understands its past.

Violence on the Margins:

Local Power, Spillover Effects, and Patterns of Violence in Gunung Kidul, 1965–66

Mark Winward and Siddharth Chandra

Introduction

The past decade has seen significant advances in our understanding of the 1965–66 Indonesian mass killings. Recent research, building on the pioneering work of Robert Cribb and others, has eliminated all doubt that the Indonesian Army was the primary architect of the violence.[1] Additional studies have uncovered provincial and local dynamics, documented experiences of violence including reconstructing individual massacres, described how both the military and civilian organizations unleashed and participated in the killings, illuminated the phenomenon of sexual violence, and captured local memories of the killings.[2] Taken together, these works have made a

---

[1] Robert Cribb, *The Indonesian Killings of 1965–1966: Studies from Java and Bali* (Melbourne: Centre of Southeast Asian Studies, Monash University, 1990); Jess Melvin, *The Army and the Indonesian Genocide: Mechanics of Mass Murder* (New York: Routledge, 2018); Geoffrey Robinson, *The Killing Season: A History of the Indonesian Massacres, 1965–1966* (Princeton: Princeton University Press, 2018); Grace Leksana, "Collaboration in Mass Violence: The Case of the Indonesian Anti-Leftist Mass Killings in 1965–66 in East Java," *Journal of Genocide Research* 23, no. 1 (2021): 58–80.

[2] John Roosa, *Buried Histories: The Anticommunist Massacres of 1965–1966 in Indonesia* (Madison: University of Wisconsin Press, 2020); Greg Fealy and Katharine McGregor, "Nahdlatul Ulama and the Killings of 1965–66: Religion, Politics, and Remembrance," *Indonesia* 89 (2010): 37–60; David Jenkins and Douglas Kammen, "The Army Para-commando Regiment and the Reign of Terror in Central Java and Bali," in *The Contours of Mass Violence in Indonesia, 1965–68*, ed. Douglas Kammen and Katharine McGregor (Honolulu: Asian Studies

critical contribution to establishing accountability for the killings, demonstrating how the killings unfolded on the ground, and describing how different groups of individuals experienced and remember this period.

A growing number of scholars have built on this body of work by drawing attention to variations in the intensity of violence across time and space. Douglas Kammen and Faizah Zakaria, for example, compare ratios of killings to detentions across seven provinces, noting that higher rates of killing were more common in provinces in which civilian opposition to the PKI was concentrated within a single rival political party.[3] Robinson argues that the disposition of local commanders was instrumental in conditioning the intensity of violence: in areas in which the army had sufficient troops to move unilaterally against the PKI, killings were either relatively few, as in West Java, or comparatively high, as in the case in Aceh.[4] In a series of studies, Chandra examines how road access and support for political parties opposed to the PKI were associated with higher levels of population loss, while Winward focuses on how gaps in military intelligence capacity led to differing levels of arrests and killings in Java.[5] In general, comparative explanations of violence have focused on either the provincial or subdistrict (*kecamatan*) level.[6]

This study contributes to the growing number of comparative studies by examining population change in the smallest administrative units in Indonesia: the *desa* and *kelurahan* (village or urban neighborhood).[7] The violence of 1965–66 resulted not only in the death of an estimated half million communist party supporters, but also in waves of migration away from areas experiencing particularly horrific violence to those that promised refuge for people fearing persecution.[8] Previous studies of such change, using similar methods to those in this paper, have examined population change at the subdistrict (*kecamatan*) level.[9] By focusing on population change at the level of the *desa*,

Association of Australia in association with University of Hawai'i Press, 2012); Annie Pohlman, *Women, Sexual Violence and the Indonesian Killings of 1965–66* (New York: Routledge, 2015); Baskara T. Wardaya S. J., ed., *Truth Will Out. Indonesian Accounts of the 1965 Mass Violence*, translated by Jennifer Lindsay (Clayton: Monash University Publishing, 2013); Mery Kolimon, Liliya Wetangterah, and Karen Campbell-Nelson, *Forbidden Memories: Women's Experiences of 1965 in Eastern Indonesia* (Melbourne: Monash University Publishing, 2015); Putu Oka Sukanta and Jennifer Lindsay, *Breaking the Silence: Survivors Speak about 1965–66 Violence in Indonesia* (Clayton, Victoria: Monash University Publishing, 2013).

[3] Douglas Kammen and Faizah Zakaria, "Detention in Mass Violence," *Critical Asian Studies* 44, no. 3 (2012): 441–66.

[4] Robinson, *The Killing Season*, 150.

[5] Siddharth Chandra, "New Findings on the Indonesian Killings of 1965–66," *The Journal of Asian Studies* 76, no. 4 (2017): 1059–86; "Glimpses of Indonesia's 1965 Massacre through the Lens of the Census: The Role of Trucks and Roads in 'Crushing' the PKI in East Java," *Indonesia* 108 (2019): 1–21; Mark Winward, "Intelligence Capacity and Mass Violence: Evidence from Indonesia," *Comparative Political Studies* 54, no. 3–4 (2021): 553–584.

[6] Kammen and Zakaria, "Detention and Mass Violence"; Robinson, *The Killing Season*; Winward "Intelligence Capacity"; Chandra, "New Findings"; "Glimpses of Indonesia's 1965 Massacre."

[7] *Kelurahan* refers exclusively to urban environs. For the sake of clarity, this paper refers to both *kelurahan* and *desa* as "*desa*," as they are of similar administrative size.

[8] Cribb, *The Indonesian Killings*, 12; Chandra, "New Findings on the Indonesian Killings"; "Glimpses of Indonesia's 1965 Massacre"; Vannessa Hearman, *Unmarked Graves: Death and Survival in the Anti-Communist Violence in East Java, Indonesia* (Singapore: National University of Singapore Press, 2018); Robert Hefner, "The 1965 Violence in Upland East Java: A Reassessment," mimeo (Boston: Boston University, 2021).

[9] Chandra, "New Findings on the Indonesian Killings"; "Glimpses of Indonesia's 1965 Massacre."

we are able to construct a more fine-grained analysis of estimates of population change coinciding with the violence than any comparative study to date. Each *kecamatan* is composed of approximately 10–12 *desa*, depending on population, allowing us to observe spatial patterns of population change that can be attributed to the 1965–66 killings with a high level of detail. We conduct this analysis in Gunungkidul, a regency (*kabupaten*) within the Special Region of Yogyakarta (Daerah Istimewa Yogyakarta, or DIY), for which we had data for 144 *desa*.

The *kabupaten* of Gunungkidul is an especially interesting case for this type of analysis for five reasons. First, it is adjacent to two areas that experienced significant violence: Yogyakarta City to the west and the primarily rural Klaten regency to the north (see Figure 1).[10] This makes it likely that there were substantial spillover effects from those two areas into Gunungkidul, either through groups from those areas engaging in cross-border violence, populations fleeing from those areas, or both. Second, there have been few systematic studies of violence in rural areas of Indonesia. Most studies of the killings have focused instead on violence in mid-sized cities and towns and their environs, such as Kediri in East Java or Negara in Bali.[11] In the provinces of Central Java and Yogyakarta in particular, little is known about rural patterns of violence. Existing studies on the violence in DIY have focused primarily on Yogyakarta City, leaving its neighboring rural *kabupaten* unexplored.[12] Third, the communist party was a dominant force in Gunungkidul. Yogyakarta as a whole was viewed as a PKI "base,"[13] and across the four rural *kabupaten* of DIY, the PKI gained its highest vote share in Gunungkidul. In the 1957 regional elections, for example, the PKI received 123,268 votes, or 51 percent of the total (Gerinda, the party that came in second, was able to secure only 23 percent of the vote).[14] These statistics suggest the presence of large numbers of PKI supporters and, therefore, potential victims in the region. An implication of this observation is that areas in Gunungkidul in which we do not observe signs of violence did not escape the violence because of the absence of communist party supporters, but very likely for some other reason. Fourth, local political tensions in Gunungkidul prior to 1965 had been sufficiently high to both have come to the attention of the military and to have galvanized anticommunist civilian organizations to collaborate with the army.[15] Notably,

[10] Mathias Hammer, "The Organisation of the Killings and the Interaction between State and Society in Central Java, 1965," *Journal of Current Southeast Asian Affairs* 32, no. 3 (2013): 37–62.

[11] Kent Young, "Local and National Influences in the Violence of 1965," in *The Indonesian killings of 1965–1966: Studies from Java and Bali*, ed. Robert Cribb (Clayton, Victoria: Monash University, Centre of Southeast Asian Studies, 1990), 63–99; Hermawan Sulistyo, *Palu arit di ladang tebu: Sejarah pembantaian massal yang terlupakan (Jombang-Kediri 1965–1966)* (Jakarta: Kepustakaan Populer Gramedia bekerjasama dengan Yayasan Adikarya IKAPI dan Ford Foundation, 2000); I. Ngurah Suryawan, *Ladang Hitam di Pulau Dewa: Pembantaian Massal 1965 di Bali* (Yogyakarta, Jakarta: Galang Press, 2007).

[12] Mark Woodward, "Only Now Can We Speak: Remembering Politicide in Yogyakarta," *Sojourn: Journal of Social Issues in Southeast Asia* 26 (2011): 36–57; Mark Winward, "Capture from below: Civil-Military Relations during Indonesia's Anticommunist Violence, 1965–66," *Indonesia* 106 (2018): 111–36.

[13] Woodward, "Only Now Can We Speak"; Winward, "Capture from Below."

[14] Daerah Istimewa Yogyakarta. Panitya *Pemilihan Daerah. 1958. Buku Peringatan Panitia Pemilihan Daerah: Pemilihan Anggauta Dewan Perwakilan Rakjat Daerah Tahun 1957* (Jogjakarta: Panitya Pemilihan Daerah [P.P.D.] Daerah Istimewa Jogjakarta, 1958).

[15] Juliette Sendra, "History from the below and on-the-ground Experiences of 1965 Repression's to the Suharto's New Order: The Case of Two Javanese Villages of Gunungkidul Region," Paper presented at the inaugural American Institute for Indonesian Studies—Michigan State University (AIFIS-MSU) Conference, June 2021, 3–7.

the area had also experienced fighting between communist militia and the nascent Indonesian army during the independence struggle of the 1940s.[16] Together, these factors predisposed Gunungkidul to the significant violence the area experienced in 1965–66, an observation underscored by recorded mass graves in the region. And fifth, as we discuss below, Gunungkidul is divided into three topographical zones, each of which experienced its own distinct pattern of population change during 1965–66, raising the question about the degree to which topography-associated factors may have influenced patterns of violence.

As the subsequent analysis will show, demographic changes coinciding with the violence of 1965–66 in Gunungkidul are consistent with a combination of spillover effects from neighboring areas and the internal dynamics of the violence. The spillover effects, observed most prominently in the northern *desa* of the *kabupaten*, likely reflect the large-scale violence in the neighboring *kabupaten* to the north, Klaten. They are consistent with segments of the population of Klaten fleeing to some of the hilly and remote *desa* of northern Gunungkidul to seek refuge. Such a dynamic can account for the pattern of one-time increases seen in a number of northern *desa*. To the south of this east-west strip of *desa* lies a group of *desa* in the vicinity of Wonosari, the principal urban area of Gunungkidul, where we observe a pattern of one-time population loss. We attribute this pattern to a combination of previous tension and the availability of both civilian and military personnel willing to move against communist party supporters. We also find clusters of population losses that we attribute to combinations of spillover effects and previous communist activism and that are spatially proximate to sites of mass execution. Finally, in the more remote southeastern and southwestern *desa* of Gunungkidul, we again see population gains consistent with refuge-seeking by those fleeing violence elsewhere. While the southwestern *desa* may have experienced spillover refuge-seeking from the neighboring *kabupaten* of Bantul and the City of Yogyakarta, both of which experienced heavy violence, the *desa* in the southeastern part of Gunungkidul likely formed refuges for people from the Wonosari area and, perhaps, to a lesser degree, from other more distant areas including the city of Yogyakarta.

The remainder of this manuscript proceeds as follows. First, we describe the situation in Gunungkidul leading up to the killings. Second, we provide a brief overview of the 1965–66 killings, with an emphasis on the central part of Java. As DIY is geographically located within this region and fell within the purview of the same military provincial command (the Diponegoro Command) as the neighboring province of Central Java, we postulate that patterns of killings in Gunungkidul are likely to resemble those in Central Java as a whole. Third, from these two sections we derive a set of hypotheses about patterns of population change. Fourth, we describe our research methods and data. The fifth section presents our results, while the sixth provides additional discussion.

Gunungkidul

Located east of Yogyakarta City and southwest of Surakarta, Gunungkidul was a relatively poor agricultural *kabupaten* in the years leading up to the killings.

---

[16] Estu Dwiyono, "Peranan Askar Perang Sabil (APS) Dalam Operasi Penumpansan Pemberontakan PKI di Kabupaten Gunungkidul Tahun 1948" (Undergraduate thesis, Universitas Negeri Yogyakarta, 2012), 100–4.

Geographically, the *kabupaten* consisted of three zones.[17] The north zone, including the *kecamatan* (sub-districts) of Patuk, Gedangsari, Nglipar, Ngawen, Semin, and northern Ponjong, were, for the most part, mountainous. The central zone, consisting of the comparatively densely populated *kecamatan* of Playen, Wonosari, Karangmojo, central Ponjong, and Semanu, was the most fertile of the three regions and was marked by relatively level land stretching from the east almost to the western boundary of the *kabupaten*.[18] The south zone, including the *kecamatan* of Saptosari, Paliyan, Girisubo, Tanjungsari, Tepus, Rongkop, Purwosari, Panggang, southern Ponjong, and Semanu, were part of the limestone karst belt of southern Java, marked by highly uneven land dotted with caves (*luweng*) and difficult to farm. This region also frequently experienced drought. Of the four rural *kabupaten* of DIY, Gunungkidul was considered to be the most food-insecure, in large part due to constraints on irrigation construction and poor soil quality. Despite these agricultural challenges, the majority of Gunungkidul's population worked within the agricultural sector. About half of this population worked on small plots of less than half a hectare. Fajar Pratikto characterizes power relationships between elite landlords and much of the peasantry as feudal in nature.[19]

Gunungkidul experienced significant conflict between communist supporters and other groups in the decades prior to the 1965–66 mass killings. On September 18, 1948, during the Indonesian independence struggle, the PKI broke from the revolutionary government, seizing the town of Madiun, located some seventy miles to the northeast of Wonosari, the principal town in Gunungkidul. The following day Sukarno, head of the revolutionary government, denounced the PKI, claiming it had staged a revolt against the revolutionary government. Over the next three months, the Indonesian Army and auxiliary militia would crush the Madiun revolt, arrest its participants, and execute the majority of its leadership.[20]

The suppression of the Madiun revolt and the break between the PKI and Indonesian revolutionary movement provided an opportunity for the Indonesian government to purge communist elements from the movement and to disarm PKI-affiliated militia. In the preceding years, the Yogyakarta area had seen sporadic clashes between "red" militia and those affiliated with other political streams, especially following the arrival of the Siliwangi division of the Indonesian Army in 1948.[21] Madiun provided the necessary pretext for the army to sideline, disarm, and outright eliminate several of these militia. In Gunungkidul, joint operations between the military and militia opposed to the PKI clashed with red militia in the areas of Semin, Nglipar, Ponjong, Semanu, and Wonosari.[22]

---

[17] See, for example, Fadjar Pratikto, *Gerakan Rakyat Kelaparan: Gagalnya Politik Radikalisasi Petani* (Yogyakarta: Media Pressindo, 2000), 29–31; Biro Statistik Kabupaten Gunung Kidul, *Kabupaten Gunung Kidul Tingkat II: Gunung Kidul Dalam Angka Tahun 1980* (Yogyakarta: Hasil Kerja Sama Pemerintah Daerah dan Kantor Statistik), 4, cited in Kandar Ii Rubi, "Kondisi Sosial Ekonomi Masyarakat Gunungkidul Masa Revolusi Hijau (1970–1974)" (S1 thesis, Universitas Negeri Yogyakarta, 2014), https://eprints.uny.ac.id/21351/.

[18] Dewi Ragil Pangesti, "Modernisasi Pertanian di Kabupaten Gunungkidul Tahun 1960–1984: Dari Krisis Pangan Hingga Ketahanan Pangan" (undergraduate thesis., Universitas Negeri Yogyakarta, 2014).

[19] Fajar Pratikto, *Gerakan Rakyat Kelaparan. Gagalnya Politik Radikalisasi Petani* (Yogyakarta: Media Pressindo, 2000), 8, 33.

[20] George Kahin, *Nationalism and Revolution in Indonesia* (Ithaca, NY: Cornell University Press, 1970).

[21] Kahin, *Nationalism and Revolution*.

[22] Estu Dwiyono, *Peranan Askar Perang Sabil (APS) Dalam Operasi Penumpansan Pemberontakan PKI di Kabupaten Gunungkidul Tahun 1948* (Undergraduate thesis, Universitas Negeri Yogyakarta, 2012), 100–4.

Among the militia supporting the army was the Army of the Sabil War (APS), an Islamic militia composed primarily of Muhammadiyah members.[23]

Following independence, Gunungkidul became a bastion of PKI support within Yogyakarta. By the time of the 1955 elections, the PKI was able to secure 47% of the vote, easily enough for first place.[24] This support increased in the 1957 regional elections, in which the PKI's vote share rose to 51 percent.[25] From this vote share, the PKI was able to secure eighteen of thirty-five seats in the local legislature (Dewan Perwakilan Rakyat Daerah, DPRD).[26] Organizations affiliated with the PKI were also able to gather considerable support in Gunungkidul, especially the Indonesian Peasant Front (Barisan Tani Indonesia, or BTI), which advocated for the rights of poor farmers that made up the majority of the population of Gunungkidul.[27] In general, the PKI and BTI attracted substantial support in poor rural areas. According to Pratikto: "In almost all the poor villages in Gunungkidul, the village officials and their farmers were fanatical party supporters."[28] In particular, the subdistricts (*kecamatan*) of Karangmojo, Ponjong, Rongkop, Semanu, and Panggang were known as major PKI bases within the *kabupaten*. A large number of teachers in Gunungkidul were affiliated with the PKI, as were the local political leaders (*pamong desa*) in rural areas.[29] Finally, increased PKI activism in Indonesia beginning in 1964 resulted in substantial recruitment campaigns in Gunungkidul, almost certainly raising party membership and affiliation further.[30]

In Gunungkidul, a key civilian rival of the PKI was the Indonesian National Party (Partai Nasional Indonesia, or PNI). While the shares of votes it garnered in the 1955 and 1957 elections, 11 percent and 9 percent, respectively, were paltry in comparison to the corresponding vote shares for the PKI, the PNI was the party of the traditional Javanese elite and, as such, wielded considerable influence in DIY as a whole.[31] The PKI's dominance within the ranks of the *pamong desa* worried local bureaucrats and administrators (*pamong praja*), who were politically close to the PNI. Unlike *pamong desa*, *pamong praja* were appointed, and Government Law No. 1 of 1957 attempted to gradually subordinate the *pamong desa* to elected local governments.[32] Growing PKI and BTI membership posed a threat to the position of those civil service leaders and to the PNI

---

[23] Dwiyono, *Peranan Askar Perang Sabil*.

[24] Alfian, *Hasil pemilihan umum 1955, untuk Dewan Perwakilan Rakjat (D. P. R.)* (Djakarta: LEKNAS, 1971).

[25] Daerah Istimewa Yogyakarta. *Buku peringatan Panitia Pemilihan Daerah : pemilihan anggauta Dewan Perwakilan Rakjat Daerah tahun 1957* (Jogjakarta: Panitya Pemilihan Daerah [P.P.D.] Daerah Istimewa Jogjakarta, 1958).

[26] Pratikto, *Gerakan Rakyat Kelaparan*, 81.

[27] Törnquist, Olle, "Pengantar Edisi Bahasa Indonesia: Setelah Berselang 30 Tahun" ["Thirty years after: preface to the Indonesian edition"], in *Penghancuran PKI* (Depok: Komunitas Bambu, 2011), vii–xxvi. (Indonesian edition of revised original English edition with new introduction of *Dilemmas of Third World Communism: The Destruction of PKI in Indonesia* [London: Zed Books, 1984]).

[28] Pratikto, *Gerakan Rakyat Kelaparan*, 87.

[29] Pratikto, *Gerakan Rakyat Kelaparan*, 87, 106.

[30] Juliette Sendra, "History from the Below and on-the-Ground Experiences of 1965 Repression's Due to the Suharto New Order: The Case of Two Javanese Villages of Gunungkidul Region," paper presented at the American Institute for Indonesian Studies – Michigan State University (AIFIS–MSU) conference, 2021.

[31] Herb Feith, *The Indonesian elections of 1955* (Ithaca, NY: Cornell Modern Indonesia Project, 1957).

[32] Millidge Walker and Irene Tinker, "Development and Changing Bureaucratic Styles in Indonesia: The Case of the Pamong Praja," *Pacific Affairs* 48, no. 1 (1975): 60–73.

pamong desa.[33] Within Gunungkidul, the majority of top positions in the local government administration were held by PNI members, as they had been prior to the PKI's electoral successes in 1955 and 1957. In at least some areas, such as *kecamatan* Ngawen, the PNI could block PKI appointments such as village heads, leading to political conflict that was ongoing at the time of the 1965–66 killings.[34] PNI support was greatest in Wonosari, Rongkop, Ngawen, and Nglipar.[35]

In addition to its competition with the PNI, the PKI faced significant challenges from Yogyakarta's Islamic political organizations: Nahdlatul Ulama (NU) and Muhammadiyah. Yogyakarta city is the birthplace of Muhammadiyah, a reformist Islamic movement founded in 1912. The Muhammadiyah-affiliated militia had confronted communist militias in Gunungkidul during the revolution, and Muhammadiyah and the PKI organized competing demonstrations against each other in Yogyakarta city in the years leading up to the mass killings, especially in Kota Gede, the southeastern-most *kecamatan* of Yogyakarta city that borders Gunungkidul.[36] Indeed, Muhammadiyah members would comprise an important part of the civilian militia organized by the army para-commando regiment (RPKAD) in Yogyakarta during the mass killings.[37] While Muhammadiyah was primarily urban, the main religious boarding school (*pondok pesantren*) of the rurally oriented Nahdlatul Ulama (NU) was located in Wonosari. Along with Wonosari, Islamic groups in general were strongest in Playen, Ponjong, and Karangmojo.[38] Following the passage of the Basic Agrarian Law of 1960[39] and its subsequent slow implementation, attempts by the PKI to unilaterally implement stalled land reforms by occupying and redistributing the estates of major landlords (*aksi sepihak*) prompted violent opposition by groups such as NU, whose membership included many such landowners, as did the elite of the PNI. In 1964, one such attempt at unilateral land reform occurred in Gunungkidul, in Wonosari, in which seventy farmers occupied lands. Land was also redistributed in Rongkop, Tepus, Paliyan, and Semanu, with no reports of violence in the process.[40] In contrast, the neighboring regency of Klaten, to the north, experienced some of the most explosive *aksi* in Central Java.[41]

A final source of tension involving PKI supporters was the People's Hunger Movement known as Gerayak. In late 1963 and early 1964 the region experienced a significant famine, and by February 1964 Reuters reported that one million people in

[33] Pratikto, *Gerakan Rakyat Kelaparan*, 87.

[34] Pratikto, *Gerakan Rakyat Kelaparan*, 90–92.

[35] Pratikto, *Gerakan Rakyat Kelaparan*, 75.

[36] Mitsuo Nakamura, *The Crescent Arises Over the Banyan Tree: A Study of the Muhammadiyah Movement in a Central Javanese Town* (Singapore: Institute of Southeast Asian Studies, 1983), 125; Woodward, "Only Now Can We Speak."

[37] Winward, "Capture from Below," 127–32.

[38] Pratikto, *Gerakan Rakyat Kelaparan*, 74.

[39] Selo Soemardjan. "Land Reform in Indonesia," Asian Survey 1, no. 12 (1962): 23–30; E. Utrecht, "Land Reform in Indonesia," *Bulletin of Indonesian Economic Studies* 5, no. 3 (1969): 71–88.

[40] Pratikto, *Gerakan Rakyat Kelaparan*, 115.

[41] See Rex Mortimer. *The Indonesian Communist Party and Land Reform, 1959–1965* (Clayton, Victoria: Monash University Centre of Southeast Asian Studies, 1972); *Indonesian Communism under Sukarno: Ideology and Politics, 1959–1965* (Ithaca, NY: Cornell University Press, 1974). A number of interview respondents noted these incidents in Klaten in their recollections of this period.

Central Java were facing starvation.[42] Given existing agricultural challenges due to soil conditions, Gunungkidul suffered tremendously during the famine.[43] Gerayak was formed by local BTI cadres in January 1964, and their first action was to stage a demonstration against the Regent of Gunungkidul, KRT Djojodiningrat, to demand improved conditions for the local populations.[44] Other actions by Gerayak included asking wealthier individuals for money or food. At times, these demands for money and food could turn violent. Pratikto distinguishes Grayak from Gerayak, the former referring to attempts by elements of the movement to rob Gunungkidul's wealthier inhabitants. This prompted significant backlash, and local security forces repressed the movement by mid-1964.[45] Gerayak was first organized in the *kecamatan* of Semanu and Playen, while its leader was the village head from Ponjong. Gerayak conducted two mass actions, both of which led to arrests, in Wonosari, while a village head in Semugih-Rongkop was also arrested.[46]

The Indonesian Killings in Central Java and Yogyakarta

The pretext for the Indonesian mass killings was the September 30th Movement, in which a group of junior officers and members of the PKI's Special Bureau kidnapped and killed six high-ranking generals and one junior officer.[47] The movement, which claimed to be acting in the defense of President Sukarno, called for the establishment of revolutionary councils throughout Indonesia. Beset by poor planning, the movement quickly collapsed. Major General Suharto, the highest-ranking combat officer not targeted by the movement, quickly rallied loyal troops in the capital, and troops aligned with the movement surrendered within twenty-four hours. On October 10, Suharto announced the formation of Kopkamtib, a parallel chain of military command to be used for restoring order and security. On October 14, he was named as the new army commander. It is likely that Suharto had already begun moving against the PKI by this time, as revealed by instructions relayed to the military command in Aceh instructing it to annihilate the September 30th Movement just prior to midnight on October 1.[48]

In Central Java and Yogyakarta the army high command was faced with a significant shortage of reliable combat troops. Following the September 30th Movement's initial radio broadcast, five of the seven infantry battalions in Central Java and Yogyakarta announced their support for the movement, including the battalion (Korem 072) stationed in Yogyakarta.[49] Moreover, a number of otherwise loyal troops had been deployed outside the province due to the confrontation over Malaysia, including the

[42] Christian Gerlach. *Extremely Violent Societies: Mass Violence in the Twentieth-Century World*, (Cambridge: Cambridge University Press, 2010), 49.

[43] Pratikto, *Gerakan Rakyat Kelaparan*, 124.

[44] Pratikto, *Gerakan Rakyat Kelaparan*, 138–40.

[45] Pratikto, *Gerakan Rakyat Kelaparan*, 144.

[46] Pratikto, *Gerakan Rakyat Kelaparan*, 130–42.

[47] John Roosa, *Pretext for Mass Murder: The September 30th Movement and Suharto's Coup d'État in Indonesia* (Madison: University of Wisconsin Press, 2006).

[48] Melvin, *The Army and the Indonesian Genocide*, 110–37.

[49] Jenkins and Kammen, "The Army Para-commando Regiment," 78.

entirety of the fourth infantry brigade and two battalions of the fifth infantry brigade.[50] By October 1, the total number of reliable combat-ready troops in Yogyakarta and Central Java was only 1,200–1,500—in two provinces with a combined population of over 20 million.[51] The military command at Yogyakarta was one such deployment that declared their support for the September 30th Movement. To overcome the lack of reliable combat troops, Suharto dispatched the mobile para-commando regiment (RPKAD) from West Java under the command of Colonel Sarwo Edhie to lead the anti-communist campaign in Central Java and Yogyakarta. Lacking sufficient troops of their own, the RPKAD would train huge numbers of civilian militia to identify, arrest, and sometimes execute suspected communists.[52] The RPKAD arrived in Central Java on October 17 and in Yogyakarta on October 20.

Violence in Central Java and Yogyakarta tended to have a distinct pattern. First, the RPKAD would arrive in a major urban center and stage a mass rally attended by non-communist civilian organizations. Attendees, supported by the army, would then parade to the local PKI headquarters or an affiliated organization, ransack it, and, in some cases, burn it to the ground. These directed riots were also usually accompanied by an initial wave of mass arrests. Following these initial demonstrations, remaining security forces and civilian militia, with occasional direct support of the RPKAD, would continue a campaign of mass arrests, interrogation, torture, and disappearances in the area. Often, security forces would rely on civilian organizations for information on communist sympathizers in a given area, tasking them with creating lists, identifying houses, and, at times, screening detainees.[53] The RPKAD established its temporary base of operations in Kartasura, a suburb of the city of Surakarta. With its access to vehicles, the RPKAD was able to keep two-thirds of its manpower on the roads at all times, allowing them to round up large numbers of suspected communists and encourage sustained local collaboration despite their relatively small numbers.[54]

The pattern described above applies to the urban environs in Central Java and Yogyakarta. However, there has been little sustained inquiry into violence in rural areas, especially in these regions. This is somewhat surprising, given that most anecdotes of large-scale violence refer to rural areas.[55] Given that the RPKAD appears to have focused its efforts on urban areas, we know little about patterns of violence outside their environs.[56]

---

[50] Harold Crouch, *The Army and Politics in Indonesia* (Ithaca, NY: Cornell University Press, 1978), 143–44.

[51] Hammer, "The Organisation of the Killings," 3.

[52] Crouch, *The Army and Politics*, 150–52; Jenkins and Kammen, "The Army Para-Commando Regiment," 88–94; Winward, "Intelligence Capacity," 570.

[53] Abdul Wahid, "Counterrevolution in a Revolutionary Campus: How Did the '1965 Event' Affect an Indonesian Public University?," in *The Indonesian Genocide: Causes, Dynamics and Legacies*, ed. Katharine McGregor, Jess Melvin, and Annie Pohlman (New York: Springer, 2018), 157–78; Hammer, "The Organisation of the Killings," 54–58; Winward, "Capture from Below," 129; "Intelligence Capacity," 570–72.

[54] Hammer, "The Organisation of the Killings," 45.

[55] Kurniawan et al., eds., *The Massacres: Coming to Terms with the Trauma of 1965* (Jakarta: Tempo, 2015); Robinson, *The Killing Season*, 122.

[56] See also Staf Pertahanan Keamanan [Defense and Security Staff] 1966. 40 Hari Kegagalan 'G30S' [*Forty Days Failure of G30S*].

Data and Methods

The focus of our analysis is the change in population in the various *desa* of Gunungkidul that can be attributed to the violence of 1965–66. In order to estimate the one-time population change associated with the violence, we used *desa*-level counts of population for each of 144 *desa* in Gunungkidul from the censuses of 1961, 1971, and 1980.[57] The following description is a brief summary of the method used to calculate this change in population. A more detailed description that appeared in earlier research on a related topic is provided in the Technical Appendix.[58]

First, using the population counts from 1971 and 1980, we calculated the rate of population growth between these two data points using the standard exponential growth curve demographers use to model population trajectories. The underlying assumption is that there were no major one-time shocks to the population during this decade, and therefore the trajectory of population growth was smooth, as shown by the solid red line in Figure 1. This calculated growth rate was then adjusted upwards to reflect the higher population growth in the 1960s and used to estimate the population of each *desa* before and in the immediate aftermath of the anti-communist violence.

We used the adjusted *desa*-specific rate of population growth to extrapolate the 1971 census back in time to 1966 to obtain the post-violence population (green dashed line—note that the adjustment is not shown in Figure 1). Next, using the population from the 1961 census,[59] we projected the population forward in time to 1965 using the same adjusted *desa*-specific rate of population growth (blue dashed line) to obtain the population on the eve of the killings. The difference between the pre- and post-violence populations, shown by the black vertical dotted line, represents the "missing" population for each *desa*. This variable represents one of the key outcomes for analysis in this paper.

Given the nature of the data (i.e., three population counts, one for each of the three censuses), a number of assumptions were made in order to arrive at estimates of the one-time population change attributable to the violence. These include:

1. A steady rate of population growth for each *desa* between the 1971 and 1980 censuses. Note that this rate incorporates into it systematic long-term rates of fertility, mortality, and net migration that would occur in normal times. While this assumption may not have held for each of the 144 *desa* in this study, we were unable to find cases of large one-time population shocks in any of the *desa* during this time period. Therefore, it is safe to assume that, in most if not all the *desa*, the population grew in a fairly smooth manner and that patterns that appear to persist across multiple *desa* are probably robust to the occasional violation of this assumption.

---

[57] Indonesia. 1983. *Penduduk Kabupaten Gunungkidul: Hasil Sensus Penduduk 1961, 1971 & 1980 Dilengkapi Hasil Sensus Over All 1968*. Wonosari: Kantor Statistik Kabupaten Gunungkidul.

[58] See also Chandra. "New Findings on the Indonesian Killings," Technical Appendix, pp. 1085-86.

[59] The only pre-1965 census for independent Indonesia was conducted in 1961. While a detailed census was also held during the late colonial era (see Departement van Economische Zaken. 1930-1936. *Volkstelling 1930*. [Census of 1930], 8 volumes [Batavia, Indonesia: Landsdrukkerij]), the intervening demographic upheaval of the Japanese occupation and World War II more generally render the data from this census unusable for the purpose of estimating a smooth pre-1965 population growth trajectory.

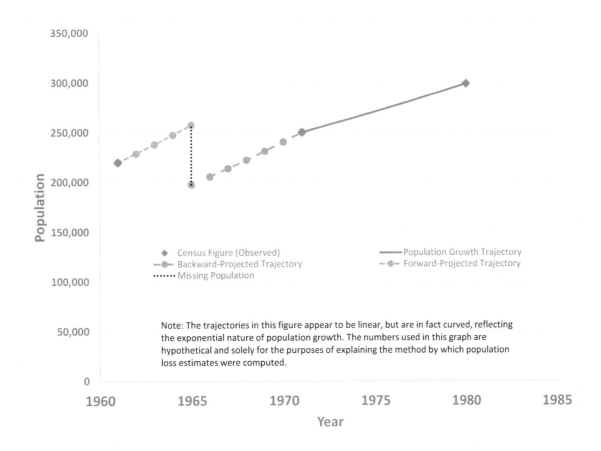

Figure 1: Calculation of population loss associated with the violence of 1965–66.

2. A higher rate of population growth in the 1960s, both before and after the break in the trajectory in 1965–66, than in the 1970s. There is a large literature on the demography of Indonesia in the 1970s, and all of it corroborates the notion that the rate of population growth fell across Java, including in Yogyakarta and Gunungkidul, as the result of the family planning programs that the Suharto regime implemented in the 1970s. In accordance with this observation, we took the *desa*-specific population growth rate estimated for 1971–80 and uniformly adjusted it upward for each *desa* for the 1960s.[60]

---

[60] See the Technical Appendix. The adjustment factor was 0.2 percent per year, which is lower than the factor of 0.3 percent that would be obtained under the assumption that population growth slowed immediately after the killings of 1965–66. There is some evidence of such a slowdown, which gathered strength in the 1970s as the government family planning initiative was implemented across Java. Importantly, estimates comparing rates of population loss across *desas* are unaffected by the choice of the adjustment factor. As discussed above, because only one pre-1965 census was conducted in independent Indonesia, it was not possible to use pre-1965 census data from multiple censuses to directly compute a pre-1965 population growth rate.

3. The only significant one-time shock to the population between the 1961 and 1980 censuses occurred in 1965–66, corresponding to the mass violence in the region. This assumption justifies the smooth forward projection of population from 1961 and the smooth backward projection of population from 1971.

It is important to note that the "missing population" reflects three underlying drivers of population change: deaths, births, and net migration. Therefore, the gap in population coincident with 1965–66 should not be interpreted as the number of deaths that occurred in any particular *desa*. However, because a violence-prone region would experience a simultaneous elevation in deaths, depression in births, and net out-migration, a large gap in the negative direction is suggestive of severe violence in that region. Second, even though there was likely significant violence across the region, we should not necessarily expect to see drops in population across all *desa* in Gunungkidul. It is possible that displacement from more violent regions resulted in migration to regions perceived to be safer and that receiving regions may have seen increases in population even if they experienced violence, because an influx of refugees from other violent areas may have more than compensated for population losses due to violence.

To explore spatial patterns of population loss associated with the violence of 1965–66, we plotted the *desa*-specific estimates of population loss on a *desa* map of Gunungkidul. This map provided several clear insights into the spatial nature of population loss and how these patterns align with the prior literature on the violence in Gunungkidul. Aligning with observations made in prior work on other parts of Indonesia, we focused on two related factors that are likely to have clear spatial manifestations. Both factors lead back to the Indonesian Army and the civilian opponents of the PKI, which worked hand-in-hand to carry out the massacres. We posit that the distance of a *desa* from hubs of organizational strength of the Indonesian Army and the civilian opponents of the PKI, coupled with the accessibility of the *desa* from those hubs, was a key factor in shaping outcomes in the various *desa* of Gunungkidul. This insight in turn predicts two types of influences on village-level outcomes: influences internal to Gunungkidul and influences spilling over from neighboring areas into the *desa* of Gunungkidul. Key locations in this regard are, first, Wonosari, the capital of Gunungkidul. Located at the center of the *kabupaten* and accessible by a road running west to east from the city of Yogyakarta, Wonosari, which was also the seat of the local military district command (*Komando Distrik Militer* or *Kodim*), was both a center of organizational strength for the Indonesian Army and easily accessible by road. A second potential source of a spillover effect is the city of Kartasura to the north of Gunungkidul. Selected as a base for operations of the Special Forces of the Indonesian Army in its campaign to destroy PKI strongholds in the neighboring *kabupaten* of Klaten and Boyolali, both PKI strongholds, Kartasura and its southern environs, experienced significant levels of violence. Therefore, one might expect a spillover effect from Kartasura and Klaten, which abuts the northern boundary of Gunungkidul. Finally, the city of Yogyakarta, located due west of Gunungkidul, was connected to Wonosari by road. A stronghold of both the Indonesian Army and a number of political parties opposed to the PKI, we might expect to see spillover effects from the violence and the organizational strength of PKI opponents in the city of Yogyakarta.

In order to measure the effects of different potential operational basis for the killings, we calculated the straight-line (Euclidean) distance between the center of Kartasura and the centroid of each *desa* using ArcGIS.[61] We did the same for Yogyakarta city and Wonosari. To test for associations between the different variables, we computed simple correlation coefficients.[62]

Results

Figure 2 is a map of the 144 *desa* of Gunungkidul showing our estimates of the one-time change in population attributable to the violence of 1965–66. Two phenomena stand out. First, a belt of *desa* running from the east to the west of the central part of the *kabupaten* shows moderate to large percentage losses in population. This belt also extends south to the central coast of the *kabupaten*. Second, clusters of *desa* showing one-time gains in population are visible in the southeastern and southwestern corners of Gunungkidul as well as in the northern and especially the northeastern area of the *kabupaten*.

Figure 3 is a scatter plot of the one-time change in population in the *desa* against their distance from Wonosari, the centrally located capital of the *kabupaten*. There is a general tendency, seen in the upward-sloping trend line in Figure 3, for *desa* closer to Wonosari (i.e., on the left side of the graph) to show larger population losses or smaller population gains than the *desa* that are more distant from Wonosari (on the right side of the graph). The correlation between distance from Wonosari and one-time population change is positive ($r = 0.34$) and statistically significant, i.e., there is a less than 1 percent chance that the pattern in the graph is coincidental.

Finally, Figure 4 is a graph of estimated population loss in the *desa* plotted against distance from Kartasura, the local center of operations of the RPKAD during its campaign against the PKI located north of Gunungkidul on the outskirts of the city of Surakarta. The observations in Figure 4 are color-coded according to the three zones of Gunungkidul described by Pratikto, i.e., the northern, central, and southern zones with forty-four, forty-seven, and fifty-three *desas*, respectively.[63] Unlike Figure 3, which shows a uniformly upward trend, Figure 4 displays a curvilinear relationship, with (a) losses increasing with distance from Kartasura among the *desa* of the northern zone (blue dots, downward sloping blue trend line showing a negative and statistically significant [$p < 0.0001$] correlation of $r = -0.46$), (b) heavy losses and no particular relationship with distance from Kartasura for the *desa* in the central zone (red dots, flat red trend line, correlation of -0.04 that is not statistically significant), and (c) losses decreasing with distance from Kartasura for the *desa* in the southern zone (green dots, upward sloping green trend line showing a positive and statistically significant correlation of 0.51).

Discussion

In this section we discuss our results in light of existing accounts of political tension and violence in Gunungkidul and the surrounding areas. We note especially the concentration

---

[61] Esri Inc. 2019, ArcGIS Pro (Version 2.4.2), accessed May 22, 2023, https://www.esri.com/en-us/arcgis/products/arcgis-pro/overview.

[62] Correlation coefficients are very closely related to regression coefficients and convey the same evidence for or against associations between variables as regression coefficients do. The main difference between a correlation and regression coefficient is the factor by which it is scaled.

[63] Pratikto, *Gerakan Rakyat Kelaparan*, 29–30.

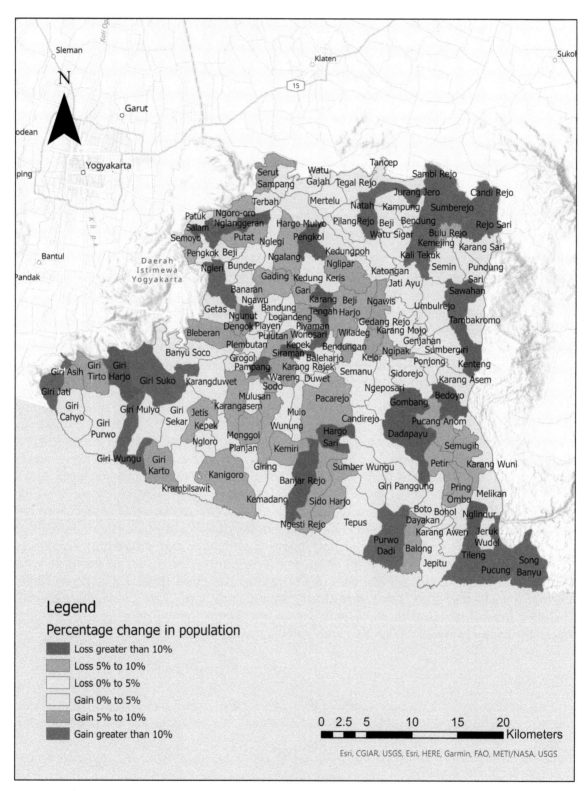

Figure 2: *Desa*-level estimates of population loss in Gunungkidul
(expressed as a percentage of total population).

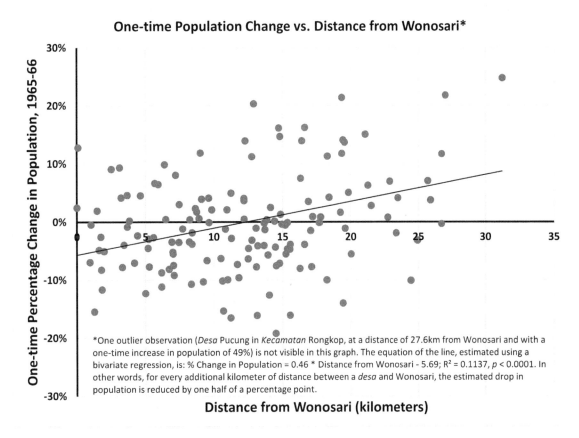

Figure 3: Estimated one-time *desa*-level population change attributable to the violence of 1965–66 (in percentage terms) vs. distance from Wonosari.

of population loss in the vicinity of Wonosari, as well as trends in each of the three zones shown in Figure 4. In the south zone we see population losses directly south of Wonosari, as well as in the more eastern *desa*. The exceptions are the far southeast corner, which like the similarly remote southwest corner, saw one-time gains in population that we attribute to an influx of refugees fleeing violence.[64] In the central zone we see the greatest level of population loss, especially near Wonosari, where PKI activism had been high in the vicinity of the road leading to Yogyakarta city. In the north zone we generally see fewer drops in population, again with the exception of the *desa* close to Yogyakarta city. We note especially high population gains in northeastern Gunungkidul, which we attribute to refugees fleeing violence from neighboring Klaten.

As shown in Figure 3, population losses tend to be greater in the *desa* closer to Wonosari. The most likely reason for this is that the security infrastructure and personnel

---

[64] These patterns of mass internal migration to avoid violence have been noted in a number of violence-prone areas, including Central Java more broadly and East Java. Chandra "The Indonesian Killings of 1965–66"; Hefner, this volume; Hearman, *Unmarked Graves*.

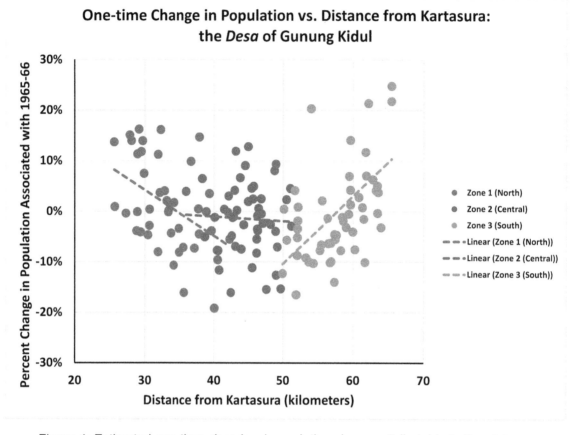

Figure 4: Estimated one-time *desa*-level population change attributable to the violence of 1965–66 in percentage terms vs. distance from Kartasura.

responsible for orchestrating the violence in Gunungkidul were disproportionately concentrated in this location. The local military command for Gunungkidul (Kodim 0730) is located within Wonosari. Even if the majority of troops had been transferred out of the region, Wonosari still contained the types of necessary facilities for organizing local security forces, making their presence likely more ubiquitous near its environs. In addition, the prison at Wonosari was used to house detainees suspected of ties with the PKI.[65] Wonosari also experienced significant political tensions, which may have led to greater civilian collaboration with the army. Wonosari had one of the only recorded *aksi* in the Special Region of Yogyakarta, and Gerayak protests in Wonosari also led to a number of arrests.[66] Elsewhere in Indonesia, these types of political tensions, in particular around land reforms, were a powerful force motivating civilian organizations to collaborate with the army during their purge of the PKI. This is true both in East Java and in the neighboring *kabupaten* of Klaten.[67] Moreover, Wonosari was the only area of

---

[65] Sendra, "History from the Below."

[66] Pratikto, *Gerakan Rakyat Kelaparan*, 115, 141.

[67] Mortimer, *Indonesian Communism under Sukarno*; Crouch, *The Army and Politics*; Fealy and McGregor, "East Java and the Role of Nahdlatul Ulama"; Hammer, "The Organisation of the Killings."

Gunungkidul in which Nahdlatul Ulama had a significant following.[68] In general, NU was a major ally of the army in its campaign against the PKI, and its central board had issued directives to participate in "crushing" the communist party as early as October 9.[69] For these reasons, it is likely that Wonosari was a crucial staging area for violence in Gunungkidul. Indeed, several respondents cited by Juliette Sendra characterize Wonosari as a hub of violence.[70]

Figure 4 illustrates the differing patterns of violence in the south, central, and northern zones of Gunungkidul. In the south and central zones, population losses tend to be concentrated in the eastern *desa* located closer to Kartasura, especially within the *kecamatan* of Semanu, Ponjong, and Rongkop. These include the *desas* of Dadapayu, Gombang, and Bedoyo. This pattern of population loss aligns in part with patterns of elevated political tension and prior PKI-related activism. For example, in the aftermath of the land reform legislation of 1960, which placed a ceiling on the amount of land that could be owned by landowners, there had been some redistribution of lands in both Semanu and Rongkop. In addition, Gerayak largely originated from this eastern cluster of *desa*. Along with Playen (immediately west of Wonosari), Semanu was one of the *kecamatan* in which Gerayak originated. Moreover, a major Gerayak leader was a Village Head from Ponjong, and at least one other official from Rongkop was arrested as part of the protests.[71] More broadly, Pratikto describes this area as a PKI base, while Sendra notes how local village heads were tasked by the army to identify and turn in local PKI supporters.[72] More recent NU reconciliation efforts also targeted this area, underscoring how violence here was likely significant.[73] Moreover, there is a major highway running through Gunungkidul (Jalan Nasional 3) that would have enabled easy access to these eastern regions by mobile troops such as the RPKAD; the RPKAD were a mechanized unit that maintained a consistent presence on the roads, often checking on the progress of anti-communist violence and providing "encouragement" and support when necessary.[74] This combination of access by the main architects of violence in the Central Java/Yogyakarta region and previous tensions that would have flagged PKI activism in the region likely explain higher levels of population loss in this area.

In the southern zone we also see clusters of one-time increases in population in the southeastern-most and southwestern-most areas of Gunungkidul. The reasons for these increased population gains are likely similar: these two corners of Gunungkidul are difficult to access. They are located far from major roads and are sparsely populated. In addition, they are characterized by difficult terrain featuring limestone caves and varying

[68] Sendra, "History from the Below," 3.

[69] Fealy and McGregor, "East Java and the Role of Nahdlatul Ulama," 117.

[70] Sendra, "History from the Below." More recently, Wonosari has also seen NU initiatives aimed at reconciliation and assisting former leftists (see Rini Yustiningsih, "Luweng Grubug, Saksi Diskriminasi Korban 1966," September 30, 2012, *Solopos.com*. An archived version is available at http://kebumenypkp65 .blogspot.com/2012/09/luweng-grubug-saksi-diskriminasi-korban.html). This appears to be part of a broader effort of grassroots reconciliation by a younger generation of NU activists in the region (Katharine McGregor 2009, "Confronting the Past in Contemporary Indonesia: The Anticommunist Killings of 1965–66 and the Role of the Nahdlatul Ulama," *Critical Asian Studies* 41, no. 2 (2009): 195–224.)

[71] Pratikto, *Gerakan Rakyat Kelaparan*, 114, 130–43.

[72] Pratikto, *Gerakan Rakyat Kelaparan*, 87; Sendra, "History from the Below," 6.

[73] Yustiningsih, "Luweng Grubug."

[74] Hammer "The Organisation of the Killings."

elevation, making them ideal places of refuge for those fleeing violence orchestrated primarily by a mechanized force and its supporting militia units. This pattern also matches that observed in other locations such as East Java, in which remote upland communities often saw significant jumps in population due to the arrival of refugees fleeing the anti-communist violence.[75]

An additional cluster of population loss extends directly south from Wonosari, encompassing part of the central and southern zones. There are likely two interrelated reasons for greater population loss in these areas. First, an important secondary road network extends directly south of Wonosari. As such, it is likely this area—accessible by road and close to Wonosari—would have seen more consistent anti-communist activity. Second, a major execution site, Luweng Grubug, lies in the area southeast of Wonosari. Located in Pacarejo, Luweng Grubug is a deep cave to which the army brought detainees for execution. Underscoring the importance of road networks, witnesses recount that the detainees would arrive via truck, with sometimes multiple truckloads of detainees arriving in an evening. They were then forced to walk to the location, where they were either pushed down into the cave network or shot. While the nearby hamlet of Jetis was placed under curfew, the sounds of the executions could be easily heard.[76] It is likely that, in an area in which there were mass executions of detainees, a greater percentage of the population would flee the area than would otherwise be the case. Recall that our measure of population loss implies not just deaths but also out-migration. Even if victims were being brought from other locations, it is not unreasonable to expect some additional out-migration in those areas in which the army was especially active or present.

An additional cluster of *desa* showing losses in population lies at the western end of both the central and northern zones, at the point where the main road from Yogyakarta city enters Gunungkidul. It is likely that the increased violence in these *desas* represent a spillover effect from the city itself. Yogyakarta city experienced significant violence during this period, especially in the southeastern section of Kota Gede.[77] Indeed, Woodward estimates that as many as 20 percent of the men in some areas were killed.[78] Here, civilian militia assisted the army and, at times, acted unilaterally, on foot.[79] The westernmost *desa* of Gunungkidul would have been easily accessible from Yogyakarta city due to their proximity to neighborhoods like Kota Gede.

Finally, within the northeastern corner of Gunungkidul, there is a cluster *desa* showing one-time population gains. This phenomenon is somewhat surprising given that this area was located closest to Kartasura, the base of operations of the RPKAD to the north of Gunungkidul. We attribute these gains to spillover effects of the violence in the neighboring *kabupaten* of Klaten. The northeastern portion of Gunungkidul borders Klaten *kabupaten*, an area that had both huge numbers of PKI supporters and

---

[75] Hefner, this volume; Chandra, "Glimpses of Indonesia's 1965 Massacre."

[76] Hari Susmayanti, "Gua Grubug, Saksi Pembantaian Mergerikan PKI di Gunungkidul," *TribunJogja*, October 2, 2013. https://jogja.tribunnews.com/2013/10/02/gua-grubug-saksi-pembantaian-mengerikan-pki-di-gunungkidul

[77] Winward, "Capture from Below."

[78] Woodward, "Only Now We Can Speak," 48.

[79] Winward, "Capture from Below."

experienced especially high levels of violence.[80] It is plausible, and indeed likely, that there would have been significant out-migration from Klaten during this period, and as a mountainous area, northeastern Gunungkidul would have been an attractive place for refuge. Indeed, this region of Gunungkidul has had a history of migration from Klaten.[81]

Conclusion

This paper is a preliminary analysis of patterns of violence in Gunungkidul in 1965–66, viewed through the lens of the census. Unlike previous spatial studies, we systematically describe and compare population loss at the level of the *desa* and *kelurahan* and in doing so, provide a detailed spatial analysis of the violence of 1965–66 in this region. As this analysis takes place in a rural *kabupaten* adjacent to two areas of relatively high violence (Klaten and Yogyakarta city), our study allows us to examine how a combination of spillover effects from these neighboring areas combined with local conditions to create particular patterns of population change in the region. Our analysis is also one of the first to systematically examine violence in a more rural setting at the level of the *desa*.

We identify four spatial patterns of abrupt population change in the region that we attribute to the violence. First, we see greater population losses closer to Wonosari, which we attribute to Wonosari's status as a regional hub for anti-communist forces. Not only is Wonosari home to Kodim 0730, but security forces also detained suspected communists within this more urban environment. In addition, Wonosari was and remains an area of strength for politico-religious organizations in Gunungkidul, and Islamic militias were among the staunchest allies of the RPKAD in the Yogyakarta region. Second, the areas in the northern zone of Gunungkidul closest to Kartasura display large one-time gains in population that diminish with increasing distance from it. While it is possible that these gains reflect refuge-seeking by people fleeing the Wonosari area, it is more likely that they resulted from people escaping the violence in neighboring Klaten, which was located close to the RPKAD's regional base of operations in Kartasura. While the mountainous terrain in northern Gunungkidul would have offered some refuge for people from Wonosari as well, our qualitative findings suggest that fleeing south was a more popular option for those residing in Gunungkidul at the time.[82] And third, supporting the above assertions, we also see large gains in population in the southeastern and southwestern areas of Gunungkidul farthest from Kartasura. Fourth, we also note clusters of population loss in areas where PKI activism was especially strong; in areas near Yogyakarta city, which was an epicenter of violence; and where we identify sites of mass execution. Conversely, we note population gains in remote areas, suggesting that these locations provided refuge for those fleeing violence.

Our study represents one of the first attempts to understand violence in Central Java and Yogyakarta in a rural environment. We find that patterns of rural violence broadly resemble that of more urban environs insofar as we see evidence of greater violence in

---

[80] Hammer, "The Organisation of the Killings," 1, 10.

[81] See Robert Hefner, "Hindu Reform in an Islamizing Java: Pluralism and Peril," in *Hinduism in Modern Indonesia: A Minority Religion between Local, National, and Global Interests*, ed. Martin Ramstedt (London: Routledge, 2004), 93–108.

[82] Sendra, "History from the Below"; Confidential Interview 005b with anticommunist activist by authors, Yogyakarta, March 2016.

more urbanized areas, with their concentration of security infrastructure and potential collaborators. This underscores some of the similarities of patterns of violence and that this pattern is reflective of a military campaign. Our study also underscores the need for additional field research in the Gunungkidul area. It appears that the region was an area of spillover violence and refuge-seeking from neighboring regions, notably Klaten and Yogyakarta. Its general proximity to Yogyakarta city, home to numerous survivor and activist organizations, should make Gunungkidul a productive region for additional research, providing important and much-needed insights into the violence in the more rural and remote areas of Central Java and Yogyakarta.

The Perpetrator's Allegory

Historical Memories and the Killings of 1965

Kar-Yen Leong

Introduction

When the Suharto administration fell in 1998 a flurry of books, memoirs, and even some documentaries were produced revealing details of the 1965 killings. Nearly 500,000 to one million suspected members of the Indonesian Communist Party or the Partai Komunis Indonesia (PKI) were murdered in pogroms that spread across the archipelago. Suharto's New Order regime then pushed Southeast Asia's best-kept secret into a dark crevasse. Stating that the actions taken were necessary to save the nation from the PKI's "insolence," these pogroms also created a new underclass of former political prisoners who required state monitoring to control the latent dangers they posed. These former political prisoners (*eks-tapol*) and their descendants, the state deemed, were the "perpetrators" wishing to harm the Indonesian body politic. Therefore, when Joshua Oppenheimer released his Indonesian documentaries, *The Act of Killing* and *The Look of Silence*, Indonesian audiences saw for the first time a "different" kind of perpetrator, murderers who mercilessly killed alleged "enemies of the state" and yet continued to revel in actions they believed to be justified.

Oppenheimer's aged perpetrators discuss the best way to spill the least amount of blood from their executed victims. Audiences abroad found the visceral "performance" of Anwar Congo and his cohort shocking, but in Indonesia, the reaction was more muted. Initially limited to private screenings, the film eventually found its way to the internet and then began circulating on local university campuses. This earned the ire of groups such as the Fron Pembela Islam (Islamic Defenders Front) as well as the Fron

Anti Komunis Indonesia (Indonesian Anti-Communist Front). Despite the efforts of these groups and the state to obstruct the documentary's screening, it nevertheless brought a particularly violent episode of Indonesian history into the spotlight after nearly five decades of silence.

In other countries with similar violent histories, scholarship on the post-conflict or post- authoritarian environment has taken a forensic turn. Mass human rights violations are considered criminal cases that necessitate evidence through "witness statements," oral historical, or archival records and even human remains. Exhumations and the reappearance of ". . . broken bodies and their position in the landscapes and architectures that saw them broken and buried, are central to the legal, political, and affective aftermath of human-made disasters around the world" (Bondergaard, 2017, p. 1).

The process of digging up the dead, making what was once invisible visible again, has had a significant impact on the sociopolitical dynamics of these countries. Given the rising amount of "undeniable evidence" due to this forensic turn, the boundaries of the field have been further expanded toward another direction: perpetrators. An indication of this is the growth in publications such as the *Journal of Perpetrator Research* as well as a burgeoning number of edited volumes on perpetrator studies (Knittel & Goldberg, 2020; Anderson & Jessee, 2020). This, however, is where the Indonesian case study diverges. Two decades after the fall of Suharto's New Order, Indonesia remains amnesiac over the killings, continuing to deny the scale of the massacre (for the most part referred to only as a "tragedy") and has refused all efforts to deal with it. Even exhumation efforts have been thwarted by groups claiming to protect Indonesia from a possible zombie PKI "resurrection" (Miller, 2018; McGregor, 2012). Nonetheless Indonesia's democratic transition has provided the necessary space in the public sphere by allowing more disparate voices to appear. Oppenheimer was possibly the necessary catalyst, prompting the Indonesian media to seek out the executioners, known as *algojo* or butchers, following the release of his documentaries.[1]

There are also parallels to be found in countries that have similarly experienced mass human rights violations. In his breakthrough documentary Cambodian filmmaker Rithy Pan forces former Khmer Rouge cadres to be confronted by their victims in a form of cinematic *j'accuse*. This encounter between victim and perpetrator creates a space binding both parties in the memory of mass violence decades after the fact (Sanchez-Biosca, 2018). The effect of the auto-genocide had rendered mute the ability of language to describe or even to understand the event. Nonetheless the affect, or the afterlife, of the violence continues to live through their bodies. Former torturers act out their past through muscle memory and Khmer Rouge leaders sit uneasily as the pictures of their victims are placed before them. Affect scholars state that bodies are ". . . always thoroughly entangled processes and importantly defined by their capacities to affect and be affected" (Blackman & Venn, 2010, p. 8).

Thus my research asks this question, how does the act of killing or witnessing killing affect them? The answer, I posit, appears in the "nuances" and "multiplicities" in terms of how these individuals dealt with the aftermath of the killings. While not wanting to

---

[1] BBC Indonesia's Heyder Affan has been extensively following these alleged murderers in their twilight years. See Affan (2015).

whitewash their crimes, I argue that these perpetrators were also victims who, under the circumstances, were forced to be complicit. The life of these crimes did not just stop at that very moment. They were committed in close quarters, where murderers were often familiar with their victims, sharing living spaces, environs, and family ties with them. Therefore, victims and perpetrators were often interconnected, with some perpetrators being forced commit murders in the fear that they too could be at the receiving end of a machete or rifle. I believe that it is this close intimate space that has made discussions or the acknowledgment of these crime so difficult for Indonesians. To date this enforced form of silence has not allowed the Indonesian people or even the state to come to terms with the violent past. Therefore, I state in this paper, the need to express the past manifests itself in a different way, beyond silence.

Framework

The analysis conducted in this paper is based both on primary and secondary sources. The former consists of interviews conducted during fieldwork in central Java, with multiple trips taken between the city of Jogjakarta, the provincial capital of Semarang, and its surrounding areas. The interviewees are made up of an alleged perpetrator as well as two bystanders who witnessed the executions of suspected members of PKI. I also feature in this paper interviews of perpetrators conducted by journalists from a prominent Indonesian language periodical. The paper includes a survey of literature as well covering the perpetrator imaginary.

The paper follows a framework that is centered on the notion of affect but is also partially skewed toward the idea of "embodied accountability." In a fascinating paper by Igreja (2019) on Mozambique, he describes how mass violence left behind an accountability gap within the local environment. In an environment where continuous conflict and the lack of institutions have pushed the burden of accountability onto local communities, he states that through the presence of the supernatural, faith healers, spirits, and possessions become part of a repertoire of what Igreja terms embodied justice. Impunity and the inability to judicially deal with violations forces the body to become a channel demanding justice. Bodies, as such, contain within them values. Therefore, I will be utilizing this framework, incorporating the concepts of embodied justice and moral bodies, to understand the affect the killings have had on the executors and even bystanders' decades after the event.

Perspectives on Perpetrators

In this section I will provide a survey on sources of Indonesia's own body of "perpetrator literature" in order to draw out the kind of relationship the authors had with individuals known to have committed human rights violations. One of the earliest confessionals of a historical actor is from Pipit Rochijat, who was actively working against the PKI due to the indignities his father suffered at the hands of PKI members. Rochijat also details how his contemporaries were actively involved in the murder of suspected PKI members. His life, however, took a turn when he was himself arrested when the army became more "hands on" in dealing with remnants of the PKI. Forced into self-exile it is interesting to note how Rochijat develops a more nuanced and critical stance toward the 1965 killings when enrolled in university studies in Germany. Removed from its claustrophobic political environment, he even dabbles in Marxist thought, reflecting and eventually becoming critical of his comrades who had perpetrated the killings, even asking whether he was, ". . . PKI or not." This shifting of frames of reference found in Rochijat's writing in coming to terms with his own experiences and role in the killings is at the core of this paper. Could other *pelaku sejarah* or historical actors also have shifted their frames of reference over the many decades following the events of 1965? The appearance of so-called perpetrators as protagonists for the first time shattered the myth of the PKI as Indonesia's public enemy number no. 1, shocking audiences with their admission of torture and murder.

Consequently, the perpetrator's "presence" then led to the expansion of 1965 scholarship beyond that of historical, biographical, and autobiographical accounts limited only to political victims. However, the perpetrator's allegory through the medium of documentary brings about countless critical issues. As Canet (2020) states, ". . . this shift in focus could prove highly problematic . . .," in that, ". . . foregrounding the perpetrator's point of view could elicit a kind of emotional engagement that may undermine the viewer's moral judgement . . ." giving rise to the ". . . potential for subverted judgement and moral slippage" (p. 160). Nonetheless, Carnet states that the perpetrator's allegory can serve as a "educational tool" acting as "prophylaxes against future occurrences and work towards conflict resolution." Nevertheless, perpetrator studies in Indonesia remains a nascent field, with Oppenheimer's productions being the primary sources of reference. This raises several important points in our understanding of the 1965 killings. While these twin documentaries offer a specific frame in which to contextualize the dynamics behind the killings, the focus on perpetrators has the potential to reveal the micro-level processes at work. Whether moral or legal judgements are passed on to these individuals, or if portrayed as killing machines perpetrating heinous acts, ". . . violent collective action is not—at least not just—the product of an individual. The individual is always already part of a social field with various interdependent structural positions and relationships, as well as an ideological and historical formation" (Bultman, 2020, p. 5). Thus in "representing" perpetrators, a space opens potentially allowing for a better understanding of their motivations and perhaps even the "afterlife" of their actions.

The perpetrator's narrative as such has been oft used in the study of mass human rights violations with the classic example being Arendt's (2006) study of Adolf Eichmann during his trial. Arendt was then able "pick apart" his actions revealing to her readers how banal a "murderous monster" could be. In the following decades, as countries began transitioning from authoritarianism to democracy, researchers began incorporating more perpetrator narratives, trying to understand the motivations for their actions. From such academic endeavors, Arendt and scholars researching perpetrator narratives from Latin America to South Africa discerned a pattern where many of the individuals in these crimes were "acting" in a bigger scheme. Behind their actions, most of the perpetrators often thought of themselves not as brutish violators of human rights but rather as fulfilling their "duty." As Payne (2020) states, ". . . they seem to emerge from a particular kind of socialization that convinced perpetrators to carry out abuses in the first place" (p. 132). Or that even under "normal" circumstances they would present themselves, ". . . as the good spouse, parent, neighbour, friend, making it unimaginable that they could commit atrocity . . . ." And that ". . . we are constantly surprised when they do not appear in that gruesome image" (Payne, 2020, p. 134).

Perpetrators are in this sense playing specific roles required of them under specific "ideological state apparatuses," appearing to be just as "normal" as other functioning individuals under such regimes. However, as the New Order meta-narrative erodes, the perpetrators' role as a historical actor changes as well, with the Indonesian landscape becoming awash with an increasingly diverse set of narratives. For researchers this means accessing a greater amount of information in what has been a "silenced" event in Indonesian history. Therefore films, documentaries, and interviews with these perpetrators give academics greater reach in understanding the dynamics of the killings and more importantly its effects. Audiences then face ageing killers ruminating and dealing with the consequences of their past crimes. It is here that we are confronted with grisly confessions of how to kill, efficiently described in detail by elderly ageing men. What is fascinating however is that these killers are engaging in new roles, repenting for their past crimes, shedding tears for their victims. This has been an issue of contention and a major source of criticism of Oppenheimer's work, with some researchers accusing the auteur of "humanizing" what are essentially criminals.[2] The moral hazard in doing so creates the possibility of perceiving these perpetrators to be "just like us," thus running the risk of deemphasizing the suffering of the victims. Nevertheless, many other scholars have advocated engaging with them to better understand the dynamics underlying their actions (Straus, 2017; Schmidt, 2017). Prompted by this I look at the notion of space and intimacy shared by both victim and perpetrator. This close, intimate space, even in the aftermath of the killings, continues to define the relationship between victim and perpetrator, shaping the present in which they live in.

Deutsch and Yanay (2016) state that ". . . intimacy is a complex psychic reality with at least two different and conflicting yet connected passions. Intimacy can arouse hate as much as love, horror of the other as much as desire, working not as an either/or pendulum movement but simultaneously and at once" (p. 22). What leads to violence lies in the fact that ". . . intimacy can arouse (particularly in men) a killing rage in cases of feeling extreme dependency, crises of masculine identity or a loss of control over the other" (p. 23).

In Bali, many of the family members of victims continued to live among their victimizers, giving rise to conditions where the former remained in constant fear of the latter. Therefore intimacy, closeness, was an inherent condition during and even after the events of 1965, cemented by silence and also denial. For decades the destruction of the PKI and the violence meted out against individuals associated with the PKI was a foundational national discourse that justified a more than three-decade-long authoritarian regime. Silence was a part of the institutional makeup of the Suharto's New Order regime. Despite how unspeakable the events might seem, the scale of the killings left behind hauntological legacies that ". . . might start with a feeling that there is something more to say, and with a feeling that there is something more to say, and with the feeling of being unsettled or wanting to unsettle" (Blackman, 2015, p. 27). Can this silence be expressive of something deeper? Can the silence speak? Here I state these silences are ". . . disclosed in atmospheres, fleeting fragments and traces, gut feelings and embodied reactions and in felt intensities and sensations" (p. 25). Because the physical

---

[2] An extensive and diverse set of viewpoints were set out in a special edition of *Critical Asian Studies,* "Indonesia Roundtable: The Act of Killing," vol. 46, no. 1 (2014).

violence was ultimately over bodily control and domination, victims were often cowed into silence, but the muteness surrounding the killings spilt over into the realm of the unspoken and of bodily reactions.

Affectivity

Returning to Igreja's (2019) research on post-conflict Mozambique, he points to the close relationship spirits and humans have transitioning from war to peacetime. In his close study of one village, spirits of those who died in the country's civil war return to possess those supposedly responsible for their deaths, thus mitigating guilt and responsibility. Memories of wars past then, specifically the war dead, literally invade the bodies of the living, becoming physical embodiments of the suffering and the atrocities committed. In that sense, as these possessions take place, the body becomes a centerpiece of past and present as it struggles to reflect the ruptured social ties within that given society.

The aftereffects of these conflicts and wars run so deep that in the case of Mozambique, the state was structurally unable to deal with it. This leaves faith healers to mitigate the psychological fallout from decades-long violence as they attempt to "exorcise" the spirits of conflicts from their human hosts. In many of these post-conflict societies, specialized spirit healers are important as they access familiar local vocabularies' attempts to mend scarred psyches. But what is also equally fascinating is Igreja's (2019) notion of embodied accountability, which refers ". . . to bodily predicaments that evolve and become crucial to initiating struggles to right wrongs related to past violations perpetrated in contexts of family and community relations. At the root of embodied accountability is a relational conception of the body and personhood . . ." (p. 784). This embodied accountability, taking shape through possessions, afflicts the body of the perpetrator as well as the perpetrators' kin. Guilt and a strong sense of complicity, therefore, is passed from one generation in visible, embodied ways, as these healers mete out a spiritual form of justice where the perpetrators and family members must reveal the scope of their actions within the context of the village. The faith healer then engages in deal-making with the spirit and leaves when it has achieved its goal. This, I believe, is a way in which "heat" is dissipated and released from the bodies of afflicted perpetrators through the theater of possession.

Close Encounters

In the literature on the killings of 1965, much work has been done on the nature of violence that occurred during the event. However there has never been a close look at the dynamics between the researcher and the *pelaku sejarah* or historical actors, which they have become so heavily engaged with. What perceptions then do these academics develop after being exposed to some of the shocking revelations made by the very people their research has come to rely on? The close psychic space shared between researcher and perpetrator, therefore, offers the possibility of revealing insights not only into the ethical issues behind such encounters but also how researchers "manage" and navigate their roles around a still deeply taboo topic in Indonesia.

In Bali where Parker (2003) based her ethnographic research, the killings were ". . . a difficult subject to research and write about. My few informants were usually either murderers, people who were complicit in murder or fearful observers" (p. 66).

She then points an accusatory finger at an entire "generation" of Balinese having perpetrated crimes against humanity and yet have ". . . resumed normal life, having gone unpunished and have been allowed to avoid taking public responsibility for their violence" (p. 66). Parker shifts between the responses of her interlocutors admitting to committing heinous acts and her own sense of morality in listening to the accounts of murder. For her their acts of extreme violence were based on a need to avenge the deaths of officers allegedly murdered by the PKI. But the scale of the ferocity and the spread of the violence is in no way commensurate with the seven deaths in Jakarta. This was for Parker ". . . a painful enigma . . ." (p. 77). While Parker explains that the violence stemmed from socioeconomic tensions inflamed by the ideological conflicts and efforts at land reforms, it should in no way absolve the murderers of their sins. She adds that macro-level explanations have ". . . an excusing effect . . ." where the ". . . individual is absolved from taking full responsibility for the inhumane act, while circumstances, society etc. are more diffusely blamed" (p. 77).

In her groundbreaking study of the 1965 killings in Aceh, Melvin's (2018) perpetrator interviewees presented her what she referred to as a "surreal" experience with former death squad leaders where she states, ". . . I also came to realise, as so many before me, quite disconcertingly at first, the humanness of such individuals. They were not monsters" (p. 77). But at the same, they spoke ". . . openly and boastfully. They considered themselves national heroes. Their greatest regret was that they had not received more recognition for their actions" (p. 18). This raises an important question as to why so many of these perpetrators continue to believe that their actions were beyond reproach. To understand this, we can also turn to the equally field-defining writings of Winward (2018), where he found that logistical limitations forced the army, specifically the RPKAD, to enlist civilians in a murderous spree. Unlike East Java where groups linked to religious organizations were already "pre-disposed" to act, the Suharto-linked RPKAD had to give the extra push by lifting both moral and legal prohibitions. Winward states that ". . . buoyed by the absence of negative consequences, and assured of additional status should they escalate their participation, members of pre-existing groups from within this community moved to organized, violent behaviour—including executions—that could only partially be controlled by the army" (p. 136). This then prompted civilian groups to pinpoint suspected PKI members to the RPKAD and to ultimately engage in the physical destruction of fellow Indonesians. How then do we reconcile the "humanness" of single individual perpetrators and the acts committed as members of a group? The unique method employed by documentary filmmaker Joshua Oppenheimer could perhaps provide answers to this question. During his foray, Oppenheimer was able to build a high level of rapport between himself and his interlocutors, whom in their younger days had been executioners who then disposed of the bodies of their victims in rubber plantations and in the many rivers that flow across the island of Sumatra. Because of his proximity to the ageing *jagal* or butchers, he was able to discern from their initial bravado a side of their personality that was hitherto hidden. Like in the case of Parker (2003) and Melvin's research, Oppenheimer's interlocutors were also of the belief that their actions were justified, with the military egging them on with the necessary "encouragement." Nonetheless the analysis needs to be pushed further in that genocide, ". . . its genesis and manifestation[,] can only be understood when boiled down to the individuals who constitute it, their actions and the relations they have to each other" (Williams, 2018, p. 18).

Oppenheimer's fieldwork enabled him to do so by embedding himself among the perpetrators he studied, turning them into his collaborators as he incorporated them into his film project. Convincing them that his film was on the success of anti-communism, his collaborators lowered their guard, exposing themselves and forcing the perpetrators to look in a mirror darkly reflecting on their past as killers. It was later revealed that their crimes continued to haunt them as they were literally followed by the vengeful spirits of their victims. Throughout his observations of these *jagal*, he was able to watch them reminisce about the role they played in the genocidal campaign that spanned across most of Indonesia. In these private moments of repose and silence, Oppenheimer was able to catch these aged killers wrestling with anxiety and the gravity of their actions. Nonetheless Oppenheimer's research/film reveals the humanness of the perpetrators struggling with their memories of sadism, murder, and massacres. Oppenheimer raises important methodological questions in his discussions of silence as a reaction among these perpetrators. This loss of speech signifies an inability to convey the complex internal negotiations ongoing within the perpetrator. In van Roekel's (2020) work among former soldiers of Argentina's Dirty War, her intimate conversations were often marked by revelatory moments of silence. These moments of repose laid bare the contradictions experienced by these soldiers as they narrated their stories in the face of a changed political environment that condemned rather than celebrated their actions, exposing uncertainties in them that can then be observed as the embodied past emerges from them.

Humanizing the Enemy

The killings were the most intense toward the later part of 1965 in the eastern half of Java. Active in the massacres was NU's multipurpose *Ansor* Front, better known as *Banser*, a sub-group within the organization that served as its "vanguard." According to a prominent NU kyai, or religious teacher, Yusuf Hasyim, who was then an *Ansor* leader, ". . . the only source of Islamic power remaining was NU's youth wing *Ansor*" (Hasyim, 2007, p. 16). NU, during that period, was an extremely influential organization with religious schools and institutions sewn deeply into the social fabric of rural East Java. Thus, the PKI was seen as an active competitor in the battle for hearts and minds, which sometimes lead to heated physical confrontations between the two groups. Hasyim (2007) states that, ". . . we believed that we had to fight fire with fire; if the Communists acted in a certain way, we had to confront them with similar tactics. From Hitler's work we learned how to counteract a threatening force by building up our own base of power. So, in this regard, *Banser* was almost the same as Hitler Youth, its name inspired by the famous Panzer divisions" (p. 17). Nevertheless, the equation for Hasyim was quite simple, ". . . one could kill or be killed." The political tensions during that period were palpable, and this was made more so by the fact that the PKI was often made out to appear foreign or unclean. This is primarily based on the alleged past crimes of the PKI and that they were "atheists." In the years following 1965, those who survived the killings spent more than a decade incarcerated as political detainees all throughout the archipelago. After their release in the later part of the 1970s, these *eks-tapol* continued to be referred to as coming from "unclean environments." It was also conveniently used by the state not only to stigmatize the *eks-tapol* but also to label anyone who opposed its policies and dictates. The binaries of clean/unclean, atheist/non-atheist, communist/non-communist formed the basis of the killings and later forms of state violence. There were to be clear distinctions based on a notion of disgust, where those in the "wrong" categories were seen as being contaminated by the communist virus and therefore to be treated as filth. They were to be constantly monitored as "latent dangers" for fear of polluting other more innocent Indonesians.

In one rare interview, an East Javanese executioner stated that his first victim was killed at the behest of a military officer. "He asked me to kill a PKI member I did not know. End this person's life without spilling a single drop of blood from his body," he said. I didn't know where the PKI member was from. Without thinking too much, I took hold of a long piece of rattan which had already been prepared. I hit the back of his neck several times. After making sure that he was dead, I dragged his body out to the beach where it would be flushed out to sea" (Samsi, 2012). Interviewed in the regency of Lumajang, Mochamad Samsi (2012) stated that he became accustomed to his "duties" during two months between the end of 1965 and 1966. "I was frequently asked to 'guard' these execution sessions. There was once some of my friends and fellow executioners encountered a PKI member who could recite Quranic verses. They became hesitant but I told them he was just pretending to escape his death. I then finished him off. This action of mine dispelled all doubt from my friends. I remembered the words of a Nahdlatul Ulama (NU) cleric: it would be wrong to kill a lizard before killing these unbelievers." The blood of unbelievers was, for this willing executioner, something meant to be spilled in a purification ritual. However, this was only one part of the repertoire. The bodies of their victims were often dumped into the sea, rivers, ravines, sinkholes, and mass graves dug deep in Java's forests.

These killing sessions, however, did not always go as planned. An individual identified only as Chambali explains that his "journey" of becoming an executioner began as a "religious calling." "From all the youths in Rengel, I was the only one willing to become an executioner, in killing PKI members. I felt that affairs with the PKI were not just over differences in ideology but that it was more like a religious war. Kill or be killed. If they were not to be killed now tomorrow, they would do the same to us. They would destroy our religion" (Chambali, 2012). Chambali (2012) was "stationed" at a nearby ravine between 70–100 meters deep. Representatives from the police, army, as well as the regent's office came to explain that their victims were enemies of the state and, on that very night, he witnessed his first killing. "In a matter of seconds, another young man slit the throat of his victim. Blood flowed heavily from his throat. The lifeless body was then pushed into the ravine. Throughout the night, the PKI men were one by one thrown into the ravine. . . . I had mixed feelings. My body was shaking, my stomach was unsettled, making me vomit. I locked myself in the house for several days" (Chambali, 2012).

On his first night as a potential executioner, Chambali (2012) was brought back to the same spot where he was to execute several PKI members who were tied and waiting at the edge of the ravine. "My hands were shaking as I placed the machete on the neck of a man who was already kneeling. And . . . serr . . . my intentions were pure . . . may Allah forgive me." But it was his memory of a particular victim on one of his excursions that remained with him. "From all of those who were executed that night there was one who escaped death. I asked him if he was Muslim and he answered yes. He answered: yes, I am Muslim. I then asked him, if you are Muslim can you recite the Islamic declaration of faith, and he recited it confidently. My body shook and the machete fell from my hand into the ravine. Those who saw this fell silent. I was then asked to leave the execution site" (Chambali, 2012). Victims or suspected PKI members were often made up of different faiths, most being Muslims, even though some were not so "devout." The "unbeliever" then reverts back to being human when told to recite Quranic verses.

The "atheist" imagery created by religious groups and the army dissipates, and the executioner's body reacts to that. Arising from this is a powerful sense of ambivalence that can be "read" from the body of the perpetrator as a kind of "embodied" text. Scarry (1987) argues that physical pain enacted through torture decimates language, allowing the torturer to "write" onto the body of the tortured whatever text is required of the regime. I state that the physical reaction arising from the executioner in a disgusted response before or even after committing the killing disrupts the regime's meta-narrative. The disgust response, I believe, follows a logic founded on a moral revulsion toward their act of killing, producing an affect deeper than the hatred of the "other." Social psychologists such as Staub (1989) have claimed executioners under Nazi rule experienced moments of intense physical discomfort when murdering their captives. However according to critics, such an argument is flawed, given that, ". . . disgust is an unreliable moral emotion because of its nature and evolutionary history. At its core disgust is a defense mechanism against toxins and disease that through our evolution came to play many roles and functions . . . the main problem with disgust is that it has a conspicuous tendency to distort and misguide our moral judgements" (Munch-Jurisic, 2014, p. 281). As such, disgust or abhorrence as an affect is not necessarily bound to morality but possibly motivates genocidal violence through revulsion or hatred of an object. Nonetheless, what I pay attention to in my paper are the moments in which the perpetrator and victim share before the death of the former. There is a pattern among executioners testing the victim's Islamic credentials by asking them to recite its declaration of faith. For both Samsi (2012) and Chambali (2012), each did so to see if their victims were true Muslims, and their ability to do so shocked them. They were in fact murdering "fellow" Muslims, and it was that moment of intimacy, as their victims spoke their final words, that momentarily ruptured the nature of their "holy war." Arising from this is a sense of physical revulsion and aversion not so much toward the murdered but rather toward the act of killing. In the next section I will feature a case study of a member of the security forces I was able to interview during the period of my fieldwork.

His Name Is W

Though 75 years of age, Pak W still struck me as strong and mobile. He moved in an animated fashion without any need for assistance and his mind was sharp and clear. My friends and I found his house within a community of retired personnel paramilitary soldiers. We were then invited to the front of his house, where we sat and began the interview properly. His home was simple and spartan but looked as if he was in the process of moving. "I will be moving away soon as my son is asking me to stay with him," Pak W said.

In the beginning, Pak W was wary and wanted to know the reason why we wanted to speak to him. After stating that we were interviewing him as part of an oral history project, he began to open up a little more in terms of talking to us. He had been a veteran of encounters in the restive province of Papua, fought in the former province of Timor

Leste, and came from a family with a long police tradition. The accommodations he had been given were compensation for the services rendered to the nation. But they were also to make way for a new headquarters building meant for the same unit he had served with. His home and that of his unit were also located 15 minutes away from a detention center meant for PKI members and another facility that had transformed from a grain storehouse to that of a prison facility. The city in which he lived was an "active hub" during the events of 1965 as a "screening center" for suspected PKI members. That a large of contingent of his unit was placed there comes as no surprise, as it was considered a major counterinsurgency unit during those years and even up until the end of the Suharto era in 1998.

During the events of 1965, he was still considered junior but was nonetheless sent out on an important mission to a site not just an hour or so from where he lived and was stationed. The site was located within a deep part of a forest in an area made up of rubber plantations that now has been turned into a nature reserve. Within a six-minute walk from the main road is a rest area where travelers feast on fruits. "That night we went out there in a truck with several of us within a unit. There were 40 prisoners who came along with us whose hand were bound together at their thumbs. Then they were marched and then told to stand in front of two pits which had already been dug. They were also tied up in a such a way that we could ensure that if one fell the others would follow," he said.

Some of the prisoners came from Ambarawa but he was unsure of where the other had come from. "We used SKS rifles and shot at them at the back of the head," he added. "We then used a machine gun to ensure that the mission was 'done.' Some of them even pleaded with me to bring some their belongings back to their families but I could not," he added. "There was even one of them whom pleaded with me saying that he had not yet been shot." While he was unfazed by all this, there were some younger members of his detail who faltered in what they were supposed to do.

Noticing a crucifix above the entrance, I then asked him if he had ever wondered if the individuals he executed on that day were bad people. "What I did that day was part of my duties, I had no other choice as it was instructed to me by the state. I have no idea over the kinds of the ideologies they had. I didn't know if they were bad, and I didn't know if they good or bad. It's just like how we are told to follow the Ten Commandments and therefore we should just do what we have been told to do as it is our duty," he stated. After completing the executions, he was asked to join an event in a village further down the road not far from the site of the execution, but he did not feel comfortable. "I could not eat anything. I felt 'hot,'" he added. When I asked him what he meant, he declined to elaborate. After the interview, I learned that, a few years back, students had approached him for an interview where it seemed that he spoke openly about what he did that night and that they had travelled to the very same spot where had executed the PKI members.

My contacts told me, however, of late that the people living in town were looking at him differently, saying things about him. Toward the end of the interview, he was more open about showing a picture of him in uniform and of the accolades he had received during his time of service. Pak W provides a fascinating study of an *aparat negara* or a state agent, whom, despite his training and even with his family background, reacting the way he did during the execution. His logic as an instrument of state carrying out his duties nevertheless did not jive with his bodily response following his actions. Even with his professional training, which differed from the bystanders and the local executioners described in the earlier parts of the paper, he also spoke of a gag reflex right after the act itself. But like the "bystanders" I showcased in the previous sections of the article, he continued to live among sites of violence that contained the memories of his actions, given the town he lived in was part of a larger ecosystem that began with "screening" and ended with death.

Bystanders

In my research, mass graves feature prominently in the stories and narratives of my interlocutors. But after 2001, there has been no reported attempt at exhumations, at least in Java. What is present, however, are intimations and indications of where a suspected mass grave is located. The only way one would know whether a particular place is a mass grave is through its use as a site of pilgrimage either for punters in their search for lottery numbers or through visits made by families believing their relatives to be buried there. In a small village on the outskirts of Central Java's provincial capital, I chanced on such a site and was also fortunate enough to find witnesses who were able to relate to me their stories. These two octogenarians were, however, responsible for burying at least 12 bodies in a mass grave two meters deep. Located in a densely wooded area, the site was a perfect place to keep a crime hidden.

Here, one of them, a Pak Sopi, explains, ". . . me and another friend of mine had to bury the dead for four hours. There were originally four of us but the other two couldn't deal with the sight, got physically sick and just went away. There was skin, bones and body parts scattered all over the place. It has also just rained heavily, so, they were everywhere." According to him, the mass graves had already been dug, and it was known among the villagers what the holes were for. He was not informed and only knew of their function when he had to work with the detritus of human parts scattered throughout the area by both bullets and heavy rain. Sopi lives a mere 15-minute walk from where the killings took place. Many years after the incident, Sopi could still hear "echoes" from the area. "I would pick corn there as I used to have a small plot of land in that area. I would go near the site to hunt for wild boar and then I would hear the sound of people laughing. I would look closer but there would be nothing. People would say to me 'wow you are courageous to go there,'" Sopi said. Now he no longer goes and does not speak of the place either to his children or grandchildren. "It would scare them," he states.

For another witness, Supir, his experiences were much more visceral. According to him, the local village leadership as well as local government and the security forces knew of the execution. Supir then was asked along with a local "tough" to watch as well as to assist. Twelve prisoners were brought to the execution site late at night. They were loosely tied to make it easier for them to be brought down from a truck and then moved over to where they were to be executed. Asked what his role was, Supir merely stated that he was responsible for holding up a flashlight. "Some of them were asked to say their last words; some were saying things to themselves; some were praying and then there was a woman who was reciting Islamic prayers. When they started, I didn't know what kind of weapon was used but it was loud, and it just kept repeating itself. Some of them didn't die immediately, like the lone woman in the group and when the fell in they kept groaning. So, the soldiers went 'dobel,'" Supir said. When pressed further what he meant by the term "dobel," it was that the soldiers "doubled" their rate of fire to ensure that the condemned were indeed dead. "Before they died some were also crying, calling out for their fathers and mothers," Supir said. When they were done, the bodies were left there to be buried by someone. When asked about what happened next, the two soldiers then asked him and his friend to share a late-night snack of *sate*, but he was unable to eat. "I couldn't eat much, and I became sick for a whole week. I could not leave the house," he added. After the event, he never went near the place again. Even during a memorialization ceremony at the site, he was only able to stand at the edges of the crowd.

The "life" of the site, as happened with Sopi, continued to stay with him. After the events, one of the two soldiers involved in the killings remained in the village and became a part of the local leadership. This soldier would continue to visit his friend and would even occasionally drop by to see him. The executioners, in their role as the "eyes and ears" of the state, continued to have a visible presence in the village, asserting its authority. The fact that both Sopi and Supir stayed their entire lives in the villages haunted by these events and living in the presence of the executioners helps explain why "changing" the New Order logic was so difficult. The presence of these executioners ensured that both victims and bystanders in the community remained silent for fear of being accused of being either communists or their sympathizers. In the years following the killings of 1965, the army adopted the *dwi fungsi* mandate that allowed it to extend into villages throughout Indonesia to "observe" and "discipline" its citizens. The role of the security forces was not external defense but social control. This power was in turn premised on the defeat and the suppression of the PKI. So, for areas where there had been executions and mass graves, silence was the only option, as speaking up would also mean being accused of being PKI. Though silenced, traces of the past remain, and these traces bind perpetrators, witnesses, and victims together.

Feeling the Heat

Rasa is an important element in the Javanese traditional notion of personhood. Akin to the Western idea of "emotion," if it were to be overwhelmed together with other elements, including *budi* (thought) and *nafsu* (passion), then a person is likely to be become unwell. To retain good health, one must be able to balance their *lahir* and *batin*, representing the inner psychic and outer physical aspects of an individual. But if an imbalance were to occur, the causes can be attributed to ". . . the accidental or intentional introduction of foreign elements into the bodies, exposure to evil or simply inappropriate types of power, the actions of spirits, passion or sorcery" (Woodward, 2011, p. 84). As Woodward (2011) further explains, ". . . most common ailments result from the presence of too great or too small a quantity of one of the elements comprising the physical body" (p. 84). Placed into the context of the Javanese worldview, the "heat" referred to by Pak W and Sopi and Supir is the "affect," which remained with them following their acts. In moments of closeness, the contact between perpetrator and even bystander caused an imbalance within the context of their personhood in Java. The affect, *rasa*, seared into their memory continues to linger decades after these events. However, the "criminogenic" structure of the Suharto regime and successive post-reform governments persisted in "normalizing" the killings. As such, perpetrators, bystanders, and victims continue to live within an environment where the anti-communist narrative has undergone little change. The physical landscape itself is a constant reflection of this bloodied past, as if forming a prison around these individuals and the communities they live in. It is not uncommon to hear of reports of possession by the spirits of the victims due in part to the "heat," which makes them more vulnerable due to ". . . accidental or intentional introduction of foreign elements into the bodies, exposure to evil or simply inappropriate types of power, the action of spirits, passion or sorcery" (Woodward, 2011, p. 84).

But just like many ailments, traditional belief systems often offer cures for such maladies. For instance, healers from the Malay peninsula provide cleansing when one's "winds" become contaminated (Laderman, 1993). Similarly Balinese dukuns return balance to the body by cooling down excess heat (Hobart, 2003). This aspect is also shared with healers in the far reaches of western Indonesia's Nusa Tenggara Timur. Like many places throughout Indonesia, the western half of the island of Timor was not spared from the violence of 1965. The killings were primarily done by groups associated with the churches in Timor as well as local police units.

In the works of Kolimon (2015), herself being the descendant of a perpetrator, she describes how decades after the killings of 1965, the effects remain with those complicit in the massacre. Based on research conducted in the province of Nusa Tenggara Timor, she states that in her interviews, these perpetrators continued to feel guilt over their actions. Even though the perpetrators were certain that PKI members were prepared to murder them, they nonetheless wanted to cleanse the "heat" that arose from their murderous actions. Some of these perpetrators chose "traditional" means or sought comfort in the church, as they ". . . felt that he had done something against the will of God." (Kolimon, 2015, p. 45) Kolimon adds, ". . . even though the New Order indoctrination sought to construct a positive image of them as being warriors, they were nonetheless wrought with guil . . . . however, because of an unsupportive political situation, that sense of guilt was unable to give rise to actions such as apologies, the rehabilitation of the victims and reconciliation between the victim and perpetrator. Therefore, the perpetrator continues to live in guilt and cannot be freed from their psychic burden." (p. 46). Kolimon's father served as a member of the local constabulary, and his role as a perpetrator began when handed a list of names of suspected communists he was tasked with arresting. After the arrests, he was then ordered to execute his captives and to dispose of their bodies into a mass grave the condemned had dug themselves. According to Kolimon, ". . . my father believed that he was serving the nation by doing all this. He was proud of his actions." Nevertheless, Kolimon spoke also about the trauma felt by herself and her family as the heat from his actions followed him home. She states, "trauma is not only felt by the victims but also by the perpetrators and their family. We have to learn to deal with this trauma. We have seen how returning war veterans do not have space to tell their stories. Therefore, they are more prone to acting violently within this environment. I have experienced it myself. I have seen how easily he can be triggered, and we end becoming victims of violence." The affect of these violent acts often flows to the following generation in the most intimate ways. Since there is no way for the perpetrator to "exteriorize" the memory of their acts, in the case of Kolimon, the violence is reenacted again and again on the younger generation. The interior space of the family provides the only output for violent memories past, in the absence of a larger public "theater".

In comparison, Argentina's transition has also been caught in the grip of a "pact of silence" where discussions about the role of perpetrators in its "Dirty War" continue to be avoided. However, several descendants of perpetrators have embarked on "confessional" journeys in navigating the waters of the past and unearthing hitherto buried family secrets through the genre of documentary. Zylberman (2020) states in his study that descendants did so as a way to reflect on the contradictory presence of a loving grandfather who, at the same time, was complicit in human rights violations. Another documentary, Zylberman states, is prompted by the abuse suffered at the hands of a father bringing the violence home in the wake of torture and killings. Here I state that bringing this issue out into the open is possibly not allowing the effects of the past to fester in the private lives of those within these families. The intimacy of violence between perpetrator and victims can cast a shadow over the immediate surroundings of the family.

In a study of the descendants of political victims, Leong (2021) states that the enclosed space of the family often becomes claustrophobic and oppressive, leaving behind scars and then becoming part of a mnemonic DNA handed down to the following generation. This could possibly be why there has been a number of confessionals appearing in Indonesia in the past few years written by the descendants of former political prisoners (Sukanta, 2016; Marching, 2017). When suppressed, it would appear that they would want their experiences of having suffered trauma and pain to be revealed to the world, to make the private and the intimate public. This is also similarly so for Kolimon (2012) and the descendant of another perpetrator, also from West Timor, in a documentary produced in Indonesia. As Indonesia democratizes, these marginalized groups become intent on being "seen," performing their liminality in many different forms ranging from puppet theater (Lis, 2018) to choir groups (Hearman, 2016). While it is not the intent of this paper to delve into the theoretical aspects of performativity, it nevertheless does attempt to understand why individuals or even groups need to bring private intimate aspects of their lives into the public. I will proffer an analytical viewpoint in the next section of this paper.

While there is an apparent lack of will in dealing with the killings of 1965 at the macro level, it is interesting to note that under the Indonesian government's auspices, a "caring program" or *program peduli* was initiated in communities affected by the 1965 killings. By incorporating local notions of "cooling" in the eastern Indonesia regency of Sikka, the program brought together groups still haunted by the legacy of the violence under rituals known as *gren*. Descendants and the communities they live in, through *gren*, account for the past as well to "placate" the land, which still hides remains of those killed that year. Its report states that, ". . . the ritual is to cool the land. It must be done because the land on which these ritual communities reside on have seen much violence and bloodshed especially amongst families. The violence was said to have left behind an 'angry' environment causing drought, disease and failed crops" (Sunarno, 2020, p. 27). Of the three different *gren* rituals carried out, one was conducted by a man suffering from the guilt from his father's role as a killer. The report states, ". . . here the narration on the 65/66 incident entered the fray and became the main focus. A son, whose father in the past had killed suspected PKI members, suffered from pains, disease, an unbalanced state of mind and bad crops" (p. 27).

Physical and bodily manifestations of the past necessitated communal rituals of confessions and interaction with the land, which in turn "enacted" a performance for events unspoken of for more than five decades. Thus, bodily affects in a sense created a bridge into a liminal historical epoch, allowing access to the muted expression of guilt and shame. The body politic, which held the New Order in place and which, to a certain extent, continues to exist in present Indonesia, is slowly having to give way to the affect felt by not only victims but also perpetrators if not their descendants. Affect, according to one definition, ". . . arises in the midst of *in-betweenness:* in the capacities to act and to be acted upon" (Seigworth & Gregg, 2010, p. 1). By acknowledging *in-betweenness* thus labels such "communist/atheist," "perpetrator/victim" begins then to lose it binary power, which have for so long left communities and individuals trapped among the ghosts of the past. From this arises potentially a politics of sights, with the need to be seen or the need to have certain experiences among marginal groups in Indonesia to engage in a politics of sight. Developed during his time conducting research in a slaughterhouse, Pachirat (2011) states that the politics of sight concerns ". . . organized, concerted attempts to make visible what is hidden and to breach, literally or figuratively, zones of confinement in order to bring about social and political transformation . . ." (p. 236).

Conclusion

Post-*reformasi* Indonesia has been dominated by contestations through performances vying for attention among a national audience in a landscape that is no longer dominated by a single overarching metanarrative. This is akin to Indonesian historian Asvi Adam Warman's concept of a "straightened history," where multiple historical universes exist in consonance with each other. Even if such narratives might appear morally disagreeable, attention to bystander narratives and even those who played a direct role in the murder of suspected PKI members are important. The intimate last moments these individuals shared with the dying left an indelible mark on them, affecting those in the following generations. Therefore, there is an important need to acknowledge the impact decades of silencing has had on them. Within their narratives are perhaps what we can discern to be tentative steps in making visible that the violence of 65/66 affected all in deep ways. Ways that then seek release, through telling or even through rituals. We must, however, be quick to realize that these rituals are not necessarily similar to the many attempts at truth and reconciliation processes "required" in transitional justice processes. Nonetheless, paying close attention to affectivity, emotions, and the workings of the intimate world will give us greater insight perhaps into eroding decades of silence. As Indonesia celebrates another *Hari Pancasila Sakti*, it becomes more obvious that there needs to be a serious retelling of its story if it is to end the strangle of ghosts' pasts on its imagination.

References

Affan, H. (2015, October 1). Jumat Pagi Bersama "algojo pemburu" PKI. BBC. https:// www.bbc.com/indonesia/berita_indonesia/2015/10/150922_indonesia_lapsus _penolakanmasyarakat
Anderson, K., & Jessee, E. (2020). *Researching perpetrators of genocide.* University of Wisconsin Press.

Arendt, H. (2006). *Eichmann in Jerusalem: A report on the banality of evil.* Penguin Classics.

Blackman, L. (2015). Researching affect and embodied hauntologies: Exploring an analytics of experimentation. In B. T. Knudsen & C. Stage (Eds.), *Affective methodologies: Developing cultural research strategies for the study of affect* (pp. 25–44). Springer.

Bøndergaard, J. H. (2017). *Forensic memory: Literature after testimony.* Springer.

Buckley-Zistel, S. (2006). Remembering to forget: Chosen amnesia as a strategy for local coexistence in post-genocide Rwanda. *Africa, 76*(2), 131–150.

Bultman, D. (2020). Evidence and expert authority via symbolic violence: A critique of current knowledge production on perpetrators. *Journal of Perpetrator Research, 3*(1), 2017–213.

Canet, F. (2020). Introductory reflections on perpetrators of crimes against humanity and their representation in documentary film. Continuum: *Journal of Media and Cultural Studies, 34*(2), 159–179.

Chambali. (2012, October). Orang itu lancar mengucap syahadat. *Tempo, 1–7,* 68–69.

Deustch, D., & Yanay, N. (2016). The politics of intimacy: Nazi and Hutu propaganda as case studies. *Journal of Genocide Research, 18*(1), 21–39.

Ferrandiz, F., & Robben, A. C. G. M. (Eds.). (2015). *Necropolitics, mass graves and exhumations in the age of human rights.* University of Pennsylvania Press

Fujii, L. A. (2009) *Killing neighbour: Webs of violence in Rwanda.* Cornell University Press.

Goffman, E. (1986). *Frame analysis: An essay on the organisation of experience.* Northeastern University Press.

Hasyim, Y. (2007). Killing communists. In J. McGlynn & H. Sulistiyo (Eds.), *Indonesia in the Soeharto Years: issues, incidents and images* (pp.16–17). KITLV Press.

Hearman, V. (2016). Hearing the 1965-66 Indonesian anti-communist suppression: Sensory history and its possibilities. In J. Damousi & P. Hamilton (Eds.), *A cultural of sound, memory and the senses* (pp. 142–156). Routledge.

Hobart, A. (2003). *Healing performances of Bali between darkness and light.* Berghahn Book.

Igreja, V. (2019). Negotiating relationships in transition: War, famine and embodied accountability in Mozambique. *Comparative Studies in Society and History, 61*(4), 774–804.

Knittel, C. S., & Goldberg, Z. (Eds.). (2020). *The Routledge international handbook of perpetrator studies.* Routledge.

Kolimon, M. (2015). Para Pelaku Mencari Penyembuhan: Berteologi Dengan Narasi Para Pelaku Tragedi '65 di Timor Barat. *Jurnal Ledalero, 14*(1), 34–59.

Kolimon, M. (2020). *The invisible heroes: Warisan memori 65* [Video]. Narasi TV. https://www.youtube.com/watch?v=2tqxNa_vZsQ

Laderman, C. (1991). *Taming the winds of desire: Psychology, medicine and aesthetics in malay shamanistic performance.* University of California Press.

Leong, K.-Y. (2021). Speaking across the lines: 1965, the family and reconciliation in Indonesia. *Kritika Kultura, 37,* 6–26.

Lis, M. (2018). The history of loss and the loss of history: Papermoon puppet theatre examines the legacies of the 1965 violence in Indonesia. In K. E. McGregor & J. Melvin (Eds.), *The Indonesian genocide of 1965: Causes, dynamics and legacies* (pp. 253–268). Springer Link.

Marching, S. T. (2017). *the end of silence: Accounts of the 1965 genocide in Indonesia.* Amsterdam University Press

McGregor, K. (2012). Mass graves and memories of the 1965 Indonesian killings. In D. Kammen & K. McGregor (Eds.), *Contours of mass violence in Indonesia, 1965–1968* (pp. 234–262). NUS Press.

Melvin, J. (2018). *The army and the Indonesian genocide: Mechanics of mass murder.* Routledge.

Miller, S. (2018). Zombie communism? Democratization and the demons of Suharto-era politics in contemporary Indonesia. In K. McGregor, J. Melvin, & A. Pohlman (Eds.), *The Indonesian genocide of 1965: Causes, dynamics and legacies* (pp. 287–310). Palgrave Macmillan.

Munch-Jurisic, D. M. (2018). Perpetrator disgust: A morally destructive emotion. In T. Brudholm & J. Lang (Eds.), *Emotions and mass atrocity: Philosophical and theoretical explorations* (pp. 142–161). Cambridge University Press.

Oppenheimer, J. L. (2004). *Show of force: Films, ghosts and genres of historical performance in the Indonesian genocide* [Unpublished doctoral dissertation]. University of the Arts London.

Oppenheimer, J. L. (Director). (2012). *The act of killing*. Final Cut For Real Productions.

Oppenheimer, J. L. (Director). (2014). *Look of silence*. Why Not Productions.

Pan, R. (Director). (2003). *S-21: The Khmer Rouge death machine*. Arte France Cinema.

Parker, L. (2003). *From subjects to citizens: Balinese villagers in the Indonesian nation-state*. Nordic Institute of Asian Studies.

Pachirat, T. (2011). *Every twelve seconds: industrialised slaughter and the politics of sight*. Yale University Press.

Payne, L. A. (2020). Unsettling accounts: Perpetrators' confessions in the aftermath of state violence and armed conflict. In S. C. Knittel & Z. J. Goldberg (Eds.), *The Routledge international handbook of perpetrator studies* (pp. 130–141). Routledge.

Rochijat, P. (1985) "Am I PKI or non-PKI?" Indonesia Vol. 40 pp. 37–56

Samsi, M. (2012, October). Haram Membunuh Cicak Jika Belum Membunuh Kafir. *Tempo, 1–7*, 66.

Sanchez-Biosca, V. (2018). The perpetrator's mise-en-scene: Language, body and memory in the Cambodian genocide. *Journal of Perpetrator Research, 2*(1), 65–94.

Scarry, E. (1985). *The body in pain: The making and the unmaking of the world*. Oxford University Press.

Schmidt, S. (2017). Perpetrators' knowledge: What and how can we learn from perpetrator testimony?" *Journal of Perpetrator Research 1*(1), 85–104.

Seigworth, G. J., & Gregg, M. (2010). An inventory of shimmers. In G. J. Seigworth & M. Gregg (Eds.), *The Affect Theory Reader* (pp.1–28). Duke University Press.

Staub, E. (1989). *The roots of evil: The origins of genocide and other group violence* Cambridge University Press.

Straus, S. (2017). Studying perpetrators: A reflection. *Journal of Perpetrator Research, 1*(1), 28–38.

Sukanta, P. O. (2016). *Cahaya Mata Sang Pewaris: Kisah Nyata Anak Cucu Korban*. Ultimus.

Sunarno, N. (2020). *Membangun Jembatan Bagi Inklusi Sosial: Catatan Refleksi atas Pendekatan Kebudyaan dan Kelansiaan pada Program Peduli Pilar HAM dan Restorasi Sosial*. Indonesia untuk Kemanusiaan Melalui Program Peduli with support from the Asia Foundation.

van Roekel, E. (2020). Getting close with perpetrators in Argentina. In K. Anderson & E. Jessee (Eds.), *Researching Perpetrators of Genocide* (pp. 115–136). University of Wisconsin Press.

Williams, T. (2018). Thinking beyond perpetrators, bystanders, heroes: A typology of action in genocide. In T. William & S. Buckley-Zistel (Eds.), *Perpetrators and perpetration of mass violence: Action, motivation and dynamics* (pp. 17–35). Routledge.

Winward, M. (2018). Capture from below: Civil military relations during Indonesia's anti-communist violence 1965–66. *Indonesia, 106*, 111–136.

Woodward, M. (2011). *Java, Indonesia and Islam*. Springer.

Zylberman, L. (2020). Against family loyalty: Documentary films on descendants of perpetrators from the last Argentinian dictatorship. *Continuum: Journal of Media and Cultural Studies, 34*(2), 1–14.

Glimpses of Indonesia's 1965 Massacre through the Lens of the Census

The Role of Civilian Organizations in the Mass Anti-Communist Killings of 1965–66 in East Java

Siddharth Chandra and Teng Zhang

It is reported that thousands to millions of people, especially activists from the PKI or its affiliated organizations—or those who were suspected of being connected with them—were killed or disappeared during those incidents. Much research has covered these bloody events, but the government itself has not yet conducted an investigation or accorded the events official recognition. Nevertheless, Abdurrahman Wahid, the Chair of the PBNU, humbly and openly apologized to the families of the 1965 victims for the role of NU's Banser in the incidents.[1]

---

[1] A. Khoirul Anam, A. Zuhdli Muhdlor, Abdul Mun'im DZ., Abdullah Alawi, Ahmad Baso, Ahmad Makki, Akhmad Muhaimin Azzet, Alamsyah M. Djafar, Ali Usman, Hairus Salim HS, Hamzah Sahal, Heru Prasetia, Iip D. Yahya, M. Imam Aziz, Miftah Farid, Mukafi Niam, Nur Kholik Ridwan, Syaifullah Amin, Tri Chandra Aprianto, Ulil Adshar Hadrawi, *Ensiklopedia Nahdlatul Ulama: Sejarah, Tokoh, dan Khazanah Pesantren*. vol. 1. (Jakarta: MataBangsa and PBNU, 2014), 180. Translated from "Dilaporkan ribuan hingga jutaan orang, terutama para aktivis—atau mereka yang diduga terkait dengan—PKI dan onderbouw-nya, terbunuh atau hilang dalam peristiwa itu. Banyak penelitian yang mengungkap peristiwa berdarah ini, tetapi pemerintah sendiri belum melakukan investigasi dan menyampaikan pengakuan resmi. Meski demikian, terkait dengan

Introduction

In the early hours of October 1, 1965, seven Indonesian Army officers, including six generals, were kidnapped and assassinated. This event precipitated a regime change in Indonesia, from the Old Order ("Orde Lama"), with President Sukarno at its apex, to the New Order ("Orde Baru"), with Major General Suharto as its leader. In the months following the assassinations, the Indonesian Army emerged as the dominant political force in Indonesia, carrying out or orchestrating widespread massacres to eliminate the Indonesian Communist Party (*Partai Komunis Indonesia*, or PKI), its most potent political rival. In this campaign it was assisted by the civilian opponents of the PKI, most notably youth organizations affiliated with competing political parties. The resulting death toll, a staggering 500,000, places the Indonesian genocide in the ranks of the "largest and swiftest, yet least examined instances of mass killing and incarceration in the twentieth century."[2] The aim of this paper is to explore the role of the PKI's political rivals in the killings in East Java and spatial aspects of the PKI's resistance and response to the violence.

The violence of 1965–66 in the province of East Java is widely understood to have reflected, in part, the binary dynamics of relations between the two major cultural streams (*aliran*) in that province, the *santri* and the *abangan*.[3] Variously led or supported by the Indonesian army, *santri*-oriented organizations such as the Nahdlatul Ulama (NU) party's Gerakan Pemuda Ansor (GP Ansor or Ansor for short) and Banser (Barisan Ansor Serbaguna Nahdlatul Ulama, a subsidiary of Ansor) played a key role in the killings of their predominantly *abangan*-oriented opponents in the PKI.[4] While the army

---

peran Banser NU di dalamnya, Abdurrahman Wahid selaku Ketua PBNU, secara rendah hati dan terbuka pernah meminta maaf kepada keluarga korban 1965 tersebut." PBNU is the acronym for *Pengurus Besar Nahdlatul Ulama*, NU for Nahdlatul Ulama, and Banser for Barisan Ansor Serbaguna Nahdlatul Ulama. This statement is not entirely accurate. The government of Indonesia conducted two investigations of the killings of 1965. The first was a Factfinding Commission, Komando Operasi Tertinggi, "Laporan Resmi Komisi Pencari Fakta," Lampiran [Appendix] C, Oei Tjoe Tat. *Memoar Oei Tjoe Tat: Pembantu Presiden Soekarno*, 6th ed. (Jakarta: Hasta Mitra, 2018), 507–25. The second was the 850-page report of the National Commission on Human Rights (Komnas HAM) completed in 2012. This report has not been officially released.

[2] Geoffrey B. Robinson, *The Killing Season: A History of the Indonesian Massacres, 1965–66* (Princeton: Princeton University Press, 2018).

[3] There is a large literature on the *aliran* and *aliran* relations in Java. The best-known work on the subject is Clifford Geertz, *The Religion of Java* (Chicago: University of Chicago Press, 1963). Building on this, scholars in the 1960s and 1970s connected the cleavages described by Geertz to political party affiliation. See Margo Lyon, Bases of Conflict in Rural Java, Research Monograph No. 3, Center for South and Southeast Asian Studies (Berkeley: University of California Press, 1970), 39–43; Rex Mortimer, "The Indonesian Communist Party and Land Reform 1959–1965," *Monash Papers on Southeast Asia*, no. 1 (1972): 13–15; Robert R. Jay, *Religion and Politics in Rural Central Java* (New Haven, CT: Yale University Press, 1963). Cultural Report Series No. 12; James L. Peacock, *Purifying the Faith: The Muhammadijah Movement in Indonesian Islam* (Menlo Park, CA: Benjamin/Cummings Publishing Company, 1978). See also Robinson, *The Killing Season*, 142, 171–73 and, for a nuanced and deep analysis of identity politics in an important NU stronghold, Robert W. Hefner, *The Political Economy of Mountain Java: An Interpretive History* (Berkeley: University of California Press, 1993), ch. 7.

[4] Scholars point out that the *santri-abangan* cleavage was not a clear-cut or static determinant of political affiliation and that *santri*-oriented political parties such as the Nahdlatul Ulama in fact gained significant following among people with *abangan* backgrounds in some locations in the aftermath of the destruction of the Communist Party of Indonesia in 1965–66. See, for example, Robin Bush, *Nahdlatul Ulama and the Struggle for Power within Islam and Politics in Indonesia* (Singapore: Institute of Southeast Asian Studies, 2009), 19. However, the syncretistic approach to religion associated with the *abangan aliran* was also identified with the more secularist political parties, including the PKI. See, for example, Hefner, *The Political Economy*, 193;

led the charge in many instances and places, it is difficult to imagine that the scale at which the killings occurred could have been possible without the active involvement of a considerable segment of the civilian population. As Douglas Kammen and Katharine McGregor point out, in East Java, "much depended on the initiative of lower-level military officers and civilian forces, in particular Nahdlatul Ulama."[5] According to Leslie Palmier, ". . . the killing of PKI followers, or alleged followers, was mainly at the hands not of the Army, but of fellow-villagers."[6] Indeed, in his pioneering work, Robert Cribb mentions the role of "civilian vigilantes, most commonly drawn from youth groups associated with anti-communist political parties. Of these the Muslim youth group Ansor, affiliated with the Nahdatul Ulama, is reported to have played the greatest role,"[7] and "a majority of these [victims] perished at the hands of NU and Ansor members."[8] In addition, the "Report from East Java," published in the journal *Indonesia*, suggests that ". . . much of the initiative in the suppression was seized by the people, with the Religious groups taking the lead."[9] Of these groups "[t]he NU has been very dominerend [*sic*] [D: dominant] in these actions of the People, even to the point of "over-confidence" [E] and ignoring other parties."[10] Harold Crouch makes a distinction between towns and villages:

> Although the army usually had control of operations in the towns, religious leaders in the villages were encouraged to take their own measures. Most commonly the lead was taken by the kiyais (religious teachers) and ulamas (religious scholars) affiliated with the NU, who mobilized students from their *pesantren* (religious schools) to drag Communists, members of pro-PKI organizations, and suspects from their homes and take them to riverbanks where their throats were cut and their bodies thrown into the river. Members of the Ansor youth organization moved from area to area inciting Muslims to exterminate "atheists". . . . In some villages the massacre even extended to children . . .[11]

Of particular interest are the areas, such as Kediri, where there was a strong *pesantren* tradition and "the actions [took] the form of 'joint action' [E] between the people and

---

Peacock, *Purifying the Faith*, 94, in which "syncretistic" and "communist" are used as compound descriptors; *Muslim Puritans: Reformist Psychology in Southeast Asian Islam* (Berkeley: University of California Press, 1978), 202; Herbert Feith, *The Decline of Constitutional Democracy in Indonesia* (Ithaca, NY: Cornell University Press, 1962), 359; and Bush, *Nahdlatul Ulama and the Struggle for Power*, 8–10. Recent scholarship has problematized the *santri-abangan* dichotomy, pointing out the historical contingency of the concept. Examples of such scholarship include M. C. Ricklefs, "The Birth of the Abangan," *Bijdragen tot de taal-, land- en volkenkunde / Journal of the Humanities and Social Sciences of Southeast Asia* 162, no. 1 (2008): 35–55; and Abdul Mughits, "Berakhirnya Mitos Dikotomi *Santri-Abangan*," *Millah: Jurnal Studi Agama* 2, no. 2 (2004): 276–88, https://journal.uii.ac.id/Millah/article/view/7024/6252.

[5] Douglas Kammen and Katharine McGregor, eds., *The Contours of Mass Violence in Indonesia, 1965–1968* (Singapore: NUS Press, 2012), 16–17.

[6] Leslie Palmier, *Communists in Indonesia* (Garden City, NY: Anchor Books, 1973), 263.

[7] Robert Cribb, "Problems in the Historiography of the Killings in Indonesia," in *The Indonesian Killings of 1965–1966: Studies from Java and Bali*, ed. Robert Cribb (Clayton, Australia: Monash University Centre of Southeast Asian Studies, 1990), 26.

[8] Gregory Fealy, "Ulama and Politics in Indonesia: A History of Nahdlatul Ulama, 1952–1967" (PhD diss., Monash University, 1998), 252.

[9] "Report from East Java," *Indonesia* 41 (1986): 136.

[10] "Report from East Java," 137.

[11] Harold Crouch, *The Army and Politics in Indonesia* (Ithaca: Cornell University Press, 1988), 152.

the army."[12] This role is also captured in the entry, quoted at the beginning of this paper, in A. Khoirul Anam's *Ensiklopedia Nahdlatul Ulama*.[13] In the above context, there is an ongoing debate about the degree to which the army on one hand and the NU and its affiliated organizations on the other played a role in the killings. The consensus seems to be that the degree to which one or both organizations participated in the killings in East Java at any point in time varied by location as well as the strength and motivation of each organization in each location at that point in time.[14] Identifying spatial variations in the violence and the factors associated with these variations can, therefore, contribute to our understanding of this balance of involvement.

The aim of this paper is to explore (1) the relationship between the scope and intensity of the violence in East Java and the organizational strength of the key civilian organization in opposition to the PKI, the Nahdlatul Ulama party, and (2) spatial evidence of the PKI's resistance and response to the violence perpetrated against it. Specifically, we ask whether there is evidence of a systematic relationship between the locations of *pesantren*, which formed the organizational foci of NU, Ansor, and Banser, and estimates of one-time population change (usually loss, but occasionally gain) associated with the 1965–66 killings of members of the PKI, its affiliated organizations, and others. Following this we ask what this relationship tells us about the dynamics of the killings and their sequelae. And finally, we look for spatial evidence of the PKI's resistance and response to these events. In order to answer these questions, we use estimates of the intensity of violence in the different *kecamatan* (districts) of East Java based on census data in conjunction with data on the locations of the historically significant *pesantren*, indicative of local capacity for political mobilization against the PKI, to examine possible associations between the two variables. In addition, in order to answer the second and third questions, we complement the above analysis by comparing the various locations to which PKI remnants are known to have fled as they attempted to resist and respond to the violence with the locations of these *pesantren* to identify patterns that may shed light on the dynamics between the two opposing groups.

---

[12] "Report from East Java," 141. Indeed, according to an official history of the Lirboyo *pesantren*, located in Kediri, "When the G30S/PKI event erupted, the Lirboyo *Pesantren* became a center for the struggle of the people in the ex-residency of Kediri, with 60% of the process of crushing and cleaning up of the PKI in the Kediri residency originating from the command of Lirboyo." See Muhammad Dahlan Ridlwan, *Pesantren Lirboyo: Sejarah, Fenomena, dan Legenda* (Kediri: Lirboyo Press, 2018), 124. Interestingly, this official account is seemingly contradicted by the testimonial of KH. Thohir Marzuqi, who suggests that Mahrus, the leader of Lirboyo, restrained Banser and left the crushing of the PKI to the army (Ridlwan, *Pesantren Lirboyo*, 280). See also Ahmad Ali Adhim, *Gus Maksum Lirboyo: Pendekar Pagar Nusa* (Yogyakarta: CV Global Press, 2017), 13–16.

[13] Anam et al., *Ensiklopedia Nahdlatul Ulama*, (1981), 180.

[14] For the interchangeable roles of NU and the army, as officially recorded by NU, see Choirul Anam, *Gerak Langkah Pemuda Ansor: Sebuah Percikan Sejarah Kelahiran* (Surabaya: Majalah Nahdlatul Ulama AULA, 1990), 92; and H. Abdul Mun'im DZ, *Benturan NU PKI 1948–1965* (Jakarta: Langgar Swadaya, 2013), 115. The latter account of the killings aligns with Anam et al., *Ensiklopedia Nahdlatul Ulama*, in its presentation of the actions of Gerakan Pemuda (GP) Ansor, the youth wing of NU, as being independent of the leadership of NU, thereby appearing to absolve the NU leadership at the time of responsibility. However, in an earlier work, Anam suggests a close connection between NU and GP Ansor during the planning and execution of the killings (Anam, *Gerak Langkah Pemuda Ansor*, 91–98). For a history of GP Ansor that almost completely omits an account of the role of GP Ansor in the killings, see Erwien Kusuma, *Yang Muda Yang Berkiprah* (Bogor: Kekal Press, 2012). The title of this book can be translated as "the young who participate (activists)."

Background

The existing literature on the violence in East Java is replete with references to the role of Nahdlatul Ulama and its ancillary youth organizations, Ansor and Banser, in the killings. This dynamic grew out of long-standing antipathy between the PKI and NU, which, as the two political parties with the largest following in the province in the late 1950s, found themselves increasingly locked in competition with each other for political power.[15] This mutual antagonism was exacerbated by the passage of the 1960 Basic Agrarian Law on September 24, 1960, described as "arguably the most important piece of legislation after the Indonesian constitution."[16] The 1960 law imposed a ceiling on the size of land holdings that individuals could own, with provision for the redistribution of surplus lands and efforts by the government to ensure that every family would own at least two hectares of land.[17] When the implementation of the land reform did not proceed as desired by the PKI and its supporters, members of the PKI and its affiliated organizations, most notably the BTI (Barisan Tani Indonesia, or Union of Indonesian Farmers), carried out a series of *aksi sepihak* (unilateral actions), which aimed to seize surplus lands from large landowners and redistribute them to the poor farmers who formed the BTI membership.[18] Embedded within the overarching dynamics that pitted the NU against the PKI in East Java was the specific problem of land ownership—it was not uncommon for spiritual leaders of the *pesantren* (the *kyai*) and their families to rank among the large land owners.[19] Unsurprisingly, then, the *aksi sepihak* of the early 1960s placed PKI-affiliated organizations in direct confrontation with the leadership of the key politico-religious organizations in the province, creating the tinder for the conflagration that was to follow.[20]

The spark that led to the mass violence was the subsequent September 30/October 1, 1965 kidnapping and assassination of the senior-most generals of the Indonesian Army.

---

[15] For detailed lists of incidents preceding the 1965 killings, see Mortimer, "The Indonesian Communist Party," 48–59; Greg Fealy and Katharine McGregor, "East Java and the Role of Nahdlatul Ulama in the 1965–66 Anti-communist Violence," in *The Contours of Mass Violence in Indonesia, 1965–68*, ed. Douglas Kammen and Katharine McGregor (Honolulu: University of Hawai'i Press, 2012), 110.

[16] Anton Lucas and Carol Warren, eds. 2013. Land for the People (Athens, OH: Ohio University Press, 2013), 2. See also Rex Mortimer, *Indonesian Communism under Sukarno* (Ithaca, NY: Cornell University Press, 1974), 284–328.

[17] Lyon, *Bases of Conflict in Rural Java*, 39–43; Gerrit Huizer, "Peasant Mobilization and Land Reform in Indonesia," I.S.S. Occasional Papers, Institute of Social Studies, The Hague, 1972, 32–33; Mortimer, "The Indonesian Communist Party," 13–15; Lucas and Warren, *Land for the People*, 3.

[18] For a more detailed list of the aims of the *aksi sepihak*, see Lyon, *Bases of Conflict in Rural Java*, 53.

[19] Fealy and McGregor, "East Java and the Role of Nahdlatul Ulama," in *The Contours of Mass Violence in Indonesia, 1965-68*, 112.

[20] See Robert Cribb, "Introduction: Problems in the Historiography of the Killings in Indonesia," in *The Indonesian Killings of 1965–1966: Studies from Java and Bali*, ed. Robert Cribb (Clayton: Monash University Centre of Southeast Asian Studies, 1990), 21–22; Lyon, *Bases of Conflict in Rural Java*; Jacob Walkin, "The Moslem-Communist confrontation in East Java, 1964–1965," Orbis 12 (1969): 822–47; W. F. Wertheim, "From Aliran to Class Struggle in the Countryside of Java," *Pacific Viewpoint* 10 (1969): 1–17; "Indonesia Before and After the Untung Coup," Pacific Affairs 39, no. 1–2 (1966): 124; Nathaniel Mehr, *"Constructive Bloodbath" in Indonesia: The United States, Britain and the Mass Killings of 1965–66* (Nottingham: Spokesman Books, 2009), 48–50; *Aminuddin Kasdi, Kaum Merah Menjarah: Aksi Sepihak PKI/BTI di Jawa Timur 1960–1965* (Yogyakarta: Jendela, 2001); Robinson, The Killing Season, 144–46; Ulf Sundhaussen, *The Road to Power. Indonesian Military Politics 1945–1967* (Kuala Lumpur: Oxford University Press, 1982), 216.

The position of the army high command, communicated by means of a vigorous media campaign, was that the assassinations had been carried out in a coordinated manner by the PKI.[21] *Santri* organizations, including those formerly associated with the then-banned Masyumi Party and the NU itself, wasted no time in aligning with the army and advocating a ban on the PKI.[22] In order to mobilize the politico-religious opponents of the PKI, the army cast PKI members as "anti-religion" and "anti-god," exhorting religious people to take up arms against the communists: "The sword cannot be met by the Koran … but must be met by the sword. The Koran itself says that whoever opposes you should be opposed as they oppose you."[23] On the same date, October 8, 1965, opponents of the PKI at a rally in Jakarta called for a *Djihad* (Holy War) against the communists.[24] In the subsequent months and years, this antipathy was to be manifested in a variety of ways. For example, the NU also adopted as a goal the crushing (*penumpasan*) or destruction (*penghancuran*) of the PKI and its affiliated organizations, advocated by the army.[25] Later, a group of NU leaders, led by K. H. Munasir Ali and K. H. Yusuf Hasyim, collected signatures in support of the dissolution of the PKI because of its alleged involvement in the 1965 "coup."[26] As Gregory Fealy and Katharine McGregor conclude, "the weight of historical evidence indicates that NU was an active, rather than passive, participant in the slaughter of communists," "in many areas, *ulama* and *santri* needed little encouragement to begin violent action," "NU's involvement in destroying the PKI was planned and overseen by its central leadership," NU's leadership fomented "among grassroots groups a sense of lethal danger about communism," and "it is difficult to sustain the argument that NU was manipulated by the military into launching the bloodshed."[27]

Indeed, according to the aforementioned "Report from East Java," "[t]he NU forms the vanguard of the movement to crush the PKI and its mass organizations,"[28] and the NU's "reele potentie [D: latent, potential power] in fact lies in its *Pesantren*, which are

[21] See Michael van Langenberg, "Gestapu and State Power in Indonesia," in *The Indonesian Killings of 1965–1966*, ed. Robert Cribb (Clayton: Monash University Centre of Southeast Asian Studies, 1990), 47–49; Robinson, *The Killing Season*, 163–71.

[22] Masyumi was one of the two major Islamic political parties in East Java, the other being NU. Established in 1945, Masyumi was active until it was banned by President Sukarno in 1960. Donald Hindley, "Alirans and the Fall of the Old Order," *Indonesia* 9 (1970): 41.

[23] Stephen Sloan, *A Study in Political Violence: The Indonesian Experience* (Chicago: Rand McNally & Company, 1971), 72; "Editorial," *Angkatan Bersenjata*, October 8, 1965, quoted in Mehr, "Constructive Bloodbath," 40.

[24] Sloan, *A Study in Political Violence*, 72. See also Ulf Sundhaussen, *The Road to Power. Indonesian Military Politics 1945–1967* (Kuala Lumpur: Oxford University Press, 1981), 216. This characterization was later borne out in reports on the killings. For example, according to a confidential telegram from the US consulate in Surabaya, "… reportedly killings here in East Java have coloration of Holy War: killing of Infidel supposed to give ticket to heaven and if blood of victim rubbed on face path there even more assured." Henry L. Heyman, United States Foreign Service Telegram, Surabaya Consulate. Control No. 930A. November 26, 1965.

[25] For a detailed account of the development of the NU's position, see Gregory Fealy, "Ulama and Politics in Indonesia: A History of Nahdlatul Ulama, 1952–1967" (PhD diss., Monash University, 1998), 246–56.

[26] See Anam et al., *Ensiklopedia Nahdlatul Ulama*, 31. See also, for example, H. Mochamad Saleh, M. Abd. Aziz Dja'far, and Moch. Sarkoen, "Surat Partai Nahdlatul Ulama Wilajah Djawa-Timur No. 956/C/Tanf/VII-67," p. 2, 1967, in *Turunan* (Magetan: Sekretariat Pemerintah Daerah *Kabupaten Magetan Djawa-Timur*, 1970).

[27] Gregory Fealy and Katharine McGregor, "Nahdlatul Ulama and the Killings of 1965–66: Religion, Politics, and Remembrance," *Indonesia* 89 (2010): 59–60.

[28] "Report from East Java," 142.

under the leadership of seven large *Pesantren*."[29] The report goes on to name the *kyai* who played leadership roles in the move to destroy the PKI, highlighting the importance of the *pesantren* at Jombang. Confirming their pivotal role, at least among the neighboring *kabupaten*, Fealy and McGregor mention Jombang as a gathering place for NU leaders from Bangil, Bojonegoro, Madiun, and Pasuruan as they attempted to obtain external assistance in carrying out the killings in their respective regions.[30] Further, "the orders [to kill] came from *kiai*, especially those in the NU."[31] The degree to which these actions were coordinated with the army in some locations is also questionable: according to Ken Young, the NU affiliate Ansor in Pasuruan, for example, "did not wait on outside encouragement to act."[32]

It should be mentioned here that NU was not the only politico-religious organization that advocated for the destruction of the PKI and its allies. The more urban politico-religious Muhammadiyah organization, albeit not as powerful as the NU in East Java, was also being mobilized as shown by the messaging coming from its leadership:

> . . . it is true for Muhammadiyah, together with (the leaders) of its youth movement . . . by putting their trust in Allah, issuing this statement: THE CRUSHING OF THE GESTAPU / PKI AND NEKOLIM IS WORSHIP. . . . This worship is not only religiously sanctioned but is mandatory, it is even obligatory . . . And because this action and struggle must be done by consolidating our strengths, both mentally, physically and materially, therefore these actions and struggles are no less than a JIHAD.[33]

---

[29] "Report from East Java," 142–43.

[30] Fealy and McGregor, "East Java and the Role of Nahdlatul Ulama," 122.

[31] Fealy and McGregor, "East Java and the Role of Nahdlatul Ulama," 122–23. This assertion is supported by personal accounts as well. For example, Mochamad Samsi, a Banser member from Lumajang who acted as an executioner recalls: "I remembered the words of an NU cleric: 'you are not a real Muslim if you do not want to crush PKI members' or 'it is forbidden to kill a gecko if you haven't killed these [PKI] infidels first.'" See Mochamad Samsi, "Haram Membunuh Cicak Jika Belum Membunuh Kafir," *Tempo*, October 7, 2012, 66, translated from Bahasa Indonesia. See also Katharine McGregor, "Syarikat and the Move to Make Amends for the Nahdlatul Ulama's Violent Past," Asia Research Institute Working Paper Series No. 107, National University of Singapore, 2008, 3–4. In addition, Kiai As'ad Syamsul Arifin is said to have released the fatwa "PKI itu halal darahnya, satu jenderal harus dibayar dengan 10,000 nyawa orang PKI." See Andi Rahman Alamsyah and Bayu A. Yulianto, eds., *Gerakan Pemuda Ansor dari Era Kolonial hingga Pascareformasi* (Jakarta: Yayasan Pustaka Obor Indonesia, 2018), 118. The fatwa can be translated as "Spilling PKI blood is halal [sanctioned by Muslim law]. The life of one general must be repaid with the lives of 10,000 PKI members."

[32] Ken Young, "Local and National Influences in the Violence of 1965," *The Indonesian Killings of 1965–1966: Studies from Java and Bali*, ed. Robert Cribb (Clayton, Australia: Monash University Centre of Southeast Asian Studies, 1990), 88.

[33] Abu Mujahid, *Sejarah Muhammadiyah Bagian 3: Meliberalkan Muhammadiyah* (Bandung: Toobagus Publishing, 2013), 102 Translated from ". . . adalah benar bagi Muhammadiyah, bersama dengan (para pemimpin) gerakan pemudanya . . . dengan bertawakkal kepada Allah, mengeluarkan pernyataan ini: PENUMPASAN GESTAPU/PKI DAN NEKOLIM ADALAH MERUPAKAN IBADAT. . . . Ibadat ini tidaklah hanya bersifat sunah tetapi wajib, bahkan merupakan wajib 'ain . . . Dan karena aksi serta perjuangan ini harus dilakukan dengan mengkonsolidasikan kekuatan kita, baik mental, fisik, dan material, karena itu aksi dan perjuangan ini tidaklah kurang dari suatu JIHAD." More recent evidence supports this statement. See, for example, "Muhammadiyah Plays Down Report of Its Alleged Complicity in 1965 Massacre," *The Jakarta Post*, October 18, 2017, https://www.thejakartapost.com/news/2017/10/18/muhammadiyah-plays-down-report-of-its-alleged-complicity-in-1965-massacre.html. A similar alignment of the Muhammadiyah Party and NU is observed in Medan, North Sumatra: "1. Muhammadiah source reports that preachers in Muhammadiah mosques are telling congregations that all who consciously joined PKI must be killed. 'Conscious' PKI members are classified as the lowest order of infidel, the shedding of whose blood is comparable to killing

This messaging was, furthermore, backed by action.[34] By all accounts, however, among the civilian organizations, the NU and Ansor played the leading role in the killings in the province by design. On the heels of the October 1 assassinations in faraway Jakarta, "[I]t was agreed that . . . NU would take a leading role in eradicating the PKI . . ."[35] As a final point, members of non-politico-religious organizations were also involved in the killings in East Java, though apparently in a more peripheral role.[36]

Data and Methods

In order to explore associations between the violence of 1965–66 and the strength and organizational capability of politico-religious parties in opposition to the PKI in East Java, we collected, created, and analyzed four sets of data. These included (1) estimates of the scale and severity of the violence and their spatial variation, (2) the following of the NU party, the key political party in opposition to the PKI in East Java, across the various *kabupaten* of the province, (3) the spatial distribution of key *pesantren* in East Java, indicative of the local capacity for political mobilization against the PKI, and (4) the spatial distribution of the Project Committees (*Komite Proyek* or *Kompro* for short) of the PKI, which became post-massacre destinations for people seeking refuge from the violence and for the final resistance of the PKI.[37] In this section, first, the data and measures with which the above patterns were identified are described. Next, the methods used to examine relationships among the above patterns are explained along with an overview of the dynamics that they can reveal about the violence.

The first set of data, reflecting the scale and severity of the violence, was created by computing estimates of one-time population change associated with 1965–66. For this purpose, census counts of population at the *kecamatan* level for the *kecamatan* of East Java for the censuses of 1961, 1971, and 1980, the three censuses closest in time to 1965–66,

---

chicken. 2. Comment: This appears to give Muhammadiah Muslims wide license for killing. Policy of reformist Muhammadiah very similar to 'final interpretation' issued by conservative NU . . ." American Consul in Medan, Confidential Memo CN: 184A, December 6, 1965.

[34] See Mujahid, *Sejarah Muhammadiyah*, 111, for an example of the involvement of a Muhammadiyah member in the killings. Supporting the preeminent role of the NU in the killings, prior to this account, multiple pages in the above-referenced history are devoted to the leading role that the NU and Ansor played in the killings (104–9).

[35] Vannessa Hearman, *Unmarked Graves: Death and Survival in the Anti-Communist Violence in East Java, Indonesia* (Singapore: NUS Press, 2018), 98. For a detailed account of the role of Banser, see, for example, Abdul Hamid Wilis, *Aku Menjadi Komandan Banser (Barisan Ansor Serbaguna): Membela Pancasila—Menumpas G-30-S/PKI* (Trenggalek: Public Policy Institute, 2011), ch. 4, 133–246.

[36] Wilis, *Aku Menjadi Komandan Banser*, 106. Hearman mentions the comparatively peripheral involvement of members of Partai Nasional Indonesia (PNI) in East Java as well. The PNI was far more active in the killings in the neighboring provinces of Bali and Central Java, where it had a stronger political base. See, for example, Geoffrey Robinson, *The Dark Side of Paradise: Political Violence in Bali* (Ithaca, NY: Cornell University Press, 1995); and Siddharth Chandra, "The Indonesian Killings of 1965–1966: The Case of Central Java," *Critical Asian Studies* 51, no. 3 (2019): 307–30.

[37] Formed in the aftermath of the assassinations of the generals on the night of September 30–October 1, 1965 and the subsequent mass killings of 1965–66, the *Kompro* comprised an important component of the PKI's attempt to reorganize as "PKI Gaja Baru" ("new style" PKI). The existence of these *Kompro* and the structure of the "new style" PKI was discovered by the Indonesian Army following an uptick in crime in parts of the province and the apprehension and interrogation of PKI activists who were involved in these incidents. See Semdam VIII Brawidjaja, *Trisula Operation by the 8th Regional Military Command Brawidjaja* (Surabaya: Jajasan Taman Tjandrawilwatikta, 1972), 49–54.

were used.[38] Briefly, the population counts for 1971 and 1980 were used to compute a population growth rate and trajectory for the intervening decade.[39] Next, using this computed population growth rate, the population count for 1971 was extrapolated backward in time to the beginning of 1966, yielding an estimate of the population that would have been "observed" in the aftermath of the violence based on the 1971 and 1980 census population counts obtained after the violence. Using the same population growth rate adjusted slightly upward to reflect the more rapid rate of population growth prior to 1965, the population count for 1961 was then extrapolated forward in time to late 1965 to create an estimate of the "expected" population, or population that would have been likely to have been observed just prior to the killings.[40] The difference between the "observed" (based on post-1965 censuses) and "expected" (based on the pre-1965 census) population for a location represents an estimate of the one-time change in population associated with the violence of 1965–66 in that location. While these estimates can be expected to be negative in most cases, reflecting the widespread massacres, it is possible that, due to large-scale movements of population, some *kecamatan* would register a one-time increase in population if the mobile population entering that *kecamatan* exceeded the reduction in population due to the killings or out-migration.[41] Figure 1 illustrates the method used for computing estimates of one-time loss or gain in population associated with the killings, and Figures 2a–b show the estimates on *kecamatan*- and *kabupaten*-level maps of East Java.

The second observable fact of interest is the degree of mass political support for the NU party as well as other key political parties in opposition to the PKI (the Masyumi Party and the National Party of Indonesia [Partai Nasional Indonesia, or PNI]) across the province. The two elections closest in time and prior to 1965–66 were the national elections of 1955 and the local elections of 1957. For each of these elections, we collected data on the number of votes cast for each major party, reported by *kabupaten*, and the number of seats awarded, on a proportional basis, to each major political party.[42] These figures were converted into percentages of the total votes cast (or seats won) in the *kabupaten* to produce a spatial portrait of the strength of NU (Figure 3a) and NU and Masyumi combined (Figure 3b).

---

[38] The 1961 census is the first and only census conducted by the government of independent Indonesia that had *kecamatan*-level data on East Java before 1965. For the three censuses, see Biro Pusat Statistik, *Sensus Penduduk 1961 Republik Indonesia* (Djakarta: Biro Pusat Statistik, 1962); *Sensus Penduduk, 1971* (Djakarta: Biro Pusat Statistik, 1971–1978); *Sensus Penduduk 1971. Seri E*, vol. 13 (Jakarta: Biro Pusat Statistik, 1974); Kantor Statistik Propinsi Jawa Timur, *Penduduk propinsi Jawa Timur 1980, menurut jenis kelamin, status perkawinan dan kewarganegaraan per desa: hasil pencacahan lengkap. Sensus penduduk 1980* (Surabaya: Kantor Statistik Propinsi Jawa Timur, 1982).

[39] See Siddharth Chandra, "New Findings on the Indonesian Killings of 1965–66," *Journal of Asian Studies* 76, no. 4 (2017): 1085–86. The remainder of this paragraph closely follows that appendix, which is also attached for reference as Technical Appendix 1.

[40] For details of the use of the adjustment factor, see Technical Appendix 1, footnote 95. The absence of a second pre-1965 census precluded the direct computation of the pre-1965 rate of population growth, necessitating this approach.

[41] Siddharth Chandra, "Glimpses of 1965 through the Lens of the Census: Migration and Refuge in East Java," *Indonesia* 104 (2017): 27–39.

[42] Alfian, *Hasil Pemilihan Umum 1955 Untuk Dewan Perwakilan Rakjat (D.P.R.)* (Djakarta (Jakarta): Leknas, 1971); Biro Pemilihan. *Daftar angka-angka hasil pemilihan D.P.R.D. tahun 1957–1958* (Djakarta: Biro Pemilihan, n.d.).

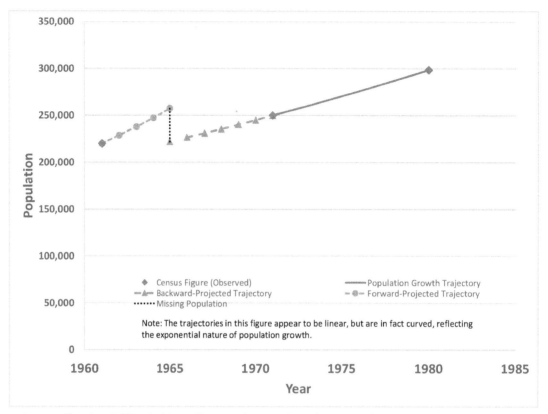

Source: Chandra, Siddharth. 2017a. "New Findings on the Indonesian Killings of 1965-66," *Journal of Asian Studies* 76(4):1056-86, Figure 1, p. 1064.

Figure 1: Illustration of the method used to compute population loss (or gain).

The third set of data reflects a more finely grained picture of the organizational strength of politico-religious opponents of the PKI in East Java by focusing on locations of the historically significant *pesantren* in the province, derived from Zamakhsyari Dhofier and listed in Table 1.[43] The *pesantren* were often co-located with branches of the youth organizations of NU, including Ansor and Banser, which have been repeatedly implicated in the killings. In addition, the *pesantren* have been associated with a high

[43] See Zamakhsyari Dhofier, *The Pesantren Tradition: The Role of the Kyai in the Maintenance of Traditional Islam in Java* (Tempe: Arizona State University Center for Asian Research, 1999), map 1, xxi. Because of the focus of Dhofier's work, the map covers the provinces of Central and East Java (with the exception of Madura). However, for the same reason, the coverage of West Java is less detailed (see Dindin Solahudin, "The Workshop for Morality: the Islamic Creativity of *Pesantren* Daarut Tauhid in Bandung, Java" [MA thesis, Australian National University, 2008], 5), and a few key *pesantren* in Madura (in Sampang, Sumenep, Pamekasan, and other locations, see H. Muhammad. Syamsuddin, *History of Madura: Sejarah, Budaya dan Ajaran Luhur Masyarakat Madura* [Bantul, Yogyakarta: Araska Publisher, 2019], 56–63) are not mentioned. In order to maintain uniformity in terms of the source and criteria for selection of the listed *pesantren*, the excluded *pesantren* of Madura were not added to the analysis. Importantly for the purposes of this paper, the results presented here remain robust to the exclusion of Madura from the analysis.

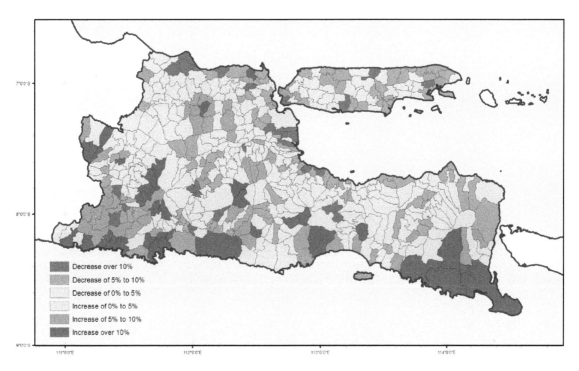

Figure 2a: Change in *kecamatan* population attributable to 1965–66.

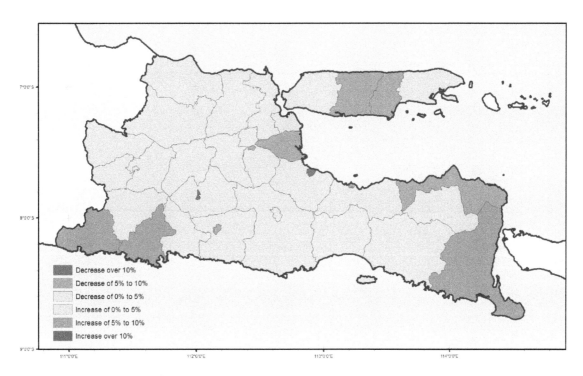

Figure 2b: Change in *kabupaten* population attributable to 1965–66.

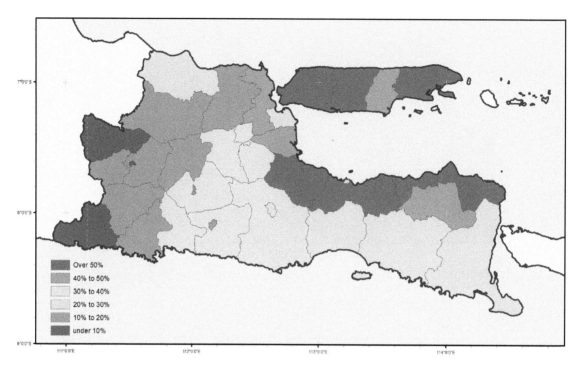

Figure 3a: Percentage of seats won by Nahdlatul Ulama (NU), 1957 election.

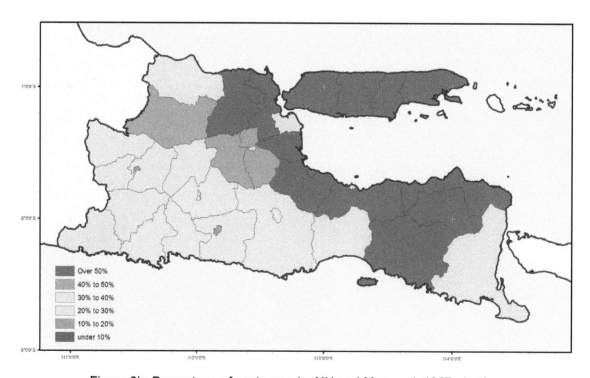

Figure 3b: Percentage of seats won by NU and Masyumi, 1957 election.

Table 1: List of *Pesantren* used in the Analysis.

Pesantren Name*	Kabupaten	Catagory**
Demangan	Bangkalan	Major
Darunnajeb	Banyuwangi	Major
Darussalam	Banyuwangi	Minor
Sedayu	Gresik	Minor
Maskumambang	Gresik	Minor
Bawean	Gresik	Minor
Jember	Jember	Minor
Tebuireng	Jombang	Major
Denanyar	Jombang	Major
Tambakberas	Jombang	Major
Rejosa	Jombang	Major
Lirboyo	Kediri	Major
Ploso	Kediri	Major
Purwosari	Kediri	Major
Lamongan	Lamongan	Minor
Lumajang	Lumajang	Minor
Malang	Malang	Minor
Mojokerto	Mojokerto	Minor
Tremas	Pacitan	Major
Pasuruan	Pasuruan	Major
Bangil	Pasuruan	Minor
Gontor	Ponorogo	Major
Probolinggo	Probolinggo	Minor
Asembagus	Situbondo	Major
Surabaya	Surabaya	Minor
Tuban	Tuban	Minor
Tuban	Tuban	Minor
Tuban	Tuban	Minor

Source: Dhofier, Zamakhsyari. *The Pesantren Tradition: The Role of the Kyai in the Maintenance of Traditional Islam in Java.* Tempe: Arizona State University Center for Asian Research, 1999.

*Where no name was provided, the name of the location (*Kabupaten*) is applied to the *pesantren*.
**Catagories as assigned by Dhofier (1999).

degree of Islamization in their respective neighborhoods,[44] suggesting the possibility of increased antipathy toward the PKI in those areas backed by a capacity for mobilization. The coordinates of these *pesantren* were located on a map and used to compute a series of locational measures on the bases of which some of the subsequent analysis was conducted (Figure 4).

While the goal of using the data from Dhofier is to capture the spatial footprint of a *"pesantren* belt," it should be noted that the *pesantren* listed in that work, displayed on the maps in this paper and used in the analysis, do not comprise the entirety of the *pesantren* in East Java at the time.[45] In fact, the number of existing *pesantren*, including the less significant and more recently established ones, was almost certainly a multiple of the number appearing in Dhofier's list. What Dhofier's *pesantren* do capture, by virtue of their historical significance and the networks within which their leadership circulated, is the spatial aspect of organizational strength of NU and ideological opposition to and potential political mobilization against rivals like the PKI. Notably, these elite *pesantren* sharply contrasted with the smaller *pesantren* that were established on the fringes of the *"pesantren* belt" in the interior of Java, for which harmonious coexistence with local (Javanist) elites and, possibly, gradual realignment in the direction of what they considered to be a proper profession of Islam were the main objectives.[46] Recognizing the key role played by military organizations in the killings, we also included a variable similar to distance from the closest major *pesantren* but reflecting proximity to district military headquarters (*Kodim*) to control for the role of the local military presence in the killings in each *kecamatan*.[47]

The fourth dataset captures the behavior of remnants of the PKI in the aftermath of the decisive reversals the party faced as the result of the 1965–66 killings. The coordinates of five *Kompro* located in East Java, identified by Indonesian military intelligence as places to which PKI members fled as the killings gathered momentum, were located on a map (Figure 4). These locations were published in a report on the military Operation Trisula, organized by the Brawijaya Regional Military Command (Komando Daerah Militer or Kodam) in East Java to root out PKI remnants in South Blitar. These data enabled analysis of the behavior of the PKI in East Java in relation to locations of strength for the NU.[48]

In order to delve into the patterns and associations of interest, two sets of analyses were conducted using the above data. The first set of analyses examined the relationship

[44] Dhofier, *The Pesantren Tradition*, 133.

[45] The notion of "two" Nahdlatul Ulamas and their spatial scope is drawn from Hefner, "Politics and Social Identity"; *Hindu Javanese: Tengger Tradition and Islam* (Princeton, NJ: Princeton University Press, 1985); "Islamizing Java? Religion and Politics in Rural East Java," Journal of Asian Studies 46, no. 3 (1987): 533–54.

[46] E-mail communication from Robert Hefner, February 16, 2020.

[47] The function of this additional "control" variable is to enable the estimation of the relationship between population change and the organizational strength of NU after taking into account (i.e., controlling for) any possible role played by a proximate military unit.

[48] See the map in *Brawidjaja, Trisula Operation*, 285. The analysis focused on the five established *Kompro* (Pandan, Blitar Selatan, K.K.A. [Kelud, Kawi, Arjuna], Semeru, and Raung-Argopuro) that were wholly located in East Java. Two *Kompro* (Kendeng and Lawu) centered across the provincial border in Central Java and a third that was not yet established (the Bendjeng Kompro, labeled *persiapan* in the map) were excluded from the analysis.

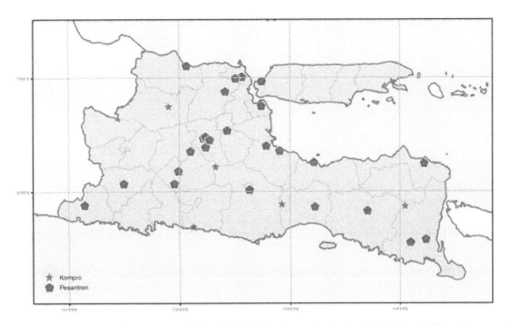

Data sources: For *Kompro*: Semdam VIII Brawidjaja. 1972. Trisula Operation by the 8th Regional Military Command Brawidjaja. Surabaya: Jajasan Taman Tjandrawilwatikta, p.285; for *Pesantren*: Dhofier, Zamakhsyari. 1999. *The Pesantren Tradition: The Role of the Kyai in the Maintenance of Traditional Islam in Java*. Tempe: Arizona State University Center for Asian Research, map 1, p.xxi.

Figure 4: Locations of historically important *pesantren* and Project Committees (*Kompro*).

between the estimated one-time change in population of a *kecamatan* attributable to the violence of 1965–66 and the organizational strength of the NU and Masyumi, the two major politico-religious parties in different places in the province.[49] For each *kecamatan*, this organizational strength was measured using two variables, the distance of each *kecamatan* from the *pesantren* closest to it (measured as the point-to-point straight-line distance between the centroid of the *kecamatan*[50] and the point location of the *pesantren*, noting that this measure emphasizes the organizational strength of NU in the neighborhood) and the share of seats won by the NU and Masyumi parties in each *kabupaten* in the 1957 election. These analyses were based on the notion that, to the extent that the politico-religious parties were hostile to the PKI and they had the following and

---

[49] While the Masyumi party had been banned in 1960, prior to the 1965 killings, it participated in the 1955 and 1957 elections. Therefore, the returns for these elections can be interpreted as an approximate indicator of the spatial distribution of support for the Muhammadiyah movement with which Masyumi's following was closely associated.

[50] The centroid of a *kecamatan* is the point inside the *kecamatan* with the "average" x (horizontal or east-west) and y (vertical or north-south) coordinates. See Wiki.GIS.com, "Centroid," 2011, http://wiki.gis.com/wiki/index.php/Centroid.

organizational means to inflict violence, locations in areas strongly supportive of these parties and in proximity to the *pesantren* would be more vulnerable to violence and, therefore, to population loss than those at a greater distance from such areas. To this end, a number of specific hypotheses were tested using both simple and partial correlation estimates.[51]

The first hypothesis test involved the relationship between support for the politico-religious parties, measured by the vote share for these parties in the 1957 election, and estimated population loss at the *kabupaten* level. The results of that test, reported elsewhere, indicated that there was indeed an association between the two variables.[52] However, since the vote shares for the politico-religious parties were measured at the *kabupaten* level, the earlier results are valid only at a very high level of spatial aggregation. There remains a need to test and validate the results using *kecamatan*-level data representing the strength of these parties to provide a more finely grained picture of this association. This study complements the prior analysis by assessing the relationship between population change at the *kecamatan* level and distance to organizational hubs for NU, represented by the neighborhood of the closest historically significant *pesantren*. If the ability to politically mobilize local communities against the PKI played a role in the severity of the violence, then we might expect to see two patterns: (1) the largest population losses in *kecamatan* in the vicinity of those organizational hubs where people were most actively involved in the killings, and (2) with increasing distance from those *pesantren*, we would expect to see diminishing losses in population (or even gains in population), which would suggest lower levels of violence with increasing distance from the hub and the kind of refuge-seeking behavior demonstrated elsewhere.[53]

To ensure that the results were robust to spatial variation in the association between organizational capacity (measured by distance from an organizational hub) and one-time population change associated with 1965–66, a geographically weighted regression (GWR) model was also estimated. The GWR model allows the relationship between one-time population changes and proximity to an organizational hub to vary depending on location. Importantly, such analysis allows for variation across hubs in the degree to which patterns of demographic change can be associated with their locations and enabling researchers to identify locations that may have been more or less closely associated with the violence than others and creating opportunities for future research.

The second set of analyses focused on a pattern that emerged in the aftermath of the killings—the relationship between the locations of the *Kompro* and the organizational hubs. The hypothesis here is that *Kompro* would be more likely to be formed the greater is the distance from the closest hub, providing a degree of protection from violence against PKI refugees by their foremost civilian political opponents. Additionally, *Kompro* would be likely to be evenly spaced across the province so as to provide greater spatial coverage as refuges and points of reorganization for fleeing PKI members and sympathizers. In

---

[51] A simple (bivariate) correlation estimate provides information about an association between two variables that is very similar to that of a simple (bivariate) regression. A partial correlation is similarly analogous to a multiple regression, which seeks to provide information about an association controlling for at least one other variable.

[52] See Chandra, "New Findings on the Indonesian Killings," Table 2, 1073; Figure 6, 1071.

[53] Chandra, "Glimpses of Indonesia's 1965 Massacre."

geographic terms, we would expect to observe spatial "repulsion" between any *Kompro* and the nearby organizational hubs for politico-religious opponents as well as between any one *Kompro* and the other *Kompro* in the province.[54]

Spatial Aspects of the Data

After compiling information on the severity of the violence, the strength of the political parties in the various *kabupaten*, locations of historically significant *pesantren*, and locations of the *Kompro*, these four sets of variables were plotted on maps to obtain an overview of spatial patterns. Figures 2a–b show estimated one-time changes in population associated with the killings at the *kecamatan* level (Figure 2a) next to a map depicting the same changes at the *kabupaten* level (Figure 2b).[55] While the basic pattern in the *kecamatan*-level map mirrors that in the *kabupaten*-level map, there are some notable points of difference. Specifically, where the *kabupaten*-level maps show a general and more aggregate pattern of greater population loss in the northern coastal *kabupaten* of the province, the *kecamatan*-level map reveals significant within-*kabupaten* variation. For example, the *kabupaten* of Tulungagung as a whole shows an estimated population loss of between 0 and 5 percent. However, the *kecamatan*-level map of Tulungagung reveals a stark difference between the *kecamatan* in the vicinity of the city of Tulungagung on the eastern side of the *kabupaten*, five of which experienced population losses in excess of 5 percent, which is consistent with large-scale violence, and the *kecamatan* in the more remote southern and western parts of the *kabupaten*, five of which experienced one-time population *gains* of over 5 percent, consistent with refuge-seeking.[56] The points here are, first, that *kecamatan*-level analysis can reveal important nuances that are not visible at the *kabupaten* level and second, that these nuances may materially contribute to our understanding of the violence and responses to it.

Figures 3a–b show spatial aspects of the strength of the Nahdlatul Ulama party, measured as the share of seats won in the 1957 election (Figure 3a) and the combined strength of the two major politico-religious parties, the NU and Masyumi (Figure 3b).[57] As has been discussed in an earlier study, the NU party enjoyed an especially strong following in a horseshoe-shaped band of *kabupaten* including Madura and the northern

---

[54] Here, "repulsion" refers to the tendency for a *Kompro* and a *pesantren* or for two *Kompro* to be located far away from each other. See the technical appendix for details of how repulsion can be defined and measured and how it is used in this study.

[55] A version of the *kecamatan*-level map appeared as Siddharth Chandra, Raechel White, and Camille North, "Indonesia: the Killings of 1965–66 in East Java," *Inside Indonesia*, September 26, 2019, https:// www.insideindonesia.org/images/Edition136/Infographic_Population_Change.jpg; Siddharth Chandra, "Mapping the 1965–66 killings in East Java," *Inside Indonesia*, September 26, 2019, https://www .insideindonesia.org/archive/articles/mapping-the-killings-of-1965-in-east-java (page discontinued). Versions of the *kabupaten*-level map appeared in Chandra, "New Findings on the Indonesian Killings" and as Siddharth Chandra, Raechel White, and Camille North, "Indonesia: the Nahdlatul Ulama Party and the Killings of 1965–66 in East Java," *New Mandala*, September 30, 2019, https://www.newmandala.org/ wp-content/uploads/2019/09/Infographic_New_Mandala_East_Java_Kabupaten_English.pdf; Siddharth Chandra, "Mapping the 1965–66 killings in Java," *New Mandala*, September 30, 2019. https://www .newmandala.org/mapping-the-1965-66-killings-in-java/.

[56] Chandra, "Glimpses of 1965."

[57] A version of the map of the share of seats won by NU in 1957 appeared in Chandra, "New Findings on the Indonesian Killings," Figure 4b, 1069.

coast of East Java from Gresik in the west to Panarukan[58] in the east. Adding the seat share of Masyumi to that of NU expands the region of strength of the two major politico-religious parties into the interior of the province along the Brantas River valley through Kediri to Tulungagung and Trenggalek, south through the Bromo-Arjuno volcanic region to Jember, and along the north coast westward to Lamongan, Tuban, and Bojonegoro.

Figure 4 shows the locations of the historically significant *pesantren* depicted in Dhofier.[59] The key regions in which these *pesantren* are located are, first, along the north coast of East Java in the vicinity of Madura and, second, up along the Brantas River valley to Kediri and beyond. There are, in addition to these two key belts, a few historically significant *pesantren* scattered across the southern *kabupaten*, including Pacitan, Lumajang, and Banyuwangi. Finally, Figure 4 also shows the locations of the five rural *Kompro* centered in East Java. These were obtained from the report on Operation Trisula prepared by the Brawijaya Regional Command (*Kodam*) of the Indonesian army.[60]

Population Reduction and Proximity to *Pesantren*

Two sets of relationships were analyzed using statistical methods. The first was the relationship between one-time changes in the population of a *kecamatan* and the proximity of the *kecamatan* to the closest historically significant *pesantren*. To the extent that proximity to the *pesantren* meant greater exposure to a potentially hostile community with the ability to mobilize and, therefore, to the possibility of violence, two patterns should be observable. First, *kecamatan* in or near which there were communities that were involved in the violence should show drops in population. And second, the relationship between the distance of a *kecamatan* from the closest *pesantren* (representing the distance from such potentially hostile communities) and population change in that *kecamatan* should be positive (that is, the farther away is a *kecamatan* from a community that was involved in the violence, the less negative [or more positive] should be the one-time change in population) if that community was involved in the violence. A comparison of Figure 4, the map showing the locations of the key *pesantren* in East Java, with Figure 2a, the *kecamatan*-level map showing population loss, shows that these *pesantren* were located in areas that experienced losses as well as gains in population. Viewed as a group, however, the *kecamatan* in which these *pesantren* were located experienced an average drop in population of 1.3 percent, compared with a much smaller average drop in population of 0.5 percent in *kecamatan* that did not have key *pesantren*.[61]

---

[58] The name of Panarukan was changed to Situbondo in 1972. See S. H. Sudharmono, "Peraturan Pemerintah Republik Indonesia Nomor 28 Tahun 1972 Tentang Perubahan Nama dan Pemindahan Tempat Kedudukan Pemerintah Daerah *Kabupaten Panarukan* 28/1972." 1972, https://www.bphn.go.id/data/documents/72pp028.doc.

[59] Dhofier, *The Pesantren Tradition*, xxi.

[60] Brawidjaja, *Trisula Operation*, 285. Two additional *Kompro*, located in neighboring Central Java close to the provincial border, are also displayed in this map.

[61] Summary statistics on the two groups of *kecamatan* are presented in the table below:

Type of *Kecamatan*	Average Population Change	Number of *Kecamatan*	Standard Deviation	Median Population Change
With key *Pesantren*	1.33%	25	0.087	−2.40%
Without Key *Pesantren*	−0.48%	465	0.071	−1.00%

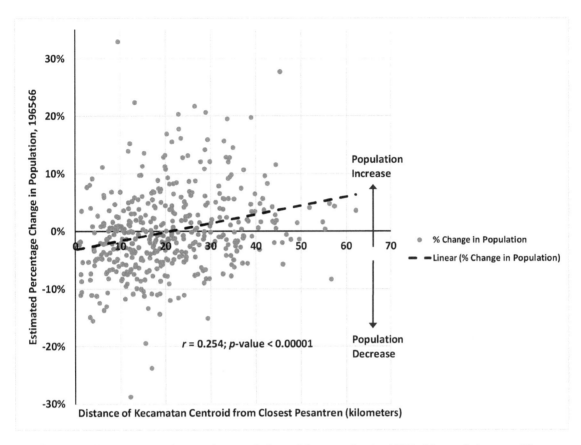

Figure 5: Percentage change in population of *kecamatan* in 1965–66 vs. distance of the centroid of the *kecamatan* from the closest historically important *pesantren*.

Figure 5 is a scatter plot of the estimated change in population for each *kecamatan*, mapped in Figure 2a, against the distance of the centroid of that *kecamatan* from the closest *pesantren* for the 432 *kecamatan* on the mainland of East Java.[62] The plot shows a positive relationship, suggesting that the greater the distance of a *kecamatan* from the *pesantren* closest to it, the less negative (or more positive) the change in its population.[63] Including the political support for the NU alone or for the NU and Masyumi combined as an additional variable, measured by the vote share in the 1957 election (the NU's vote

---

[62] Madura, which was a major NU stronghold as demonstrated by the vote share of NU in the 1957 election, had only one historically significant *pesantren* according to Dhofier (see Dhofier, *The Pesantren Tradition*, Map 1, xxi). However, other accounts suggest that there were a number of additional *pesantren* of significance on this island. Recognizing this discrepancy while keeping the criterion of uniformity of sources of statistical data in mind, the *kecamatan* of Madura are excluded from Figure 5.

[63] The correlation coefficient of 0.25 was statistically significant at the 1 percent level, indicating that the observed relationship is unlikely to be a chance one.

share was 30.4 percent; Masyumi's vote share was 9.9 percent) demonstrated that these variables too were associated with population loss, as suggested in an earlier study.[64]

While this finding suggests that, on average, greater proximity to politico-religious organizational hubs was indeed associated with greater reductions in population, it would be a mistake to infer from this finding that the locations of *all* such hubs were equally associated with these population reductions. Indeed, much of the evidence suggests the contrary, indicating the need for a more finely grained examination of this association.[65] In order to identify spatial variations in the relationship between population reduction and proximity to these hubs, therefore, geographically weighted regression was used. Briefly, GWR estimates a separate relationship for the neighborhood of each *kecamatan*, thereby giving greater weight to the data for that *kecamatan* and its neighbors and little or no weight to the data for distant *kecamatan*. In this manner, 432 relationships were estimated, one centered on each *kecamatan*. This procedure enabled a focus on whether particular clusters of *kecamatan* appear to be "hot spots" for population reductions that are associated with proximity to politico-religious hubs, a finding that would motivate further research into politico-religious mobilization as a factor in the killings in those neighborhoods.

Figures 6a and 6b show the *kecamatan* for which the GWR revealed a relationship between distance to the closest politico-religious hub and population loss, with the locations of the *pesantren* superimposed on them. The colored *kecamatan* are the *kecamatan*, which, when used as the center for the GWR, show a relationship between distance from the closest *pesantren* and population loss, with *kecamatan* colored in red showing the largest gradient of declines in population losses with increasing distance from the closest *pesantren* and *kecamatan* colored in yellow showing the smallest gradient.[66] The dashed lines indicate the neighborhood around each of these central *kecamatan*, consisting of approximately thirty *kecamatan*, for which the relationship holds. *Kecamatan* outside the dashed lines show no evidence of the gradient in their neighborhood, nor do they belong to any neighborhood within which this pattern is observed. Figure 6a shows the results for a model with only population loss and distance to the closest *pesantren* included. Figure 6b shows the results for a similar model, but with distance to the local military district command (*Kodim*) headquarters included as an additional (control) variable.[67]

---

[64] See Chandra, "New Findings on the Indonesian Killings," 1066–80. The coefficient on the vote share for NU in the model containing the NU vote share was −0.10 (with a p-value < 0.001) and the coefficient on the combined vote share for NU and Masyumi in the model containing that variable was −0.08 (with a p-value of 0.003). The negative coefficient indicates that the higher vote share was associated with a more negative change in population (i.e., greater population loss). For vote shares, see also D. S. Lev, *The Transition to Guided Democracy: Indonesian Politics, 1957–1959* (Sheffield: Equinox Publishing, 2009).

[65] In the context of East Java, the "Report from East Java" suggests that there was a hierarchy of complicity in the killings across the *pesantren* of the province, with some *pesantren* playing a coordinating role, others playing a more localized role, and still others not mentioned at all. See "Report from East Java," 8–10. In the context of neighboring Central Java, see, for example, Gregory Fealy, "Ulama and Politics in Indonesia: A History of Nahdlatul Ulama, 1952–1967" (PhD diss., Monash University, 1998), 255.

[66] The colored areas in the map show where this pattern was both positive (i.e., closeness to *pesantren* is associated with greater population reduction or lower population increase) and statistically significant (i.e., unlikely to be a chance association).

[67] Given space constraints and the importance of the subject, detailed analysis of the role of the Indonesian Army in the killings remains outside the scope of this paper and is analyzed elsewhere. See Siddharth Chandra, "Glimpses of Indonesia's 1965 Massacres through the Lens of the Census: Spatial Aspects of

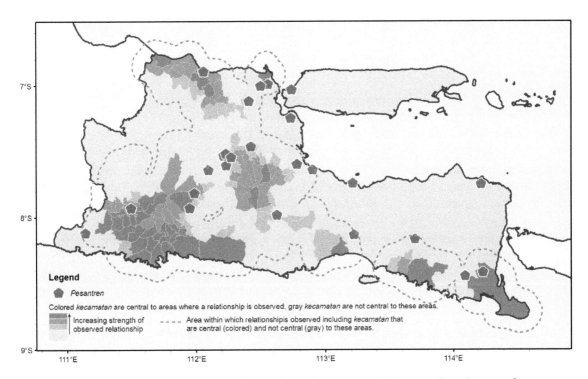

Figure 6a: Locations where population loss decreases with increasing distance from the closest historically important *pesantren* based on GWR models.

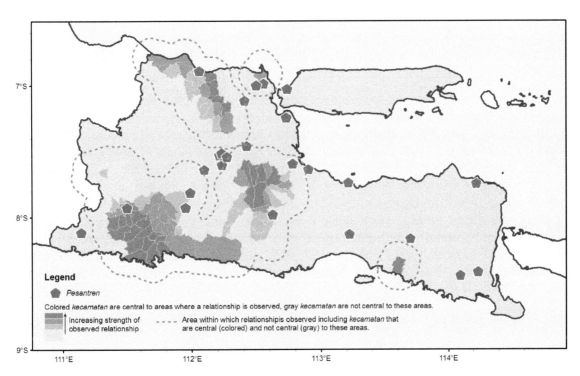

Figure 6b: Locations where population loss decreases with increasing distance from the closest historically important *pesantren* (after accounting for distance from the local *Kodim* headquarters) based on GWR models.

The logic for including distance to the local *Kodim* is that, like the politico-religious civilian organizations, it is known that the Indonesian Army was involved in the killings to varying degrees depending on the specific location. Therefore, omitting this variable could lead to inaccurate estimates of the gradient described above.

Figure 6a reveals four regions where *kecamatan* that were closer to a politico-religious hub systematically experienced greater population losses than those that were farther away from one. The largest of these regions lies in the southwestern part of the province and includes *kecamatan* from the *kabupaten* of Kediri, Madiun, Magetan, Ponorogo, Trenggalek, and Tulungagung. The second region includes *kecamatan* from the *kabupaten* of Jombang, Malang, Mojokerto, Pasuruan, and a few other neighboring *kabupaten*. The third region is centered in the *kabupaten* of Tuban in the northwestern part of East Java and includes *kecamatan* from the southern part of Lamongan, the neighboring *kabupaten* to the east. The fourth region consists of a scattering of *kecamatan* lining the southern shore of the eastern half of East Java. When distance from the local *Kodim* headquarters is included as a variable in these models (Figure 6b), the fourth of these regions no longer shows the relationship, suggesting that the three other regions (Kediri region, Tuban region, and Jombang region) are the ones with the more statistically robust relationship.

It is important to note that the gradient pattern (i.e., of decreasing population loss or increasing population gain with increasing distance from nearby *pesantren*) could occur in regions that show either losses in population or gains. *Kecamatan* identified in Figures 6a and 6b that also experienced gains in population (as shown in Figure 2a) tend to lie at some distance from the closest *pesantren* and should be interpreted as refuges for fleeing populations.[68] This is the case with some *kecamatan* in the eastern part of Bojonegoro *kabupaten* that were central to the Pandan *Kompro* (identified by Indonesian military intelligence as a regrouping point for PKI members in the aftermath of the 1965–66 killings[69]) and a cluster of *kecamatan* in the northeastern corner of Ponorogo and the northern tips of Trenggalek and Tulungagung on the eastern slopes of the Liman-Wilis volcanic complex (see the blue semicircle of *kecamatan* in the lower left part of Figure 2a).

More interesting for the purposes of this study are the colored regions in figures 6a and 6b that coincide with *kecamatan* that experienced losses in population. Table 2 contains the *kecamatan* where each organizational hub was located along with the loss or gain in population in the *kecamatan* and whether it lies in the center or neighborhood of a collection of *kecamatan* that shows the pattern of decreasing population loss as one moves away from the organizational hub based on the results of the GWR. A number of striking patterns emerge from Table 2. First, the number of these *kecamatan* that lost population (seventeen) outnumber those in *kecamatan* that gained population (seven) by a ratio of more than two to one. Second, the vast majority of *kecamatan* where *pesantren* are located (twenty-one out of twenty-four) are central to (seven) or in the neighborhood of (fourteen) areas where population decline becomes more severe with

---

the Role of the Indonesian Army in East Java," mimeo, Michigan State University, 2023. In keeping with the building consensus on the subject, that study provides evidence that is consistent with pervasive involvement of the army in the killings. As is the case with the present study, however, consistency with involvement does not prove involvement, and the findings of that paper merit further exploration as do the findings of this paper.

[68] For more on patterns of refuge seeking, see Chandra, "Glimpses of 1965."

[69] See Brawidjaja, *Trisula Operation*, 285.

Table 2: Organizational Hubs and Consistency of Local Patterns of Population Change Attributable to 1965–66 with Violence Based on Geographically Weighted Regression.

Location of Hub		Population Change in Kecamantan	Loction of *Kecamatan* in Relation to Population Loss Gradient*	
Kabupaten	*Kecamatan*		Model with No Controls	Model with Control for Distance from Local *Kodim*
Banyuwangi	Bongorejo, Cluring, Muncar	Increase > 5%	Central	No relationship
Banyuwangi	Pesanggaran	Increase > 5%	Neighborhood	No relationship
Gresik	Sedayu	Decrease > 5%	Neighborhood	Neighborhood
Gresik	Dukun	Decrease > 5%	Neighborhood	Neighborhood
Jember	Jember	Decrease < 5%	Neighborhood	No relationship
Jombang	Diwek	Decrease < 5%	Neighborhood	No relationship
Jombang	Jombang	Decrease > 5%	Neighborhood	No relationship
Jombang	Tembelang	Decrease < 5%	Neighborhood	No relationship
Jombang	Peterongan	Decrease < 5%	Central	No relationship
Kediri	Mojoroto	Decrease > 5%	Central	Neighborhood
Kediri	Kras	Increase > 5%	Neighborhood	Neighborhood
Kediri	Purwosari	Increase > 5%	Neighborhood	No relationship
Lamongan	Lamongan	Decrease > 5%	Central	Neighborhood
Lumajang	Lumajang	Increase < 5%	Neighborhood	No relationship
Malang	Malang	Decrease < 5%	Neighborhood	Neighborhood
Mojokerto	Mojokerto	Decrease < 5%	Central	Neighborhood
Pacitan	Arjosari	Increase > 5%	Neighborhood	No relationship
Pasuruan	Pasuruan	Decrease > 5%	Neighborhood	No relationship
Pasuruan	Bangil	Decrease > 5%	Neighborhood	Neighborhood
Ponorogo	Mlarak	Decrease < 5%	Central	Central
Probolinggo	Probolinggo*	Decrease > 5%	No relationship	No relationship
Situbondo	Asembagus*	Decrease > 5%	No relationship	No relationship
Surabaya	Surabaya	Decrease < 5%	No relationship	No relationship
Tuban	Tuban	Decrease > 5%	Central	Central

* If a *Kecomatan* that experienced a high degree of population loss was surrounded by other *Kacamatan* that experienced equally high or hinger degree of population loss, then no gradient will be observed and these cells will be marked as showing no relationship. The pattern holds for Proboliggo and Asembagus.

increasing proximity to the *kecamatan* when distance from the local *Kodim* headquarters is not taken into account. However, this number falls to ten out of twenty-four (two of which remain central and the remaining eight of which are in the neighborhood) when distance from the local *Kodim* headquarters is taken into account, suggesting (a) a role for these organizational hubs in these ten areas and (b) parallel and possibly overlapping associations for the *Kodim* and politico-religious hubs in the fourteen areas where this change is seen.

The above exercise provided evidence consistent with higher levels of violence in the *kecamatan* where some, *but by no means all*, of the politico-religious hubs were located by testing for spatial associations between patterns of population loss and the locations of those *kecamatan*. It underlines the importance of regional variations in the roles played by anti-PKI civilian forces across East Java.

Location of *Kompro* and Distance from *Pesantren*: A Case of Spatial "Repulsion"

A remaining question is whether the behavior of survivors of the violence was also associated with the locations of hubs of politico-religious mobilization, measured by the coordinates of the historically significant *pesantren*. With this in mind, the second statistical exercise involved examining the locations of the *Kompro* in relation to the locations of the *pesantren*. Recall that the *Kompro* (*Komite Proyek*) were rallying points for PKI members and others who were fleeing the violence in Java and hoping to regroup. The map in Figure 4 above suggests that the *Kompro* tended to be systematically located at a distance from the *pesantren*, a pattern that geographers call "repulsion."[70] Across the five *Kompro*, the shortest distance between a *Kompro* and a *pesantren* was twenty-one kilometers, while on average, the distance from a *Kompro* and the closest *pesantren* to it was thirty-six kilometers. Given the high population density of East Java and the correspondingly large number of historically significant *pesantren* identified by Dhofier (i.e., one every 1,701 square kilometers), these distances are quite large and suggest that the locations of the *Kompro* may have been deliberately selected to play an insulating role against hostility from local politico-religious organizations. However, considering that there were only five established rural *Kompro* in East Java, it is important to confirm whether the visible pattern of *Kompro* locations is a chance occurrence or an indication of a more systematic pattern.

Spatial analysis can allow us to test statistically whether the observed pattern of location of *Kompro* in relation to *pesantren* is consistent with a random scattering of locations or whether, conversely, the locations of the *Kompro* are systematically (or non-randomly) related to and therefore "repelled" by the locations of the *pesantren*. If the *Kompro* were being purposefully located at a distance from the *pesantren* and from one another, then we would expect the distances (or some measure reflecting the distances) between any *Kompro* and (1) the *pesantren* closest to it as well as (2) the *Kompro* closest

[70] For early use of the term "repulsion" in the context of spatial distribution, see R. Taylor. "Aggregation, Variance and the Mean," *Nature* 189 (1961): 732–35. In the context of geography, see, for example, K. M. Curtin and R. L. Church, "A Family of Location Models for Multiple-Type Discrete Dispersion," *Geographical Analysis* 38, no. 3 (2006): 248–70.

to it to be "unusually" or discernibly large.[71] In other words, the closer is the potential location of a *Kompro* to the *pesantren* or other *Kompro*, the greater will be the repulsion, and the *Kompro* will tend to be located where the repulsion from the *pesantren* and the other *Kompro* is the lowest. With this in mind, the analysis was carried out in two steps. In the first step, two indices, the first capturing the repulsion (which decreases with increasing distance) between each of the five *Kompro* in East Java and the *pesantren* closest to it and the second capturing the repulsion between each *Kompro* and the *Kompro* closest to it were calculated, and the average values of these two indices across the five *Kompro* were computed. An extreme pair of values for these numbers, representing *pesantren*-to-*Kompro* and *Kompro*-to-*Kompro* repulsion, would indicate that the *Kompro* were being systematically established at a distance from the *pesantren* and in a spread-out configuration. By contrast, a "normal" (or non-extreme) pair of values of this measure would indicate that the locations of the *pesantren* and of other *Kompro* were likely not factors in the location decisions for the *Kompro*.

Following this logic, in order to ascertain whether the observed pair of indices of repulsion was extreme, a Monte Carlo simulation was carried out as follows: first, five points in the province were randomly selected (simulated) to represent a random set of hypothetical *Kompro*. Next, this set of five randomly selected points was treated like a set of five *Kompro*, and pairs of indices of repulsion, one between the *Kompro* and the closest *pesantren* to each of them and the other between each *Kompro* and the *Kompro* closest to them were computed.[72] This exercise was repeated over and over (100,000 times) until 100,000 pairs of indices of repulsion (one for *pesantren*-to-*Kompro* repulsion and the other for *Kompro*-to-*Kompro* repulsion) were computed, one for each randomly generated scattering of five simulated *Kompro*. A frequency distribution of the pair of these indices was created from the 100,000 randomly generated sets of simulated *Kompro*. In the final step of the simulation, the pair of indices computed using the actual (observed) configuration of *Kompro*, shown on the map in Figure 4, was compared with the distribution generated by random configurations of simulated *Kompro* to ascertain whether the actual (observed) pair of indices of repulsion was extreme in the sense that they are in the tail of the distribution of the 100,000 values of pairs of indices generated by the simulations. The alternative possibility is that the values of the indices computed for the observed set of *Kompro* are generated often enough in random scatterings of simulated *Kompro* so as to not be distinguishable from such random configurations. A finding of extreme values of the indices of repulsion between the *Kompro* and the *pesantren* and between one another is indicative of the systematic location of the *Kompro* away from the *pesantren* and of spacing out among the *Kompro*.

Table 3 shows the likelihood that the indices generated by a randomly generated set of five *Kompro* will yield values less than or equal to the indices generated by the actual

---

[71] For a description of the different types of indices of repulsion that were used for the analysis, see Technical Appendix 2. For the rest of this paper, the word "distance" is used to refer to distance and the phrase "index of repulsion" is used to refer to an index that declines in value as distance increases, reflecting the property of repulsion. A useful analogy to understand repulsion is a pair of magnets. When like poles of the magnets are in close proximity with each other, a strong repulsive force is felt. As distance between the two like poles is increased, this repulsive force diminishes.

[72] Details of these indices are provided in Technical Appendix 2 below.

Table 3: Evidence that the observed locations of *Kompro* are consistent with repulsion from *pesantren*.

Description of Repulsion index	Probability that a randomly generated set of *Kompro* will yield values equal to or less than the observed values
Average of the reciprocal of the square of the distance,* d (or Mean ($1/d^2$))	0.012 or 1.2%
Average of the reciprocal of the distance* (or Mean ($1/d$))	0.014 or 1.4%
Reciprocal of the minimum (across all five *Kompro*) distance* (or 1/Minimum (d))	0.048 or 4.8 %

*For each index (*Kompro*-to-*pesantren* repulsion and *Kompro*-to-*Kompro* repulsion), 'distance' is the distance between *Kompro* in question and the closest *pesantren* or *Kompro* to it. For details, see the Technical Appendix.

locations for the *Kompro* for three different sets of indices. In all three cases, this was highly unlikely, occurring in less than 5 percent of the cases of randomly generated sets of *Kompro* locations. This finding is suggestive of a systematic (i.e., non-random) pattern of location of *Kompro* that factored in the distance of the closest *pesantren* from each *Kompro*.

The Location of Civilian Politico-Religious Hubs and Patterns of Population Loss

The key finding from the first exercise of this paper is the identification of multiple hubs of high politico-religious mobilization capacity, Gresik, Kediri, Lamongan, Ponorogo, Pasuruan, and Tuban, for which the estimated reduction in population attributable to the violence of 1965–66 declines as distance from the hub increases. The fact that Kediri also features prominently in anecdotal accounts of the killings lends credence to the inferential methods being used in this paper and, possibly, to the credibility of other inferences about hitherto unidentified patterns drawn from the findings. The prominent role of NU in the killings in Kediri has been repeatedly mentioned in the rich literature on this subject. For example, Fealy and McGregor summarize the work of a variety of scholars in this regard.[73] Hermawan Sulistyo highlights the roles of the NU leadership in Kediri, and Iwan Gardono Sudjatmiko, citing Harold Crouch and John Hughes, emphasizes the critical role played by the NU's Ansor youth organization in killings in Kediri.[74] The anonymous article referred to above also places Jombang at the center of

---

[73] Fealy and McGregor, "East Java and the Role of Nahdlatul Ulama," 38.

[74] Hermawan Sulistyo, "The Forgotten Years: the Missing History of Indonesia's Mass Slaughter (Jombang-Kediri 1965–1966)" (PhD diss., Arizona State University, 1997), especially ch. V, 170–225; *Palu Arit di Ladang Tebu: Sejarah Pembantaian Massal yang Terlupakan (Jombang-Kediri 1965–66)* (Jakarta: Pensil-324, 2017), ch. 5, 181–243; Iwan Gardono Sudjatmiko, "The Destruction of the Indonesian Communist Party (PKI) (a comparative analysis of East Java and Bali)" (PhD diss., Harvard University, 1992), 197–98; Harold Crouch, *The Army and Politics in Indonesia* (Ithaca: Cornell University Press, 1988); John Hughes, *Indonesian Upheaval* (New York: David McKay, 1967).

collaborative actions on the part of a number of *pesantren* and mentions the involvement of Ansor in the killings.[75] An account by an executioner (*algojo*) in *Tempo* magazine's widely read *"Pengakuan Algojo"* edition specifically mentions collaboration between the army and students from the Lirboyo *pesantren* in Kediri:

> The Kodam [regional military command] even sent troops in civilian clothing to Lirboyo [the famous *pesantren*, or Islamic School]. The military picked up and transported students in military trucks to send them to pockets [groups] of PKI members who were the targets of operations in all areas of the Kediri Residency. In the field, the military placed the students on the front lines and made them the executioners.[76]

Ponorogo has also been mentioned in the anecdotal literature, though not with the same prominence or regularity as Kediri. For example, Cribb notes that the population of Ponorogo according to the 1971 census appeared to be much lower than it should have been in relation to the 1961 census count, suggesting large-scale killings in the region.[77] In addition, the persecution of performing artists of *Reog Ponorogo*[78] that occurred as part of the anti-PKI campaign was especially devastating:

> The devastating effect of the events of 1965 on *warok* and *reog* culture is dramatically highlighted by statistics from the Department of Education and Culture. In 1964 there were 385 registered *reog* troupes in the Ponorogo regency. By 1969 the number had dropped to a mere 90.[79]

A decline of this magnitude could be reflective of large-scale killings, out-migration, or the disbanding of troupes for fear of persecution. It is also worth noting that the Gontor *pesantren* in Ponorogo was the locus of clashes between the PKI and NU in the 1940s, indicative of a prior history of violent confrontation between the two parties and, possibly, the foundation for violence in 1965–66.[80]

---

[75] "Report from East Java," 142–43. See also M. Halwan and Yusuf Hidayat, eds., *"Sang Pejuang Sejati"*: *KH. Muhammad Yusuf Hasyim Di mata Sahabat dan Santri* (Jombang: Pustaka Ikapete, 2007), 18–20, 155–57.

[76] Tim Laporan Khusus Tempo. "The Military, Students, and the Kediri Tragedy" in "Requiem for a Massacre," *Special Report Tempo* (English), October 7, 2012, http://theactofkilling.com/wp-content/uploads/2012/09/TEMPO-UK-Edition-HiRes.pdf.

[77] Robert Cribb, "Soal Statistik Korban," *Liputan Khusus Tempo* [Tempo Special Coverage], October 7, 2012, http://theactofkilling.com/wp-content/uploads/2012/09/TAOK_TEMPO_MABAZINE_article.pdf.

[78] Reog Ponorogo is a traditional dance form closely identified with the culture of the region.

[79] Ian Douglas Wilson, "*Reog* Ponorogo: Spirituality, Sexuality, and Power in a Javanese Performance Tradition," *Intersections: Gender and Sexuality in Asia and the Pacific* 2, 1999, http://intersections.anu.edu.au/issue2/Warok.html#n11. For a firsthand account of the killing of a warok artist from Ponorogo, see S. Y. Haji, "Kalau Saya Mati, Saya Mati Syahid," *Liputan Khusus Tempo* [Tempo Special Coverage], October 7, 2012, http://theactofkilling.com/wp-content/uploads/2012/09/TAOK_TEMPO_MABAZINE_article.pdf. See also Hary Sulistyo, "Representasi Konflik Politik 1965: Hegemoni dan Dominasi Negara dalam Cerpen Susuk Kekebalan karya Han Gagas," *Poetika: Jurnal Ilmu Sastra* 6, no. 1 (2018): 26–43, https://jurnal.ugm.ac.id/poetika/article/view/35611/22037.

[80] See Tim Penyusun, *Biografi K.H. Imam Zarkasyi dari Gontor: Merintis Pesantren Modern* (Ponorogo: Gontor Press, 1996), 137–45. For specific mention of conflict between the PKI and BTI and the Gontor pesantren between 1963 and 1965, see also See also M. Halwan and Yusuf Hidayat, eds. *"Sang Pejuang Sejati"*: *KH. Muhammad Yusuf Hasyim Di mata Sahabat dan Santri* (Jombang: Pustaka Ikapete, 2007), 196.

Tuban, on the other hand, has received little to no attention in the literature, suggesting the need for fieldwork to determine the dynamics of the killings in the area.[81] For example, it is possible that Kodim (Komando Distrik Militer or District Military Command) 0811, headquartered in Tuban, may have been the driver of the violence and that its location close to the *pesantren* in Tuban city is being picked up by the variable that measures the distance of the neighboring *kecamatan* from the *pesantren*. The same issue applies to the cases of Kediri, Jombang, and Ponorogo (the headquarters of Kodim 0809, 0814, and 0802, respectively). While separating the effect of Kodim locations out from the effect of the locations of civilian politico-religious hubs is difficult in these cases because the two are co-located in space, the inclusion of distance from the Kodim headquarters as a control variable did not affect the findings for Kediri, Ponorogo, and Tuban (see Figures 6a and 6b), i.e., that distance from the closest *pesantren* in those areas helps to explain the local pattern of demographic change associated with the violence. Importantly, the identification of these hot spots can provide a road map for researchers who may be interested in conducting location-specific field studies of the mass killings of 1965–66 in the future.

The second key finding in the paper is the pattern of spatial repulsion. The Monte Carlo simulations demonstrate that the locational patterns of the *Kompro* were statistically discernibly (i.e., "unusually") far away from the closest *pesantren* as well as from one another. Table 3 shows the likelihood that, for a randomly distributed set of five points (simulated *Kompro*s), they would be located at distances from the closest *pesantren* and from the closest neighboring *Kompro* that yield indices of repulsion that are equal to or less than the indices calculated using the actual (observed) locations of *Kompro*. This likelihood is below 5 percent for all three indices of repulsion used. Therefore, we can conclude that the findings are consistent with the locations of the *Kompro* being associated both with the locations of the *pesantren* and with the locations of the other *Kompro*. The first form of repulsion, *pesantren*-to-*Kompro* repulsion, suggests a possible role for the antagonism between the PKI and its politico-religious rivals, most prominently the NU. As the death toll from the violence mounted, the remnants of the PKI fled locations in which they were under threat, regrouping in relatively safe areas. These areas were systematically located at a distance from their politico-religious opponents, a pattern that is consistent with the role of politico-religious mobilization in the violence. The second form of repulsion, *Kompro*-to-*Kompro* repulsion, is a common organizational pattern, illustrating the need for an organization to efficiently cover a large spatial domain—the *Kompro* were spread out across the province so as to cover a broad swath of the province and of PKI members in the different parts of the province as they took refuge from the killings and attempted to reorganize.

Limitations

In interpreting the findings in this paper, the reader should be cognizant of several limitations of the analysis. The most important of these is the caution that, just as correlation, which the above exercises establish, does not imply causation, a demographic

[81] An exception is a recent undergraduate thesis. See Fauzan, "Peran GP Ansor dalam Menjaga Keutuhan NKRI: Studi Historis Peran GP Ansor dalam Perlawanan dan Penumpasan G 30 S/PKI di *Kecamatan* Soko Kapbupaten Tuban 1967–1968" (Undergraduate thesis, UIN Sunan Ampel Surabaya, 2015), http://digilib .uinsby.ac.id/3921/, which focuses on the Soko *kecamatan* in the south of the Tuban kabupaten bordering Bojonegoro. For the important role played by the local *kiai*, see Fauzan, "Peran GP," 57.

pattern that is consistent with the involvement of politico-religious organizations in the killings is not the same thing as proof of involvement. Furthermore, the choice of the location of the historically significant *pesantren* as a spatial indicator of the capacity for politico-religious mobilization does not prove that a *pesantren* itself was involved in the violence if such a location is associated with high levels of local violence and a gradient of decreasing violence with greater distance from it. Taken in conjunction with the available anecdotal material from witnesses and in prior research, however, the findings are in many cases compelling and suggest that any hitherto undocumented patterns highlighted above may also merit further study. Second, the use of census data and the method of estimation of population change using those data are subject to a number of assumptions,[82] the violation of which in any *kecamatan* would render the estimates of one-time population reduction (or increase) associated with 1965 in that *kecamatan* inaccurate. Third, in some sections of this paper, such as the analysis of spatial repulsion, all *pesantren* locations are treated in the same manner. To the extent that there may have been variation in the degree of politico-religious mobilization capacity in the vicinity of different *pesantren* it might be expected that locations with greater capacity would have exerted stronger repulsion on the *Kompro*, thereby justifying a disproportionate role for them in determining the location of the *Kompro*. The small number of *Kompro* and *pesantren* and the difficulty of assigning numerical values to such factors as "mobilization capacity" preclude the incorporation of this consideration in the repulsion analysis. Further, given the locations of some *pesantren* in urban areas, other variables that are also associated with urbanization, such as easy access by road, which has been shown elsewhere to be associated with population reduction,[83] may also explain some of the variation in population loss being picked up by *pesantren* and Kodim location. For these reasons, the results need to be understood as partial findings and not as findings that in and of themselves conclusively establish a role for politico-religious mobilization highlighted in this paper. To the extent that these results are backed up by the available anecdotal information, as in the cases of Kediri and Ponorogo, however, the level of confidence in the findings, the above limitations notwithstanding, is strengthened.

Conclusions

While the involvement of NU in the killings of 1965 is well-established and was acknowledged by none other than the late leader of NU and former Indonesian President Abdurrahman Wahid himself, the specifics of this involvement across space have not been explored systematically or in much depth. What we do know about NU's involvement is informed by anecdotal accounts by executioners, victims, and other witnesses, by analyses of the overarching environment in which the killings were perpetrated and of the politics and evolution of NU itself, and by historical accounts of NU, written in some instances by NU-affiliated authors. The use of systematic province-wide data from the censuses in conjunction with spatial data on organizational aspects of NU and the PKI can reveal patterns that are not apparent from the accounts while confirming (or refuting) what is known about this involvement.

---

[82] See, for example, Chandra, "Migration and Refuge," 30–32; Technical Appendix 1 of this paper.

[83] Siddharth Chandra, "Glimpses of Indonesia's 1965 Massacre through the Lens of the Census: the Role of Trucks and Roads in 'Crushing' the Indonesian Communist Party in East Java," *Indonesia* 108 (2019):1–21.

While the identification of Ponorogo and Kediri as locations for which there is a statistically demonstrable association between population loss and distance from the local *pesantren* is consistent with a role for systematic politico-religious mobilization, borne out in anecdotal accounts, in the violence, an interesting addition to this list is Tuban, where politico-religious mobilization in the killings has not received the kind of attention that has been accorded to Kediri and, to a lesser degree, to Ponorogo. The identification of the spatial repulsion, and especially the *pesantren*-to-*Kompro* repulsion pattern, complements the pattern of decreasing population loss with greater distance from the *pesantren*, a pattern that is also consistent with politico-religious mobilization as a factor in the killings.

Finally, the findings also demonstrate the danger of painting the entire NU Party with the same brush. At least insofar as cross-*kecamatan* variation in population loss can also be interpreted as being consistent with cross-*kecamatan* variations in violence, to the extent that these variations reflect variations in violent politico-religious mobilization, NU-affiliated organizations in some areas appear to have been more heavily involved in the killings than others, and it should not be surprising if future research demonstrates that some organizations played no role in the killings or even a role in protecting survivors and refugees. It is hoped that this study will stimulate such nuanced research into the role of civilian politico-religious organizations in the killings in East Java in 1965–66, thereby enhancing our understanding of this important episode in modern Indonesian history.

Technical Appendix 1

Details of the Computation of One-Time Population Change Associated with the Violence of 1965–66

NOTE: Much of this appendix, marked in double quotes, is taken verbatim from Chandra, "New Findings on the Indonesian Killings," 1063-66.

"This study uses the population loss method for estimating a one-time population shock, defined as a break in an otherwise smooth population growth trajectory, using census data.[84,85,86] Briefly, this method involves estimating population loss as the discrepancy between the "expected" population, estimated using a trajectory calculated with census data from before the shock, and the "observed" population using a trajectory calculated with census data from after the shock (see Figure 1). These two population trajectories can be extrapolated forward and backward respectively to the time at which the shock occurred, producing discrepant (or similar) estimates of the "expected" (based on the

[84] Chandra, Siddharth. 2013. "Mortality from the Influenza Pandemic of 1918–19 in Indonesia." *Population Studies* 67(2):185–93.

[85] Chandra, Siddharth, Goran Kuljanin, and Jennifer Wray. 2012. "Mortality from the Influenza Pandemic of 1918–1919: The Case of India." *Demography* 49(3):857-65. doi:10.1007/s13524-012-0116-x.

[86] Davis, Kingsley. 1951. *The Population of India and Pakistan*. Princeton, N.J.: Princeton University Press.

pre-shock trajectory) and "observed" (based on the post-shock trajectory) populations at the time of the shock. The difference between the "expected" and the "observed" population is the number of "missing" or, where there is a one-time increase in the population, the number of "surplus" people. This method is suited for the analysis of data that are collected over intervals of time, such as those from the three population censuses of Indonesia. Further details of the computations are presented in the technical appendix at the end of this article.

The availability, for each *kecamatan*, of only three observations on population, one corresponding to each of the three censuses in 1961, 1971, and 1980, necessitates a number of assumptions about population growth in order to estimate the one-time population change attributable to the 1965–66 killings. The first is that, for each *kecamatan*, there were no other major one-time intervening events that significantly disrupted the population growth trajectory. In other words, with the exception of the one-time break in the population growth curve in 1965–66, shown in Figure 1, there are no significant breaks in the trajectory between 1961 and 1980. Second, the population growth rate between 1971 and 1980 is constant and is equal to the population growth rate calculated using the census observations for 1971 and 1980, as described above. A third assumption is about the population growth rate before 1971. A simple version of this assumption would be to set the pre-1971 population growth rate equal to the post-1971 population growth rate, and to calculate the population in late 1965 by growing the population observed in 1961 at this rate. However, the vast preponderance of the literature[87] demonstrates a large drop in fertility in East Java after 1971 compared to that before 1971 as the result of a number of factors including but not restricted to the concerted Suharto-era family planning program,[88] stepped-up transmigration,[89] and the post-1965 economic stabilization. In East Java, fertility decline was particularly pronounced.[90] Added to the fact that mortality

[87] Cho, L., G. M. Feeney, P. McDonald, S. G. M. Mamas, G. McNicoll, M. Singarimbun, S. Suharto, Suyono, and R. J. Lapham. 1987. *Recent Trends in Fertility and Mortality in Indonesia*. Panel on Indonesia, Committee on Population and Demography, Commission on Behavioral and Social Sciences and Education, National Research Council. Report No. 29 and Papers of the East-West Population Institute, No. 105. Washington, D.C.: National Research Council and Honolulu: East-West Center, 8; McNicoll, Geoffrey, and Si Gde Made Mamas. 1973. *The Demographic Situation in Indonesia*. Papers of the East-West Population Institute No. 28. Honolulu: East-West Center; McNicoll, Geoffrey, and Masri Singarimbun. 1986. *Fertility Decline in Indonesia: Analysis and Interpretation*. Yogyakarta: Gadjah Mada University Press, 47; Poedjastuti, Sri. 1987. *Levels and Trends of Fertility in Indonesia Based on the 1971 and 1980 Population Censuses: A Study of Regional Differentials*. Asian Population Studies Series No. 62-E. Bangkok: United Nations Economic and Social Commission for Asia and the Pacific, 26; Quick, Sylvia D. 1979. *Indonesia. Country Demographic Profiles*. ISP-DP-18. Washington, D.C.: Department of Commerce, Bureau of the Census, Population Division, 7.

[88] Hull, Terence H. 2005. "Indonesia's Population from 1950 to 2000: Carving Out New Futures." In *People, Population, and Policy in Indonesia*, ed. Terence H. Hull, xvii-xxi. Singapore: Institute of Southeast Asian Studies; McNicoll, Geoffrey, and Masri Singarimbun. 1986. Fertility Decline in Indonesia: Analysis and Interpretation. Yogyakarta: Gadjah Mada University Press, 47; Poedjastuti, Sri. 1987. Levels and Trends of Fertility in Indonesia Based on the 1971 and 1980 Population Censuses: A Study of Regional Differentials. Asian Population Studies Series No. 62-E. Bangkok: United Nations Economic and Social Commission for Asia and the Pacific.

[89] Hugo, Graeme J., Terence H. Hull, Valerie J. Hull, and Gavin W. Jones. 1987. *The Demographic Dimension in Indonesian Development*. Singapore: Oxford University Press.

[90] McNicoll, Geoffrey, and Masri Singarimbun. 1986. *Fertility Decline in Indonesia: Analysis and Interpretation*. Yogyakarta: Gadjah Mada University Press, figure 3, 47.

rates dropped more slowly than fertility rates during this time period[91] and that average annual net migration stemming from the *transmigrasi* (transmigration) program was higher during the 1970s than it was in the prior decade,[92] this development suggests that the pre-1971 population trajectory should show a higher growth rate than the post-1971 trajectory. In Figure 1, this is shown by the steeper slope of the pre-1965 portion of the trajectory compared with the post-1965 portion of the trajectory. The same adjustment was made for the 1965–71 portion of the trajectory (not shown in Figure 1). Note that the absence of a second census before 1965 precludes the estimation of a separate pre-1965 population growth rate using pre-1965 census data. Based on the estimates provided in some of the above-cited works, therefore, an annual pre-1971 growth rate that is uniformly 0.2 percent higher than that observed for the post-1971 period was used across all *kecamatan*.[93] It should be noted that the choice of the pre-1971 population growth rate will influence the estimate of population loss by tilting the two pieces of the pre-1971 population trajectory upward or downward, thereby increasing or decreasing the gap between the "expected" and "observed" populations at the time of the 1965 killings. The comparison across *kecamatan* will, however, be stable; a *kecamatan* that shows a large loss relative to other *kecamatan* when the pre-1965 trajectory is steep will continue to show a large loss relative to other *kecamatan* even when the pre-1965 population growth rate is adjusted upward or downward uniformly across all *kecamatan*. In sum, the population loss estimates reflect the change in population unaccounted for by the growth trend and, to the extent that the assumptions of the model listed above hold, can

---

[91] Quick, Sylvia D. 1979. *Indonesia. Country Demographic Profiles*. ISP-DP-18. Washington, D.C.: Department of Commerce, Bureau of the Census, Population Division, 7.

[92] Swasono, Sri-Edi. 1986. "Kependudukan, kolonisasi dan transmigrasi" [Population, colonization and transmigration]. In *Transmigrasi di Indonesia: 1905–1985* [Transmigration in Indonesia: 1905–1985], eds. Sri-Edi Swasono and Masri Singarimbun, chap. 5. Jakarta: Penerbit Universitas Indonesia (UI-Press).

[93] Poedjastuti, Sri. 1987. *Levels and Trends of Fertility in Indonesia Based on the 1971 and 1980 Population Censuses: A Study of Regional Differentials*. Asian Population Studies Series No. 62-E. Bangkok: United Nations Economic and Social Commission for Asia and the Pacific, 26; Quick, Sylvia D. 1979. Indonesia. Country Demographic Profiles. ISP-DP-18. Washington, D.C.: Department of Commerce, Bureau of the Census, Population Division, 7. Detailed discussion of the upheavals of 1965–66 is noticeably absent from the demographic literature produced by Indonesian and western demographers during the New Order. The few estimates of population growth rates between the 1961 and 1971 censuses assume a smooth trajectory, which erases the upheavals of 1965–66, thereby contradicting the fundamental premise of the present work. Those estimates of population growth are, furthermore, almost invariably presented at the provincial level.
Absent accurate computations of the population growth rate in the 1960s or reliable data that could inform the estimation of such growth rates, the following approach was used. First, the reported 1961–1971 population growth rate for the province, which assumes a smooth trajectory, was used as a lower bound for the population growth rate. Next, the upper bound for the population growth rate for 1961–1971 was calculated by projecting the lower 1971–1980 population growth rate back in time to 1966, and then calculating the population growth rate that would be needed for the 1961 population to reach this higher number by the end of 1965. These two calculations for the population growth rate between 1961 and 1971 provided a range of population growth rates within which the actual provincial population growth rate lies. The upward adjustment of 0.2% in the growth rate is a round figure that lies within this interval for East Java. Acknowledging that it is an imprecise estimate of the actual population growth rate that can affect estimates of the numbers of 'missing' people in any location, this paper does not focus on absolute numbers of 'missing' people. Instead, it focuses on the *relative* severity of population loss or gain, which remains stable across different values of the adjustment factor within the above-described range. Where we do refer to percentage changes in population, we also focus on locations where the estimated population change (gain or loss) was greater than 5% in value, further accommodating and acknowledging any imprecision introduced by use of the specific adjustment factor.

be used as a proxy for the severity of the 1965–66 violence. As the results demonstrate, even under these strong simplifying assumptions about population growth in East Java, a compelling picture of the massacres emerges.

In this framework, the one-time change in population can be interpreted as the loss in population associated with the violence of 1965–66. While this change corresponds to the severity of population changes at the time of the killings, it comprises not only mortality (i.e., the killings), but also the two other fundamental drivers of demographic change, fertility and migration, and does not distinguish among these three key effects. It does, however, allow for and is robust to regional variations in steady ongoing demographic processes, such as constant in- or out-migration or a consistently lower or higher fertility rate in one *kecamatan* compared to another. As will be shown, in some *kecamatan*, an unexpected one-time increase in population corresponding to the 1965–66 upheavals is observed, suggesting migration from other, perhaps more troubled, *kecamatan*. In this sense, this study emphasizes the migration impacts of the violence as much as it does the mortality effects, and a large one-time drop in population can be interpreted as an indication of the severity of the killings, because the associated migration and fertility impacts will likewise be negative and very likely reflective of the severity of the violence."

Technical Appendix 2

Visual inspection of the map in Figure 4 suggests that the locations at which PKI members were regrouping[94] in the aftermath of the killings of 1965-66 (the *Kompro*, represented by yellow and red stars) were systematically located at a distance from the *pesantren* (represented by green pentagons). However, considering that only five rural *Kompro* identified by army intelligence were located within the boundaries of East Java, it is not clear from visual inspection whether the observed pattern represents repulsion. In other words, such a pattern could be 'accidental.' The aim of this technical appendix is to examine the proposition that the observed pattern of *Kompro* location represents a pattern of spatial repulsion that is statistically defensible. In order to do so, it is necessary to demonstrate that the observed pattern of location in Figure 4 is one that would be unlikely to occur if the *Kompro* were randomly distributed across the province (rather than in a systematic manner that suggests that the locations were influenced by locations of *pesantren*).

The first step in such a process entails choosing a set of measures that represent the concept of repulsion. A number of studies have measured the intensity of spatial interaction such as attraction (gravity) or repulsion using functions of distance.[95] Similar to a "pull-push" or gravity model, we use the reciprocal of the square of the distance between a *Kompro* and the nearest *pesantren* as a measure of the repulsion between a

---

[94] See, for example, Pauker, Guy J. 1969. *The Rise and Fall of the Communist Party of Indonesia*. Report No. RM-5753-PR. Santa Monica, CA: RAND Corporation.

[95] See, for example, Haynes, Kingsley E. and A. Stewart Fotheringham. 1984. *Gravity and Spatial Interaction Models*. Vol. 2. Beverly Hills, CA: Sage, 1984; Zipf, George Kingsley. 1946. "The P 1 P 2/D hypothesis: on the intercity movement of persons," *American Sociological Review* 11(6): 677–686.

Kompro and the *pesantren*. In other words, for each *Kompro*, the repulsion felt by it depends on its distance from the nearest *pesantren* as follows:

$$R_{K-p_N} = \left(\frac{1}{d_{K-p_N}}\right)^2$$

where R_{K-pN} is the measure of repulsion between Kompro and the nearest *pesantren* and d_{K-pN} is the distance between the two locations.

Next, we randomly generated 100,000 sets of five points, with each set representing a random configuration of five hypothetical *Kompro*. We confined this simulation to the island of Java because the documentation of the historically significant *pesantren* on Java provided in Dhofier appears to be more detailed and complete that the documentation for Madura.[96] After computing the repulsion measure for each of the five randomly generated *Kompro* in each set, we computed the index of repulsion between the set of five *Kompro* and the *pesantren* as

$$F_{K-p_N} = \frac{1}{\frac{1}{5}\sum_{K=1}^{5}R_{K-p_N}}$$

A larger value of indicates a stronger pattern of repulsion, produced by *Kompro* that are located, on average, at greater distances from the *pesantren* closest to them. Thus, the 100,000 sets of five simulated *Kompro* can be used to compute a simulated distribution of the index of repulsion . We also could calculate the index of repulsion for the real *Kompro* shown in Figure 4 and examine the location of this index in the distribution of indices generated by the 100,000 randomly generated sets of five *Kompro*. If the five observed *Kompro* are being discernibly (in the statistical sense) repelled by the existing *pesantren*, then we would expect the index of repulsion for the set of the five observed *Kompro* to take on a value that is smaller than that generated by the vast majority (say 90%) of the randomly simulated sets of *Kompro* that, by definition, are not affected by the same repulsive forces. Figure A1 (below) shows that the observed configuration of *Kompro* was unlikely to have resulted from a random process (i.e., the value of the index, shown by the dashed line, lies in the right tail of the distribution of indices created by randomly generating 100,000 configurations of *Kompro*).

In undertaking this exercise, a second consideration needs to be factored into the analysis. Since the *Kompro* represented the PKI's attempt to reorganize in the aftermath of the killings, we would expect them to be scattered across East Java rather than clustered in the same location to provide efficient coverage of the province. Therefore, this organizational logic suggests that we should expect to observe *Kompro*-to-*Kompro* repulsion in the same manner in which we should expect to observe *Kompro*-to-*pesantren* repulsion. With this in mind, we also calculated the index of *Kompro*-to-*Kompro* repulsion, with the individual measure of repulsion equaling

$$R_{K-K_N} = \left(\frac{1}{d_{K-K_N}}\right)^2$$

---

[96] Dhofier. 1999. *The Pesantren Tradition*.

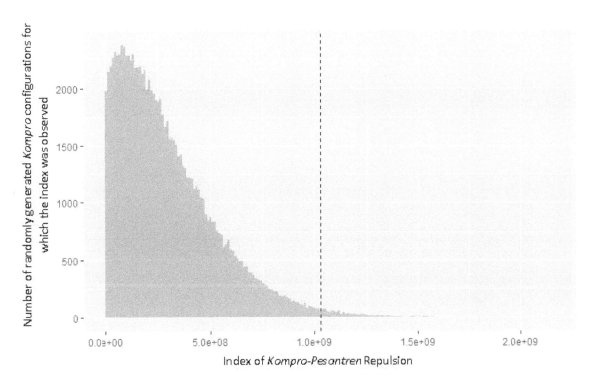

Figure A1: The value of the index of *Kompro-Pesantren* repulsion vs. the number of randomly generated *Kompro* configurations for which that value of the index was observed. The dashed line is the value of the index for the observed *Kompro* configuration. Note that the dashed line lies in the right tail of the distribution, indicating a low probability that the configuration was the result of a random process.

where R_{K-K_N} is the measure of repulsion between *Kompro* and the nearest *Kompro* to it, K_N, and d_{K-K_N} is the distance between the two locations. The resulting index of *Kompro*-to-*Kompro* repulsion for the set of five *Kompro* equals

$$F_{K-K_N} = \frac{1}{\frac{1}{5}\sum_{K=1}^{5} R_{K-K_N}}$$

If the five observed *Kompro* are being discernibly (in the statistical sense) spread out across the province, then we would expect the index of repulsion (or spacing-out) for the set of the five observed *Kompro* to take on a value that is larger than that generated by the vast majority (say 90%) of the randomly simulated sets of *Kompro* which, by definition, are not influenced by the same repulsive forces.

Finally, the two types of repulsion described above should simultaneously influence the spatial pattern of location of the *Kompro*. The 100,000 simulated groups of *Kompro* give us a bivariate distribution of repulsion between *Kompro* and *pesantren* (F_{K-pN}) and among *Kompro* (F_{K-KN}), which can be plotted on a two dimensional graph, with one dimension (on, say, the horizontal axis) representing the index of *Kompro*-to-*pesantren*

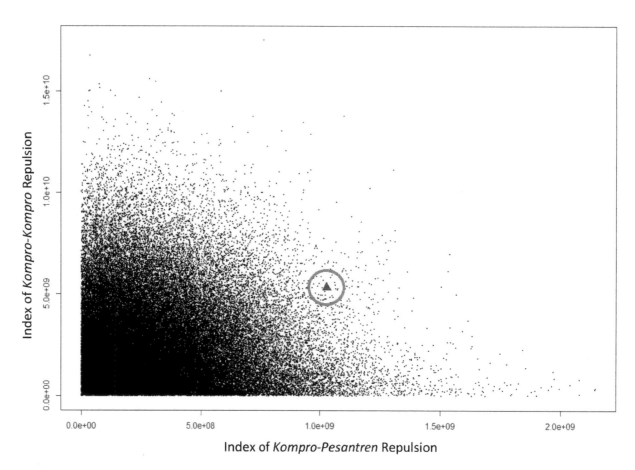

Figure A2: Index of *Kompro-Kompro* repulsion vs. index of *Kompro-Pesantren* repulsion for randomly generated *Kompro* Configurations (black dots) and the observed *Kompro* configuration (red triangle). Note that the pair of indices for the observed *Kompro* configuration lies in a sparse area, indicating the low probability that the configuration was random.

repulsion and the other dimension (on, say, the vertical axis) representing the index of *Kompro*-to-*Kompro* repulsion. An 'unusually' high value for the pair of indices would yield a point on the upper right side of this plot that is far enough away from the center so as to be judged to be an outlier. In Figure A2, this is shown to be the case.

In order to determine whether the observed pair of indices constituted an outlier, we used the convex hull method, which involves counting the number of observations that need to be peeled away from outer layers of the plot of randomly generated pairs of indices to reach the pair of indices calculated using the observed set of five *Kompro*.[97] If

---

[97] Green, P. J. 1981. "Peeling bivariate data." In *Interpreting Multivariate Data*, V. Barnett (ed.), 3-19. Chichester: Wiley.

fewer than 5% of all the points in the plot need to be peeled away in order to reach the indices for the observed set of *Kompro* (representing a p-value of less than 0.05), then the pair of indices for the *Kompro* can be judged to be outliers. This was the case not only for the repulsion index defined above ($p = 0.012$), but also for two alternate repulsion indices that we computed, one using the reciprocal of distance (rather than its square; $p = 0.014$) and the other using the minimum value of distance across all five *Kompro* ($p = 0.048$; see Table 3). We examined these two alternate repulsion indices to make sure that the results that we found for the index we chose did not depend on the choice of the specific function (i.e., the reciprocal of the square) being used to compute the indices.

The 1965–66 Violence in Upland East Java:

A Reflexive Reassessment

Robert W. Hefner

This essay draws on comparative ethnographic and historical research on the 1965–66 violence in Indonesia to reassess the course and consequences of the violence in upland areas of the Pasuruan and Malang regencies (*kabupaten*) in the province of East Java. This is a region where I carried out research in 1978–80, 1985, and during short visits in 1991, 1999, and 2005. Although my account builds on this now-distant research,[1] my broader ambition is to reframe and update my earlier analysis by juxtaposing it to recent paradigm-changing studies carried out by a new generation of scholars examining the 1965–66 violence and its aftermath. This new body of research has allowed me to reassess my earlier findings and rethink them in a way that, I hope, offers additional insights into the history and contemporary legacy of the 1965–66 violence across Indonesia as a whole.

The essay makes five main points. First, it demonstrates that, even within rural settings separated by only a few kilometers, the timing and scale of the anti-communist violence varied significantly. Second, it shows that a key influence on this variation was not merely army ambitions or the relative strength of local Muslim militias (although both of these factors were important), but the nature of the relationship between local

---

[1] Among other publications on this research, see *Hindu Javanese: Tengger Tradition and Islam* (Princeton: Princeton University Press, 1985); *The Political Economy of Mountain Java: An Interpretive History* (Berkeley: University of California Press, 1990); and "Where Have All the Abangan Gone? Religionization and the Decline of Non-Standard Islam in Contemporary Indonesia," in *The Politics of Religion in Indonesia: Syncretism, Orthodoxy, and Religious Contention in Java and Bali*, ed. Michel Picard and Rémy Madinier (London: Routledge 2011), 71–91.

Indonesian Nationalist and Communist Party (PKI) activists in the years leading up to the killings. Third, the study reveals that, in some rural communities, there was significant ambivalence in NU circles about joining in the anti-communist campaign, because NU preachers worried that participation in the killings might undercut their recently initiated programs of Islamic appeal (*dakwah*) in *abangan* villages. Fourth, the study confirms the demographic findings of Siddharth Chandra and Mark Winward concerning the scale and contemporary significance of the population movement within rural Java set in motion by the killings.[2] Fifth, and drawing on my research in Muslim NGOs and mass organizations over the past fifteen years, I suggest that although a "conservative turn" in Muslim society since the early 2000s has set back efforts to promote reconciliation between Muslim organizations and survivors of 1965–66 killings, the prospects remain for a modest but still thoughtful public discussion of the violence and its legacies.

The Violence's Diverse Embeddings

The 1965–66 killings in Indonesia have long formed a background to the Java portion of my Indonesia research. As a graduate student in anthropology writing dissertation grant applications in 1977, I had flirted with the idea of conducting research on the violence in midslope and upperslope villages in the regencies (*kabupaten*) of Malang and Pasuruan, East Java. More senior East Java ethnographers—especially, the anthropologist Robert Jay of the famous MIT "Modjokuto" project (1952–54)—had alerted me to the fact that, in some areas of eastern Java, the 1965–66 killings had been more severe in hill-country communities than in the adjacent wet-rice lowlands.[3] That had been the case in the small upland village above Pare, East Java, where Jay had conducted his dissertation research in the early 1950s, in the same years that Clifford and Hildred Geertz were carrying out research in Pare town (referred to in their publications with the pseudonym, Modjokuto).[4] One reason Jay never made a return visit to his upland Pare field site, he told me many years later (in 1991), was that so many of his field interlocutors had perished in the 1965 killings. By contrast, Clifford Geertz had conducted most of his research in urban Pare, and in conversations with me in November 1981 he told me that most of his primary interlocutors had survived the 1965–66 killings.

Pare is situated in the Kediri regency in the western portion of the province of East Java. It lies just one hundred kilometers to the west of the mountain subdistricts in the Bromo-Semeru massif where my wife (Nancy Smith-Hefner) and I eventually conducted research, beginning in 1978. Defined by the Mount Arjuna-Welirang massif that forms its

[2] See Siddharth Chandra, "Glimpses of Indonesia's 1965 Massacre through the Lens of the Census: Migration and Refuge in East Java," *Indonesia* 104 (October 2017): 27–39; "New Findings on the Indonesian Killings of 1965–66," *The Journal of Asian Studies* 76 (November 2017): 1059–86; "The Indonesian Killings of 1965–1966: The Case of Central Java," *Critical Asian Studies* 51, no. 3 (2019): 307–33; and Siddharth Chandra and Mark Winward, "Road to Perdition: Spatial Determinants of the Mass Political Violence of 1965–1966 in Yogyakarta, Indonesia," paper presented at First International Conference on Indonesian Studies, American Institute for Indonesian Studies and Michigan State University, Panel on the 1965–1966 Violence, June 25, 2021.

[3] See Robert R. Jay, *Religion and Politics in Rural Central Java* (New Haven: Yale University, Southeast Asian Studies, 1963); *Javanese Villagers: Social Relations in Rural Modjokuto* (Cambridge, MA: MIT Press, 1969).

[4] Clifford Geertz, *Religion of Java* (New York: Free Press, 1960); *The Social History of an Indonesian Town* (Cambridge, MA: MIT Press, 1965); and Hildred Geertz, *The Javanese Family: A Study of Kinship and Socialization* (Glencoe, IL: Free Press, 1961).

spine, the social ecology of the highlands east of Pare bears a striking resemblance to that of the eastern highlands of Pasuruan and Malang regency. As it turned out, however, my ethnographic research in the latter uplands did not confirm Jay's hunch that the violence in upland Pasuruan and Malang might have been more severe than that in the wet-rice lowlands, as Jay had predicted on the basis of his Pare research. On the contrary, in the mountainous subdistricts where I conducted research, the killings had not been nearly so extensive as in nearby lowland communities. In the latter territories, thousands had perished in the first weeks of the anti-PKI campaign, whereas the death toll in some twenty-five villages in the Bromo uplands to the east and southeast numbered only several hundred. In addition to differing in scale, the timing and organization of the killings also differed from the lowland territories to the west of these upland subdistricts, in a manner consistent with the sequence of events that Siddharth Chandra, Vannessa Hearman, Grace Leksana, Katharine E. McGregor, Geoffrey Robinson, and John Roosa have reported from other areas of East Java.[5]

In the NU-dominated areas of lowland Pasuruan to the north and west of the Puspo mountain subdistrict in which I did two years' dissertation research, the killings had begun in the middle of October in 1965. This was a full four weeks earlier than was the case in the regency's mountain subdistricts just twenty-five kilometers to the east. Although on October 6, 1965, NU and PKI militias had clashed in the Banyuwangi district of far eastern Java, the killings in lowland Pasuruan were among the first in East Java to be carried out in a territorially extensive manner, and they were initiated without armed forces' coordination. According to village oral histories that I collected in 1979–80 and 1985, the first victims in lowland Pasuruan perished at the hands of NU organized militias in mid-October 1965. This was a full three weeks before armed forces units arrived to coordinate a more far-reaching campaign against "counter-revolutionaries" alleged to be associated with the Thirtieth of September movement. This first phase of the killings also differed from the violence's later organization in that it involved the capture and immediate execution of alleged PKI activists rather than the victims being detained for an extended period. In this manner, rather than being trucked away for interrogation and execution in villages several kilometers from their homes (as would later be the pattern in these regencies' uplands), the lowland victims were killed in the very neighborhoods in which they resided and sometimes only minutes after being captured. Another characteristic of this first phase of the violence, also different from the later violence in the uplands, was that the mutilated bodies of some of the victims were left for display along roadsides as warning to other Thirtieth of September supporters and as a chilling harbinger of what was to come.

---

[5] See Siddharth Chandra, "Glimpses of Indonesia's 1965 Massacre," pp. 27–39, and "New Findings on the Indonesian Killings of 1965–66"; Vannessa Hearman, *Unmarked Graves: Death and Survival in the Anti-Communist Violence in East Java Indonesia* (Singapore: National University of Singapore Press, 2018); Grace Leksana, "Collaboration in Mass Violence: The Case of the Indonesian Anti-Leftist Mass Killings in 1965–66 in East Java," *Journal of Genocide Research* 23:1 (2021), pp. 58–80; Katharine E. McGregor, "Confronting the Past in Contemporary Indonesia: The Anticommunist Killings of 1965-1966 and the Role of Nahdlatul Ulama," *Critical Asian Studies* 41:2 (2009): 195–224; Geoffrey B. Robinson, *The Killing Season: A History of the Indonesian Massacres, 1965-1966* (Princeton: Princeton University Press, 2018), esp. p. 8; and John Roosa, Pretext for Mass Murder: *The September 30th Movement and Suharto's Coup D'Etat in Indonesia* (Madison: University of Wisconsin Press, 2006), p. 26. On the violence in the Jombang and Kediri regions, see Hermawan Sulistyo's remarkable, *Palu Arit di Ladang Tebu: Sejarah Pembantaian Massal yang Terlupakan (1965–1966)* (Jakarta: Gramedia, 2011).

It was only a full month later, in mid-November, 1965, that the anti-PKI violence in Pasuruan regency assumed a more regularized nature. The campaign's tighter coordination was linked to the arrival of army units charged with extending the crackdown against the PKI into territories in which the PKI had not yet been neutralized. The army units brought open-backed trucks, many "borrowed" from local merchants, to ferry large numbers of Ansor militia members to villages targeted for neutralization.[6] It was also only in this second phase of violence that upland communities in Pasuruan's southeastern highlands were included in the anti-communist operations. Up to this time, no upland community had witnessed outbreaks of violence, and none among the upland region's small network of communist activists had been detained. When the violence did finally begin in the Pasuruan uplands, its perpetrators were not local activists, but Ansor militias trucked in by the army from lowland communities fifteen to twenty-five kilometers away.[7] In striking contrast to the violence in lowland Pasuruan, after arresting alleged communists the militias transported the prisoners out of the mountain region down some fifteen kilometers to a NU-dominated village, one that hosted several of the regency's largest Islamic boarding schools (*pesantren*). According to eyewitnesses I interviewed in 1980, there the detainees were forced to dig mass graves. They were then beaten with bamboo bats, strangled with metal wire, and given a final dispatching with machete blows.

The second of the two regions in which I carried out research, the Poncokusumo subdistrict in Malang regency, lies just to the south of upland Pasuruan, in the southwestern stretches of the same Mt. Bromo-Semeru massif. In the regency of Malang as a whole, NU's institutional presence had always been far less extensive than was the case in the Pasuruan lowlands to the north. This social fact strongly influenced the timing and organization of the killings in the Malang region. In this latter territory in the early 1960s, the Indonesian National Party was by far the dominant political force. In the regency's Mt. Bromo uplands, the nationalist party's advantage was even more overwhelming. In the fifteen mountain villages in which I eventually gathered oral histories during 1978–80 and again in 1985, no less than 85–90 percent of the local population had given their vote to the Indonesian National Party in the 1955 elections. In these same villages, the share of the vote given to NU was typically 5 percent or less; the PKI share was half that.[8]

Although in both Pasuruan and Malang's eastern uplands its party machinery was weak, Nahdlatul Ulama nonetheless had a fledgling *religious* infrastructure in most of these mountain communities. It was organized around a network of mosque imams and Qur'anic study groups intent on bringing locals to a more normative-minded profession of Islam. Importantly, however, this NU-based religious infrastructure was not reinforced by village cadres dedicated to the task of party-based mobilization. In fact, in these and many other upland communities, mosque-based NU networks adopted a quietist position on political matters, fearing that partisanship in matters of party politics

---

[6] As Geoffrey Robinson has observed, this pattern of truck-transport to remote sites was a feature of the killings in many parts of Indonesia. See Robinson, *Killing Season*, p. 7.

[7] Hefner, *Political Economy*, 209–15.

[8] Hefner, *Political Economy*, 199–208.

might undercut their programs of religious appeal (*dakwah*) in these strongly nationalist communities.

There was a broader background to this attitude. In the 1950s and 1960s, all of the Muslim villages in these upland portions of Pasuruan and Malang were regarded as strongholds of the *abangan* or "Javanist" variety of Islam, organized around a synthesis of Indonesian Sufism and the indigenous Javanese spiritualities long known in Indonesia as *kebatinan*.[9] Although Muslim villagers in this region sponsored Islamic rites of passage (birth rituals, circumcision, marriage, and death) in which Islamic prayers figured prominently, mosque worship and Qur'anic studies sessions (*pengajian*) were rare. The latter were instead trademarks of the normative-minded variety of Islam known in Java as *santri* Islam. The latter was the variety of Islamic observance predominant in Pasuruan's lowlands.

The balance of religious observance in these upland communities changed dramatically, however, after the events of 1965–66. Although teaching staff became widely available across the highlands only in the early 1970s, education in state-mandated, normative varieties of Islam became compulsory for all students in public schools. In a region in which almost half of the Muslim-majority administrative villages (*kelurahan*) had never had a mosque, the Ministry of Religious Affairs in the late 1960s launched an ambitious program to provide every Muslim-majority village with at least one mosque as well as two to four small prayer houses (*musholla*). By the late 1970s, the great divide seen in the Guided Democracy era (1959–65) between *santri* and *abangan* Muslims in this upland East Java territory had diminished dramatically. By the 1990s, the adherents of a traditionalist variety of *abangan* Islam had become a decided minority in this and other areas of East Java.[10]

Years earlier in the Guided Democracy era (1959–65), electoral politics in this upland region had been overwhelmingly PNI in orientation. At the same time, however, in villages across both upland territories party-based mobilization of any sort was strongly discouraged. A recurring theme in the two hundred ethnohistorical interviews I conducted with villagers across this region in 1978–80 and 1985 was that most people regarded party-based activism as antithetical to their identities as "mountain people" (*wong gunung*). In the local social imaginary, mountain Javanese are ethnically Javanese but distinct from the class structured and politically factionalized world of

[9] For an early and still insightful ethnographic overview of *kebatinan* mysticism in Java, see Paul Stange, "'Legitimate' Mysticism in Indonesia," *Review of Indonesian and Malaysian Affairs* 20 (1986): 76–117; see also Mark R. Woodward, *Islam in Java: Normative Piety and Mysticism in the Sultanate of Yogyakarta* (Tucson: University of Arizona Press, 1989); and Timothy Daniels, *Islamic Spectrum in Java* (Burlington, VT: Ashgate, 2009). For a penetrating analysis of the evolution of Ministry of Religious Affairs policies toward kebatinan mystics, see Ismatu Ropi, *Religion and Regulation in Indonesia* (Singapore: Palgrave MacMillan 2017), esp. pp. 120–26.

[10] On the early stages of public *abanganism*'s decline, see my "Islamizing Java? Religion and Politics in Rural East Java," *Journal of Asian Studies* 46, no. 3 (1987): 533–54; for an updated analysis, see "Where Have All the Abangan Gone?" For a pan-Javanese overview of the same processes of political repression and religious decline, see M. C. Ricklefs, *Islamisation and Its Opponents in Java c. 1930 to Present* (Singapore: National University of Singapore Press 2012), especially pp. 268–317. For an ethnohistorical study of similar processes of state-controls and societal Islamization in a West Javanese setting, see Chaider S. Bamualim, "Negotiating Islamisation and Resistance: A Study of Religions, Politics and Social Change in West Java from the Early 20th Century to the Present" (PhD diss., University of Leiden, 2015).

"lowland people" (*wong ngare*).[11] One especially striking feature of that social divide was the uplanders' prioritization of village harmony (*kerukunan*) and unpretentious gregariousness over party-based factionalism.

In contrast to Pasuruan, where NU dominated the religious infrastructure, in Malang city and lowland communities to its east Nahdlatul Ulama's following was significantly smaller than its PNI and Communist rivals. Even in Malang city, the Muslim-reformist organization Muhammadiyah (est. 1912) had a larger and better-organized social infrastructure than did Nahdlatul Ulama. The relatively weaker position of NU in the Malang region influenced the course of the violence in the area. In the eastern Malang lowlands adjacent to the Poncokusumo subdistrict in which I conducted a year's research, there was no first-wave assault by NU militias on PKI activists like that which had taken place in lowland Pasuruan in early October. The first attacks on communists began in Malang city rather than in the countryside, and they were launched only after October 23, 1965—which is to say after the East Javanese military command announced it was putting in place mechanisms for a well-coordinated campaign against the PKI.[12] In the *abangan*-dominated mountain subdistrict of Poncokusumo to the east of Malang where I was to later conduct research, the violence began even later, in mid-November of 1965. As had been the case in Pasuruan's eastern highlands, the campaign in the latter region had awaited the arrival of army-backed militias driving up the main (and only) mountain road from lowland Malang to the Mt. Bromo uplands. In the eyes of most uplanders, even those who had no sympthy for the PKI, the campaign to exterminate the small cadre of local communists in the uplands was the work of outsiders and antithetical to local values of harmony (*kerukunan*) and uplander solidarity.

Whereas in Pasuruan regency the civilian militias mobilized for the killings were overwhelmingly NU-based, those in Malang city were led by male youth from the Muhammadiyah, complemented by a smaller number of activists from the Catholic Student movement and Nahdlatul Ulama.[13] The most prominent of the Malang militia leaders were Muhammadiyah college graduates formerly active in the Indonesian Muslim Student Association (Himpunan Mahasiswa Indonesia, HMI). In the early 1960s, as rivalries between Muslim and communist youth had heated up nationally,[14] communist youth in Malang had organized rallies calling for the banning of the HMI and the expulsion of HMI students from college. Several of these demonstrations ended in clashes between HMI and Communist youth, often to the detriment of the HMI. As I learned in 1980 from a former HMI leader in Malang (see below), the PKI students justified the assaults by claiming that the HMI was a counter-revolutionary force complicit in the Darul-Islam rebellions underway in Aceh, West Java, and South Sulawesi. The PKI campaign had left HMI activists bitterly resentful and determined at some later point to turn the tables on their powerful rival.

---

[11] Hefner, *Political Economy*, 3.

[12] Leksana, "Collaboration in Mass Violence," 73.

[13] In their recent study of the killings in Yogyakarta, Chandra and Winward similarly report that in that city too Muhammadiyah activists comprised the core leadership for the anti-communist campaign. See Chandra and Winward, "Road to Perdition."

[14] On the situation of the HMI and student groups both prior to and after the events of September 30, 1965, see Francois Raillon, *Les étudiants indonésiens et l'Ordre nouveau: Politique et idéologie du Mahasiswa Indonesia, 1966–1974*, vol. 6 (Paris: Éditions de la Maison des Sciences de l'Homme, 1995).

Some twelve years after the events of 1965–66, as I was about to launch my dissertation research, a Malang-born HMI leader showed up at my Malang hotel room to volunteer to work as my partner in ethnographic research in the southeastern mountain territories of Malang regency. Ten years my senior, the politely mannered and soft-spoken man explained that he was a former college teacher who had lost his job at the University of Jember several years earlier as a result of his outspoken opposition to Suharto-era policies on Islam. In the years since, he had made ends meet by serving as a mountain-climbing guide and engaging in small-scale vegetable farming in the upland communities in the Malang and Lumajang regencies where I intended to carry out research.

This man, whom I will call Pak Yusuf, went on to work with me during the entire period of my ethnographic research in upland Pasuruan and Malang in 1978–80, 1985, and 1991. A thoughtful, deeply pious, and energetically intelligent man from a prominent but non-affluent Muhammadiyah family in Malang, Pak Yusuf eventually became my closest friend in East Java and remained so up through his death in 2008. Several months into our relationship, while gathering oral histories in January 1980 on sociopolitical change in the Pasuruan highlands, Pak Yusuf startled me by revealing that he had played a central role directing civilian militias involved in the anti-PKI killings in the Malang and Lumajang regencies, as well as in the "Trident Operation" (*Operasi Trisula*) against remnant PKI activists in South Blitar from June to September 1968. Pak Yusuf volunteered these facts after an interview we had conducted with a former PKI activist in Puspo village in Pasuruan regency, a man who had survived the killings. In Lumajang and South Blitar, I learned, Pak Yusuf had used his caving and mountain climbing skills to seek out remnants of the PKI taking refuge in limestone caves in both of those territories. As Chandra and Hearman have both observed, the mountain borderland between the Malang and Lumajang regencies as well as South Blitar were regions identified by Communist Party officials as *Komite Proyek* ("committee project"). These territories had not yet been opened to road building, which would begin in earnest only in the late 1970s. In the months following the outbreak of the anti-PKI campaign in October 1965, then, party survivors had regrouped in the region with the aim of eventually mounting counter-attacks on anti-PKI forces.[15] With his mountaineering skills and cordial ties to upland locals, Pak Yusuf was uniquely qualified to hunt down these PKI refugees.

In bits and pieces over the next several years, Pak Yusuf revealed that he served not just as a militia coordinator, but as an interrogator and judge in upland communities across these two East Java regencies, as well as in lowland districts south of Malang and in South Blitar, where the scale of the killings (and his role) had been even greater. As he explained to me in a five-hour conversation in April 1980 in Ngadiwono, Pasuruan, Pak Yusuf had officiated in the sentencing of more than one thousand PKI activists, condemning several hundred to their death. When I asked him whether he had regrets about his actions, he said without hesitation that he felt that the ascendant Suharto regime had used Muslim allies for its own political ends, and at least from this point of view, he had some regrets about his actions. On several occasions, too, he commented that he was often startled by the number of PKI activists who had asked to be allowed to

---

[15] See Siddharth Chandra, "Glimpses of Indonesia's 1965 Massacre," 34–34; and Vannessa Hearman, "Guerilla, Guns, and Knives? Debating Insurgency in South Blitar, East Java, 1967–68," *Indonesia* 89 (April 2010): 61–91, esp. pp. 62, 65, and 73–83.

perform Islamic prayers prior to being executed. In the overall scheme of things, though, Pak Yusuf insisted that he and his colleagues in the Muslim militias had no choice. Had they not joined the campaign, "Indonesia would have ended up like Cambodia under the Khmer Rouge." With regard to the anti-communist campaign in South Blitar in 1968, Pak Yusuf said he had even fewer misgivings, because "in that region we were sure we were dealing with dedicated communist cadres."

Although the scale of the killings in both of these upland East Java regions was more limited than in the wet-rice lowlands to their west, the political and religious consequences of the campaign were significant and enduring. The social effects were visible in everything from religious conversion and the demolition of Javanist spirit cult shrines to the inauguration of a new, "Green Revolution" economy and, with it, new national styles of status and consumption.[16] Although its effects were less immediately apparent, the pall of the killings nonetheless still hung over this upland region well into the 2000s.

An Accommodationist Communist Party

As the above description makes clear, NU militias had played the leading role in the attacks on communists in lowland areas of Pasuruan that broke out in the middle of October 1965. This example confirms Chandra's province-wide analyses of the pivotal role of NU militias in assisting the army in the detention and killing of alleged PKI activists.[17] The course of the violence in lowland Pasuruan is also distinctive because, as Leksana and Robinson have similarly reported,[18] the first incidents of mass killings occurred well before the arrival of anti-PKI army units in the region and a month before the mid-November initiation of an army-coordinated campaign in the Pasuruan and Malang highlands. When the campaign was eventually extended into these latter mountain territories, the effort was directed not by local NU militias as in lowland Pasuruan, but by army units sent to the region in trucks confiscated from alleged supporters of the PKI.

In Pasuruan regency, the trucks brought in anti-communist militias from the wet-rice lowlands and adjacent hill communities. The great majority of these civilian militias were NU-linked, Ansor youth from two large Islamic boarding schools (*pesantren*) in the subdistrict of Pasrepan, located along the main road linking the mountain subdistrict to the town of Pasuruan in the coastal plains below. In a pattern seen elsewhere in Java, as Chandra and Winward have noted,[19] the Ansor militias concentrated their efforts in villages accessible by road—typically within two to three kilometers of an asphalt road. A later and less violent mopping up operation against PKI survivors took place in the same upland territories in the middle months of 1966.

---

[16] See Hefner, *Political Economy*, 81–227.

[17] Chandra, "Glimpses of Indonesia's 1965," 29. In his 2019 article on the killings in Central Java, Chandra reminds us that "while politics in East Java was dominated by the PKI and NU, in Central Java the competition in many locations was triangular, with the PKI and NU in close competition not only with each other but also with the PNI." See Chandra, "The Indonesian Killings of 1965–1966," 314.

[18] Leksana, "Collaboration in Mass Violence," 63; and Robinson, *The Killing Season*, 151–52.

[19] Chandra and Winward, "Road to Perdition."

When the Ansor youth and their army backers arrived in a village, their procedure was to order the full staff of village officials to assemble in front of the village meeting hall. The militia leadership then explained the aims of their campaign and ordered village officials to round up and detain all PKI cadre residents in the village. As I learned from the dozens of oral histories I collected in 1979–80 and 1985, village officials were told they had just one day to complete the round up. The army and Ansor militias also told village officials that if they delayed the detention or shielded PKI individuals, the officials would be regarded as co-conspirators in the PKI's "counter-revolutionary" actions. Of equal note, the militia teams also reassured village officials that PKI detainees would not be executed in their home villages; they were to be taken out of the highlands to meet their final destiny. No killings were supposed to take place in upland communities themselves. No less remarkably, in the end none did.

Although some villagers whom I interviewed in 1980 and 1985 speculated that the detainees were taken away rather than executed locally so as to avoid sparking unrest, village officials whom I interviewed insisted that the army officers in charge of upland operations offered a different explanation. The military coordinators made clear that they understood that people in these mountain communities were good Indonesian nationalists, unsympathetic to the communist cause or the Thirtieth of September movement. In May 1985, one army official who had visited upland villages for more than twenty years told me that, while coordinating the detention of PKI activists in the area in November 1965, he realized that villagers would be "traumatized" if the killings were carried out locally. So he had recommended the policy of detainee-removal so as spare local people that trauma.

There was another striking detail to the course of the killings in Pasuruan's eastern uplands. My interviews in 1985 with the small group of NU preachers who resided in these predominantly *abangan* communities indicated that, when the preachers heard that lowland NU militias were about to extend their campaign up into mountain communities, the preachers appealed to their traditionalist brothers that they *not* do so. Years later these preachers told me that they feared that rounding up and executing communists in this upland region would damage the fragile proselytizing (*dakwah*) progress NU preachers were just beginning to make in this still predominantly *abangan* region.

In August 1985, toward the end of my second stint of research , one especially well regarded NU preacher in the Puspo subdistrict provided an unusual detail on a disagreement raging in NU circles in late 1965. In the course of our three-hour conversation late one evening, the always-dignified preacher broke down sobbing. The topic of our conversation was the local community's growing interest in NU-promoted religious *dakwah*. However, in the course of commenting on his own religious outreach in the area he abruptly changed the topic so as to explain that in November 1965 he had appealed to his lowland NU brothers not to unleash a campaign of killing in villages across the upland region. He had told his NU colleagues that he was certain that all of the local PKI cadres were poorly educated and ill-informed "followers" who understood little about communism; no less important, he explained, they were not unbelievers (*kafir*). "I know all of them personally, and none of them were atheists," he declared, talking through his tears. On these grounds, he explained, he had appealed to his lowland NU counterparts not to participate in any coordinated invasion of upland villages. By this time, however, the province-wide assault on the PKI was moving up the mountainside, and Ansor units were central to it. The preacher's appeals thus went unheard. Although this example may be something of an outlier to the broader Java pattern, Katharine E. McGregor has also shown that several prominent NU *ulama,* including Abdullah Faqih of Langitan Pesantren and KH Choiril Bisri of Rembang, forbade their students from participating in the killings. McGregor notes that Bisri "tried to dissuade the military from killing leftists on the basis that they were neighbors and only different in their ideology."[20]

In the oral histories I collected during fieldwork in 1978–80, 1985, 1991, and 2005, I was also regularly told that "almost all" of the village heads (*petinggi*) in the mountain districts of eastern Pasuruan and Malang were at first reluctant to carry out the orders for detaining local PKI activists. As noted above, none of them participated in the actual execution of cadres. The fifteen village chiefs on whom I gathered biographical information were all affiliated with the Indonesian National Party. In this upland territory, the PNI was regarded as the party of President Sukarano and all local government officials. I was often told, "In this region in those [pre-New Order] days, if you're a local village official, you're PNI."

There was, however, a deeper political logic to the upland chiefs' hesitation in the face of the anti-PKI campaign. In the years leading up to September 30, 1965, communist mobilization in upland areas of the Pasuruan and Malang regencies around Mount Bromo had never won more than a few dozen supporters in each village. Equally significant, local PKI activism tended to be low-key and nonconfrontational with regard to the PNI village establishment. Among other things, there was no upland equivalent to the PKI campaigns in nearby regions of lowland Pasuruan and Malang to press for implementation of the land redistribution scheme stipulated under the terms of the 1960 Basic Agrarian Law. Villages in these two upland regions had rates of landlessness of about 2–8 percent—among the lowest in rural Java. By Indonesian standards as well, there were few large landholders, and the overall pattern of land distribution was only moderately class stratified.[21]

Upland villagers were keenly aware of this difference in class structure between their communities and the wet-rice lowlands, where landlessness on average affected some 40–60 percent of rural households. When comparing the two regions, the uplanders habitually distinguished "lowland Javanese" (*wong ngare*) from "mountain people" (*wong gunung*) in just this way. Local Muslim villagers also maintained a sense of themselves as a people different in bearing and religious tradition from those in the lowlands. With this strong corporate self-identification, most villagers were happy to defer to the recommendations of village leaders to steer clear of mobilizational politics and vote as a bloc in support of the Indonesian National Party. This politics-aversive pattern was one that resembled what, decades ago, the anthropologist Eric Wolf had called "closed

---

[20] Katharine E. McGregor, "A Bridge and a Barrier: Islam, Reconciliation, and the 1965 killings in Indonesia," in *Reconciling Indonesia: Grassroots Agency for Peace,* ed. Birgit Brauchler (London: Routledge 2009), 216.

[21] See Hefner, Political Economy, 113–58. For a comparative analysis of class inequality and demographic growth in upland Central Java, see Jan G. L. Palte, "The Development of Java's Rural Uplands in Response to Population Growth: An Introductory Essay in Historical Perspective" (Yogyakarta: Occasional Paper, Gadjah Mada University, Department of Geography, 1984). For a broader, pan-Indonesian perspective on social class and economic change in Indonesia's uplands, see *Transforming the Indonesian Uplands: Marginality, Power and Production,* ed. Tania Murray Lee (Amsterdam: Harwood Academic Publishers, 1999).

corporate" peasant communities in Latin America, rather than socially open, heavily capitalized, and class-stratified peasantries.[22]

With the notable exception of its campaign in support of squatters on forestry lands (see below), then, local communists in the uplands limited their mobilizational efforts to a low-key and mostly unsuccessful appeal for votes in the 1955 and 1957 elections. Another area where local PKI cadres were occasionally active had to do with efforts to create an umbrella organization for the *kebatinan* mystical groups active in Malang and Pasuruan's eastern highlands.[23] Here again, however, these socio-religious initiatives brought communist leaders into alliance with rather than opposition to the upland PNI establishment. Their collaboration operated in a way that underscored the two group's joint opposition to Nahdlatul Ulama and campaigns of Islamic reform.

Although these activities in support of indigenous religious traditions brought the PKI leadership into operational alliance with PNI leaders, the same initiatives antagonized relations with local Nahdlatul Ulama leaders. Most of the mystical groups in this upland region self-identified as Muslim, albeit of a non-*santri* variety. In the culture-war atmosphere of the late-1950s, however, a minority among these movements mocked pious Muslims and promoted outright apostasy from Islam. The largest among these latter groups was an organization established in the early 1950s and known as the Javanese Budha-Visnu religion (*agama Budha Visnu Jawi*).[24] Unlike the majority of mystics in this mountain region, the Budha-Visnu group made no secret of the fact that it urged its followers to apostatize from Islam. However, its village-based leaders also took care to emphasize their commonality of culture with the broader local populace, as well as with the PNI-based village chiefs.

In November 1965, the Budha-Visnu group was to pay dearly for its advocacy of apostasy from Islam. NU militias arriving in the mountain region included the Budha-Visnu leadership among the first of its targets for capture and execution. Years later, in July 1985, in fact, Budha-Visnu survivors told me that it was only as a result of army commanders intervening to stop the killing of Budha-Visnu followers that the carnage had been curtailed. By that time, however, dozens of Budha-Visnu followers had perished. The example is a small but notable exception to Geoffrey Robinson's otherwise compelling conclusion that, "In marked contrast to many other cases of mass killing or genocide, the victims in Indonesia were not targeted because of their ethnicity, nationality, or religion."[25]

In sum, although the PKI in this upland region had involved itself in campaigns intended to protect the interests of *abangan* Muslims, they framed their appeals in ways that emphasized the common rather than opposed interests of local communist and national officials. Time and time again, the local PKI presented itself as an ally of the

[22] Eric R. Wolf, "Closed Corporate Peasant Communities in Mesoamerica and Central Java." *Southwestern Journal of Anthropology* 1, no. 13 (1957): 1–18.

[23] Hefner, "Islamizing Java"; " Political Economy".

[24] Hefner, "Islamizing Java," 538–43.

[25] Robinson, *The Killing Season*, 7.

many local PNI leaders who, since the early 1950s, had sought to preserve their *abangan* traditions on the grounds that these were a legitimately Javanese profession of Islam. [26]

There was, however, one partial exception to the nonconfrontational posture of the small PKI organization in these upland villages. The exception had to do with landless peasants who had come from the lowlands in the early republican era to squat on what state officials regarded as state forestry lands. Whereas studies of the violence elsewhere in Java have focused on the role of the PKI in mobilizing "unilateral actions" (*aksi sephihak*) aimed as seizing large landholdings so as to enforce ownership limits stipulated in the Basic Agrarian Law of 1960,[27] there were no such actions in these upland communities in southeastern Pasuruan and eastern Malang. The one campaign the PKI did launch had to do with defending the rights of landless squatters who had occupied lands previously owned by Dutch landholders, as well as those who had moved in the late 1940s onto forest lands under the management of the Department of Forestry. Several dozen squatters had pioneered these land seizures in the middle years of the Indonesian Revolution (1945–49). In the late 1950s (and beginning especially in May 1958), their numbers had been boosted with the arrival of another group of squatters, now under the direction of communist activists. Small in number, the squatter population was regarded by local villagers as outsiders but not otherwise troublesome and certainly not oppositional with regard to village leadership as a whole.

A third and far larger influx of squatters took place after October 1965 with the arrival of refugees from the nearby Malang and Pasuruan lowlands. This new wave of immigrants consisted entirely of villagers fleeing the killing then underway in lowland communities. The great majority of these individuals were members of PKI affiliate organizations in the Pasuruan and Malang lowlands. Eventually, some of these PKI refugees from the killings were identified and detained in the course of army-led campaigns. The largest of the latter mobilizations took place more than a half year later than the first wave of arrests in the mountain region in November 1965. When, in April 1966, security officials arrived in the upland area to seek out surviving PKI elements, they directed most of their attention toward the remote mountain districts south of Mt. Semeru, along the border of the Malang-Lumajang regencies. There, as in South Blitar, PKI survivors were actively regrouping and attempting to mount organized resistance.[28] By contrast, most refugees who had earlier joined the ranks of the squatter community in upland Pasuruan and Malang where I did research were interviewed by army officials and quickly released. Security officials recognized the locals were not serious PKI activists. When, thirteen years later (in February 1980) I encountered some of these survivors, most had integrated well into local society. They had built families and refashioned themselves as "mountain people" (*wong gunung*). A few had converted

---

[26] As Geoffrey Robinson has argued, and as the present essay agrees, it is imperative when speaking of *santri-abangan* tensions in rural Java to recognize that, although these social cleavages figured in later violence, the intensity of the divide cannot explain why the mass violence escalated to the degree that it did and how it took on the well-coordinated organization it displayed across broad swaths of Indonesia. See *The Killing Season*, 13.

[27] See Rex Mortimer, *Indonesian Communism under Sukarno: Ideology and Politics, 1959–1965* (Ithaca: Cornell University Press, 1974), 277.

[28] Hearman, *Unmarked Graves*, 138–70.

to Christianity, but most were more comfortable self-identifying as Muslims "in the Javanese way" (*cara Jawa*).[29]

Although most of these refugees had begun their new lives in poor circumstances, by the late 1970s and early 1980s many were getting by economically rather well. Most had better literacy and math skills than their upland neighbors and put them to use opening food stalls (*warung*) and small stores. A few also made use of their ties to friends and family in the lowlands to build long-distance trading relationships, moving upland forest and farm goods down to lowland markets. The other trademark that I encountered among many of these survivors had to do with their social personality. While the preferred social style in upland interactions was one of a gregarious egalitarianism, many of the refugee residents showed a wistful reserve and a self-conscious demeanor. Their village fellows responded to my inquiries about these individuals' past in an unfailingly consistent manner. As one villager put it, "I never hear them talk about their past. All we really know is that originally, they're from somewhere else." In social fact, almost all adult locals understood that the new immigrants were refugees from the 1965–66 killings. Rather than stigmatizing the refugees as former communists, however, most locals opted to maintain village harmony by protecting the immigrants' anonymity.

Conclusion: Varied Embeddings and Uncertain Futures

Standing back from this brief history, then, we can see that there were several reasons for the lower incidence of mass killings in these two upland regions than that which Jay had reported from his upland Pare community. First and foremost, there was an only skeletal Nahdlatul Ulama presence in both of these mountain regions. What NU networks there were dedicated themselves to proselytization while steering clear of faction-inducing political mobilization. As Chandra has observed, the regencies in East Java where political support for Nahdlatul Ulama was greatest (as measured by, among other things, the percentage of the vote given to the NU party in the 1955 and 1957 elections) tended to be "regencies that saw larger declines of population" during and after the 1965–66 violence, both as a result of mass killings and refugee flight.[30]

As noted above, in the upland subdistricts in Pasuruan and Malang subdistricts where I conducted research, the NU infrastructure was not only small—it was also politically quietist. In the 1950s and early 1960s, these upland villages were overwhelmingly *abangan* in religious orientation. Few are *abangan* in this manner today. No less significant, in mountain communities where NU preachers dedicated themselves to campaigns of religious proselytization (*dakwah*), some NU officials had reservations about taking part in or otherwise condoning the killings. Some protested loudly against

[29] On religious conversion in Java in the aftermath of the violence, see Vannessa Hearman, "The 1965–1966 Violence, Religious Conversions and the Changing Relationship between the Left and Indonesia's Churches," in *The Indonesian Genocide of 1965: Causes, Dynamics, and Legacies*, ed. Katharine E. McGregor, Jess Melvin, Annie Pohlman (New York: Palgrave MacMillan 2018), 179–95. For an earlier analysis, see Robert W. Hefner, "Of Faith and Commitment: Christian Conversion in Muslim Java," in *Conversion to Christianity: Historical and Anthropological Perspectives on a Great Transformation*, ed. Robert W. Hefner (Berkeley: University of California Press, 1993), 99–125.

[30] See Chandra, "New Findings," 1067.

Ansor militias coming into the mountain region in pursuit of communists, fearing the campaign would undercut their own *dakwah* outreach.

The situation in the wet-rice lowlands below my mountain residences in Pasuruan and Malang regencies was entirely different. Pasuruan regency had long been known as a stronghold of NU activism. Notwithstanding NU's dominance, beginning in 1960 the PKI had made headway organizing laborers in textile factories located to the south of Pasuruan city. This small mobilizational advance generated fierce resentment in lowland NU circles. By 1964, the small PKI presence in this region combined with far noisier PKI mobilizations in Banyuwangi to the east and Surabaya-Kediri to the west to raise political tensions in the Pasuruan lowlands to a fever pitch.

This combination of circumstances made for an early and especially fierce outbreak of anticommunist killings in the Pasuruan lowlands. The violence began even before the arrival of army special forces and before the East Java military command's call on October 21 for the extermination of the so-called "counter-revolutionaries" associated with the abortive left-wing officers' coup in Jakarta. As Robinson has also observed,[31] the anti-PKI campaign across much of East Java was delayed slightly because in the days following the failed Jakarta coup, the military command in East Java, though fiercely anti-communist, wished to signal its pro-Sukarno posture and avoid taking actions that might jeopardize the president's standing. Meanwhile, as Harold Crouch has also reported, Ansor, the youth wing of Nahdlatul Ulama, showed no such hesitancy. On October 10, Ansor leaders decided to "hold synchronized rallies . . . on the thirteenth at Kediri, Blitar, Trenggalek, and other towns, after which attacks would be made on PKI offices and PKI supporters would be deliberately killed."[32]

Farther south yet from the city of Pasuruan, in the verdant eastern hills of the Malang regency, NU was significantly less powerful than its counterpart in Pasuruan regency. Lacking a strong NU organization to direct the campaign, the killings in south Malang began later (in mid-November 1965) and were launched on a large scale only after the arrival of armed-forces handlers. As noted above, another difference with the Pasuruan example is that in and around Malang city, Muhammadiyah activists, including those under the leadership of my long-time friend, Pak Yusuf, played a more prominent role than did NU in coordinating the anti-communist campaign.

A second conclusion of relevance for the comparative analysis of the 1965–66 violence has to do with the population movements that took place in the course of the killings. In the midst of first wave of killings in November 1965, a large population movement took place, from lowland communities up into the mountain subdistricts of southeastern Pasuruan and eastern Malang. During my dissertation research, from 1978 to 1980, and again during a year's research in this same region during 1985, I regularly encountered refugee survivors in these areas. Although I stumbled on to refugees like this in virtually every upland community, the silence that surrounded such families made it difficult to estimate just how large this up-mountain influx had been. It is for that reason that I have been grateful for Siddharth Chandra's remarkable demographic reanalysis of the violence

---

[31] Robinson, *The Killing Season*, 151–52.

[32] Harold Crouch, *The Army and Politics in Indonesia* (Ithaca: Cornell University Press, 1988), 147.

in East Java.[33] Chandra has demonstrated that the population movement to which I was a late-arriving observer was nothing less than massive—involving thousands of people. The refugees came to the highlands not with dreams of landownership, as some had during Indonesia's independence war, but because they were terrified of the killing machine moving methodically across the Pasuruan and Malang countryside.

My third and concluding comment fast-forwards from my earlier experiences to my research on Muslim associations and citizenship in Jakarta and Yogyakarta in the 1990s and 2000s. From 1990 onward, I had relocated my research out of East Java to Jakarta. There for the next decade I carried out research among the capital's Muslim middle class, focusing on the Islamic resurgence and debates over how Muslims should engage the country's growing pro-democracy movement. I concentrated much of my research on NU and Muhammadiyah activists, a story I recounted in *Civil Islam*.[34] However, as I hinted in the preface to that book, the specter of the 1965–66 violence still haunted these urban settings. In my first public speaking engagement at a NU-sponsored seminar in Jakarta in 1991, one of the youthful activists, familiar with my research on the 65–66 violence in East Java, challenged me by asking, "In light of what you reported as to NU activists' complicity in the mass killing of communists in 65–66, do you actually believe Indonesian Muslims are capable of promoting democracy?" The young man's question was clearly directed more at his NU fellows in the room than it was me.

However, as I continued my research in Jakarta, and later, in the 2000s, in Yogyakarata, I came to realize that the issue of 1965–66 is still far from resolved in mainstream Muslim circles. In the late 1990s and early 2000s, I became close to the late Abdurrahman Wahid (1940–2009). As president Wahid attempted to effect a reconciliation between NU and survivors of the 65–66 violence. In Jakarta in 1999 and Yogyakarta in the 2000s, I also got to know Imam Aziz quite well. Mas Imam is renowned for having established an organization known as Syarikat (Masyarakat Santri untuk Advokasi Rakyat; Santri for People's Advocacy) in 2000. He did so with the support of the small but influential progressive wing of the NU in central Java (and Yogyakarta in particular), associated with the local LAKPESDAM (Committee for the Study and Development of Human Resources).[35] One of Syarikat's core ambitions was promote reconciliation between survivors of the 1965–66 killings and NU militia-members who had carried out those actions. As Katharine McGregor and Priyambudi Sulistiyanto and Rumekso Setyadi have also reported, my sense from Jakarta and Yogyakarta in the 2000s was that the Syarikat initiative was regarded unfavorably by many rank-and-file NU, as well as by an even higher percentage of pesantren-based (as opposed to university-educated) NU scholars.[36] Although Imam Aziz's position in the NU national leadership is today secure and he is hugely respected, my interviews and two 1,000-person surveys conducted in 2004 and 2006 confirmed that the Gusdurian and Azizian position on PKI reconciliation

[33] Siddharth Chandra, "New Findings"; "Glimpses of Indonesia's 1965 Massacre through the Lens of the Census."

[34] Robert W. Hefner, *Civil Islam: Muslims and Democratization in Indonesia* (Princeton: Princeton University Press 2000), xii–xvi.

[35] On Imam Aziz and Syarikat's founding, see Katharine E. McGregor, "Confronting the Past," 205–20.

[36] See McGregor, "Confronting the Past"; and Priyambudi Sulistiyanto and Rumekso Setyadi, "Civil Society and Grassroots Reconciliation in Central Java," in *Reconciling Indonesia: Grassroots Agency for Peace*, ed. Birgit Bräuchler (New York: Routledge 2009), 192–213.

remains a decidedly minority view. In fact, it seemed to me that *organized* opposition to reconciliation efforts actually grew in NU circles in the years following Gus Dur's presidency, coincident with the "conservative turn" seen in NU and Muhammadiyah circles.[37]

I will conclude this retrospective essay with a brief observation on just what is happening with regard to the 1965 issue in both NU and Muhammadiyah circles today. On one hand, the rank and file of these two organizations have been buffeted by the manipulation of anti-communist sentiments in the course of the 2014 and 2019 presidential campaigns. Although much has been made of the alleged role of the armed forces in promoting polarization around this issue, my impression is that this top-down view overlooks the fact that even in the strongly democratic wings of NU and Muhammadiyah many people disagree with efforts to apologize for the 1965–66 violence or otherwise pursue a truth-and-reconciliation pathway. A sympathetic minority feel the issue is best addressed through less "divisive" practical measures, like eliminating discrimination against the children and grandchildren of PKI survivors. In some four decades of research, and with the notable exception of friends in Syarikat, LAKPESDAM, and human-rights NGOs, I have encountered only a minority of individuals who favor a bolder approach to reconciliation.

But my second and final observation softens this first generalization about the continuing salience of anti-reconciliation sentiment. It is that among the younger generation of Indonesians, including the younger generation of NU and Muhammadiyah activists, discussion of the events of 1965–66 is no longer seen as taboo, or a matter on which there can be only one point of view. Yes, public events of a truth-and-reconciliation sort still incite opposition, sometimes along with phone-call warnings from unidentified callers, as Imam Aziz has experienced. But in universities and in Muslim intellectual circles generally, discussions of 1965–66 have become, if not commonplace, considerably less controversial.

A key condition of this new tolerance, I believe, is that it is expected that at all such events include anti-communist voices and that the proponents of these views be treated respectfully along with those advocating apology or reconciliation. For activist Indonesians hoping for a South-African style truth-and-reconciliation engagement with survivors, this approach may appear to be a half-measure at best. My sense, however, is that such discussions may actually be an Indonesian instrument for incremental progress and healing. They bring the subject of 1965–66 into the public sphere even in the absence of consensus and reconciliation and without the expectation that a full consensus will ever be possible. But events of this nature also allow a partial recognition of the fact Indonesia today is strong and stable enough to exorcise the worst ghosts of the 1965–66 violence, even while citizens agree to disagree on its precise meaning or moral truth.

---

[37] See Martin van Bruinessen, "Introduction: Contemporary Developments in Indonesian Islam and the 'Conservative Turn' of the Early Twenty-First Century," in *Contemporary Developments in Indonesian Islam: Explaining the "Conservative Turn"* (Singapore: ISEAS Publishing, 2013), 1–20. For a contrasting view that suggests, I believe convincingly, that the *political and economic* effects of pietistic trends in contemporary Indonesia are less consistently "conservative" than many analysts suggest, see Thomas B. Pepinsky, R. William Liddle, and Saiful Mujani, *Piety and Public Opinion: Understanding Indonesian Islam* (New York: Oxford University Press, 2018).

Learning Injustice:

Historical Memory of the Indonesian 1965 Genocide and Education to Young People

Sri Lestari Wahyuningroem and Dyah Ayu Kartika

Introduction

This article discusses educational initiatives involving collective memory of past gross human rights violations in Indonesia. The events referred to here are the 1965 genocide, mass violence against citizens affiliated with the communist party, and those accused of being communists in the 1965–1966 period. Tens to hundreds of thousands of people were killed, and tens of thousands of others were detained without trial by the government led by General Suharto, which marked the beginning of an authoritarian regime that lasted for more than three decades in Indonesia.

In 1998, due to the severe economic and political crisis, followed by riots in various places, Suharto finally resigned, and the transition to democracy began. Multiple elements in civil society and the state have attempted several transitional justice initiatives to resolve past wrongs, including ending the genocide 65. However, the collective memory of the incident of genocide is still being denied by the state.

Civil society is trying other ways to challenge this denial. Transitional justice approach, which at the beginning of the democratic transition seemed to be a common agenda, was slowly being sidelined and began to be abandoned by the government (Wahyuningroem, 2022). At almost the same time, civil society initiatives to present justice and truth are getting more robust and diverse (Wahyuningroem, 2013, 2019). One of the spaces used is education for young people, emphasizing historical memory, especially from survivors. These initiatives are carried out both outside of official school institutions and those that take place in school classrooms. We call this form of education historical memory education (HME), an approach to teaching that studies history as a collective memory of a particular event.

In this article, we focus on two initiatives that target young people at the tertiary level, namely the Student Human Rights School (SEHAMA), which an NGO, KontraS, initiated, and the independent initiative of several individual lecturers at universities in Indonesia. In particular, we want to know and compare the adoption of HME in informal spaces such as SEHAMA and formal education spaces such as universities. How is HME implemented, and what is its impact on collective memory related to genocide 65 in the public area in Indonesia?

This article is part of a more considerable peace and justice education project conducted by KU Leuven and Gajah Mada University in Indonesia. Along the way, we were also involved in a study conducted by Forces of Renewal for Southeast Asia (FORSEA) regarding how genocide is taught in several Southeast Asian countries, especially Indonesia. The data we use mainly comes from in-depth interviews with three members of KontraS who initiated and organized SEHAMA, three participants, two survivors of the 1965 genocide, two lecturers who used several parts of the HME approach, and one student who took part in this lecture model. This initiative's various reports and products are secondary sources of information used in our analysis.

We argue in this paper that HME has the potential to not only transform the understanding of past wrongs but also transform the political agenda among the young generation that participated in the projects. In a country where impunity and the state's denials of past human rights abuses remain strong such as in Indonesia, such potential exists as a limited space with a risk of being unsustained due to limited resources and support from elements of the state. Some of the outcomes of such initiatives include leadership and networks for participants to work on human rights issues in their careers. These outcomes can only be achieved in initiatives that directly involve individual young people compared to working through intermediaries such as schools or government agencies.

We start our discussion by outlining what we refer to as historical memory education. Even though there are numerous studies on historical memory works, few have studied the use of the approach to education. We will mainly use the framework of HME developed by Correda et al. (2018) and Schultze-Kraft (2022). Following from the discussion, we explain the historical memory of 1965 genocide within the context of state's denial especially in the education sector by maintaining the State's official narrative of the account. The next discussion will discuss how HME approach is adopted by KontraS and individual university lecturers before we assess the outcomes of such approach in the following part. Lastly, we will complete the article with a conclusion.

Historical Memory Education for Young People

In this article, we specifically look at HME carried out by elements of civil society against young people in Indonesia. HME refers to "the field within pedagogical and educational studies that reviews instructional experiences and builds educational theory regarding the healing of wounds of recent violent conflicts and authoritarian regimes, in contexts in which the victims' right to truth and non-repetition needs to be warranted through education" (Corredor et al., 2018, 3). It emphasizes the socio-structural conditions that allow conflicts and authoritarian regimes to arise, allowing historical aspects in explaining the fractures in today's democracy that led to human rights violations. This educational model emphasizes historical memory, namely how groups, collectivities, and nations construct and identify with particular historical narratives.

Historical memory is essential for several reasons in the context of a country transitioning from conflict or a form of authoritarianism that gave birth to mass violence. First, historical memory allows public acknowledgment of what happened to several citizens who were victims of mass violence and injustice. Public disclosure of the victim's experience will enable victims to act on the public narrative to make it consistent with their personal experiences and memories. At the same time, this also allows healing of the sociopolitical context, which is fundamental for full reparation, notably when transforming the public discourse is essential for restoring victims' dignity and mental health (Corredor et al., 2018; Schultze-Kraft, 2022). Historical memory is also a guarantee of non-repetition because it creates a general understanding of the paths that lead to evil and promotes social imaginations that prevent it (Bickford & Sodaro, 2010).

Historical memory applied in education has characteristics that distinguish it from historical education and other forms of peace education (Schultze-Kraft, 2022). Corredor et al. (2018) state that its uniqueness lies in meeting three different levels of memories: personal, collective, and historical. Personal memory refers to the individual's memories, collective memory refers to the shared recollections of mnemonic communities, and historical memory refers to the historical narrative constructed by expert historians and social science researchers. When these three levels are connected during instruction, students can understand how accounts at multiple levels can arise in historical memory and how they represent valid lenses to analyze conflicts.

This emphasis on historical memory serves to intervene in emotion and empathy, which then bridges the process of new knowledge of an event. This educational model believes that practicing emotional regulation and interpersonal problem-solving skills is a step toward reducing violence in a post-conflict society. In contexts of sustained conflicts and human rights violations, people learn that violence is the solution to everyday conflicts (Posada & Wainryb, 2008). Along the same line, prolonged exposure to violence produces emotional desensitization (Tarabah et al., 2015).

Emotional intervention could have an impact to improve students' agency, because agency connects individual reflection and action. *Agency* is defined here as the sense that one can control the outcomes of one's actions and decisions and intentionally influence one's circumstances in life (Schwartz et al., 2005). A basic sense of agency is necessary for political participation. However, the agency needs a complex political and historical understanding. Understanding the complexity of history is, therefore, essential to prevent evil (Corredor et al., 2018). Historical understanding complements the changes at the personal level and helps to translate empathy into effective action toward victims and agency into intelligent political participation. In this sense, a solid disciplinary understanding of history is essential in peacebuilding through education (McCully, 2011).

The historical memory we focus on in this paper involves young people, in this case, students at the higher education level, as participants. Education to reach the youth is one of the strategies civil society groups adopt to bring truth and justice to the nation's past injustices. In this context, as Ramirez and Duthie (2015) explain, education has two important goals. Firstly, it contributes to developing children's abilities and skills for participating in a country's productive and sociopolitical realms. Secondly, it enhances the capacity of citizens, especially adolescents and children, to think critically about the present and the past, so they can foresee and build a better future. In the period of democratic transition, education can be an essential vehicle for remembering the past, facilitating the transmission of memory, and promoting peace. Because of its formative potential, education can help shape new norms, mediate between competing narratives of the past, and nurture a culture of respect for human rights across generations. A fundamental aspect in this respect is that education is a sector that simultaneously reaches multiple generations (Ramirez & Duthie, 2015, p. 1).

The Missing Narrative: 1965 Massacre and History Education in Indonesia

The state still plays a big role in suppressing the collective memory of the 1965 Indonesian mass killings. Young people had very limited options to learn about the tragedy from schools as history textbooks and teachers were not allowed to show alternative narratives from the state's version. Even if there is another version of the history, public debates focus more on the perpetrators of the killing of six generals (Gerakan 30 September or G30S), other than the aftermath mass extermination.

More than 20 years after the fall of the New Order Era, Indonesian history in schools found tremendous difficulties in standing on objective facts. In 1976, pro-New Order historians under the military's influence published six books as the main reference for history education at school (Głąb, 2018). These books covered Indonesian history from ancient to contemporary Indonesia, including the killings of six Indonesian army generals in 1965, which was also known as Gerakan 30 September (the 30th of September movement). The book incriminated the Indonesian communist party as the single actor behind the killings by associating the party's name, Partai Komunis Indonesia, with the incident, making the phrase "G30S/PKI" (Gerakan 30 September/Partai Komunis Indonesia) widely accepted in Indonesia. This emphasis is important because it was concluded even with empirical debates that suggest the involvement of the entire party in the killings (Purwanta, 2016). However, the books remain the primary source of history textbooks during Suharto's reign.

The fall of Suharto and Indonesia's New Order Era in 1998 became an opportunity to reformulate the orchestrated version of Indonesian history (Leksana, 2009). Megawati Soekarnoputri, then the President of Indonesia (2001–2004) and the daughter of President Soekarno, chose to avoid a significant change in the reconciliation of victims of the 1965 tragedy. She decided to take another approach by focusing on how history is written by asking a team of historians to publish a book on this subject for teaching and educational purposes. The book was published in 2012, long after her administration finished, and there have not been many changes in the history textbook to introduce the topics to Indonesia's young generations. Nevertheless, there was an attempt to change the narrative about the incident in Indonesia's new 2004 national curriculum. Historians tried to detach the association of the G30S incident from the communist party by removing "PKI" as evidence suggesting their link remained inadequate (LIPI, 2007). The change came with a backlash from influential anti-communist actors in Indonesia, such as Yusuf Hasyim, a prominent leader of the biggest Islamic organization in Indonesia, Nahdlatul Ulama (NU); and Taufiq Ismail, a well-known Indonesian author. They reported the changes in the textbook to the parliament, problematizing the absence of the Indonesian communist party not only in the September 30th incident but also in the 1948 Madiun affairs (Adam, 2007). The parliament welcomed the report and took it very seriously. Consequently, almost all history books, including those without the 1965 incident as their subject, were banished. The parliament also pushed the Attorney General to investigate the then Head of the National Education Curriculum, Diah Harianti, and the previous head, Siskandar, for associations with the communist party. The Ministry of Education, under President Yudhoyono (2004–2014), put the term "PKI" back in the history textbooks.

The efforts to counter the hegemonic state's version in the textbook continue despite repercussions. As of 2020, the topic was first introduced and discussed with students in grade 12, the last grade in Indonesia's mandatory educational system, likely to encourage sensible debates with more mature students. The textbook includes the involvement of more actors and scenarios, from the internal disputes within the army, the intervention of international intelligence bodies, the coup by elite members of the communist parties, and the role of Suharto (Abidin & Salimi, 2021). Nevertheless, the main narrative is still problematic, leading students to reason why and how the communist party was behind the incidents and emphasizing the weakness of President Soekarno during the Cold War rather than stating the facts based on historical empirical findings (Riyandanu, 2020).

While the change in textbooks seemed grim, the implementation of the 2006 national curriculum brought new hope for more open discussion about the tragedy at school. It was an evaluation of Indonesia's educational issues, which relied mainly on the top-down approach (Leksana, 2009). The 2006 curriculum was derived from decentralization principles and encouraged teachers to decide on teaching materials and methods that work best for students. Teachers with a more critical approach to seeing the 1965 incident used it as an opportunity to introduce alternate versions of history (Abidin & Salimi, 2021). These efforts were mostly sporadic, done in silence, and in a small-scale manner since teaching alternative history came with huge consequences and challenges, including the likelihood of being associated with or labeled as communists as well as encountering complaints or threats from schools and students' parents (Pratama, 2022).

Regardless, the information explosion with technological advancement and the increased discussion on the 1965 tragedy in Indonesia's literature and pop culture raised collective consciousness among the younger generations. They do not depend on the school to learn about Indonesia's past, rather using alternative media and channels such as history education in NGOs. Human rights groups in Indonesia acknowledge the potential of education to bring about the memory of historical injustice to settle the nation's past wrongs, especially by outreach to young people (university and high school students). As part of their "dual-track" strategy, these groups adopted and implemented various strategies and targets.

Historical Memory Education Approach to Young People on the 1965 Genocide

Aulia, 32 years old, studied political science at one of the biggest public universities in Jakarta for her undergraduate study. In 2008, she took a course on human rights politics, and she encountered the term "1965 tragedy" discussed by her lecturer in some of the classes. She and her friends were initially surprised that what they knew about communist treason was being discussed openly in a significantly different perspective. She never imagined that this event of mass violence would actually victimize a large number of civilians and have a major impact both in quantity and quality to the current generation in Indonesia (Interview, March 2018). Her strong curiosity of this critical perspective on state hegemonic narratives such as the 1965 genocide eventually made her submit an application to participate in informal education outside the campus, which was known as the Student Human Rights School.

SEHAMA is an intensive informal education program organized by KontraS, an NGO established in 1998 that later became a leading organization confronting the authoritarianism of the Soeharto regime focusing on human rights issues. When transitional justice gained its momentum between 1998 to 2000, KontraS was the leading civil society organization in articulating the position that prosecutions were the best way to settle past human rights abuses, despite their skepticism about the corrupt and inept legal system in Indonesia (Farid & Simarmata, 2004). When the political elite became concerned over the international attention on human rights accountability for the serious crimes that took place in East Timor, KontraS and particularly its Chair, Munir, consistently supported the establishment of human rights court that deals with various cases of past human rights abuses, especially for cases they advocated such as Tanjung Priok, Talangsari, East Timor, Aceh, and the activists-enforced disappearance case. For KontraS, human rights court was not merely to deprive the military court of its authority in terms of human rights accountability, but to put into effect an international standard of criminal justice system that could increase possibilities of punishing high-ranking generals and decision makers by taking the command responsibility and crimes of omission into account (Suh, 2012, p. 134).

In the late 2000s, when the space for human rights accountability through prosecutions was shrinking and legal justice became far from their expectation, KontraS realized that there should be more than one strategy to achieve justice, both retributive and restorative. The commitment for regular recruitment gave the opportunity for involving younger generations of human rights activists. Recruitment systems were mostly conducted through volunteerism, targeting university students and young activists. From their engagements with student volunteers, they developed an idea to have a more systematic education on issues that they are working on (Interview with Papang Hidayat, February 2018). In 2009, they started the first SEHAMA, a three-week, full-day course for students in their last year of university study.

The program was established under the research division in KontraS. It targets university students nationally who were in their last year of their studies. The idea of establishing the school came after concerns raised by human rights practitioners and researchers on the scarcity of human rights courses taught at universities. Most of them were taught in a very legalistic approach, making human rights merely legal formal issues (Interview with Mulki, Jakarta, January 2018). SEHAMA aims at strengthening human rights perspectives among students beyond legal formal theories. Not only students learn principles of human rights but also skills and networks to do advocacies and campaigns on relevant human rights issues. The outcomes expected have been for students to work for justice and the promotion of human rights in their own locals and communities.

Each year, the school is attended by 30 selected students out of more than 100 applications ranging from Aceh, the westernmost province, to Papua, the easternmost province. Affirmative actions are given to some areas impacted with human rights issues such as Papua, Aceh, and Maluku or Nusa Tenggara Timur (NTT). KontraS designed the curriculum for university students with the ability to analyze and write academic articles or reports. The first part of the school focused on normative and theoretical aspects of human rights. This includes subjects on universal principles of human rights, transitional justice, peace and conflict, etc. Each of these subjects also included empirical cases from various countries. The second part of the curriculum focuses on Indonesia's context, including discussions of cases of past human rights abuses. Students were expected to analyze the legal system, democratic practices and mechanisms, identify challenges for human rights accountability, and so on. The third part is action. Students had to do "live-in" activity for three days in certain human rights vulnerable groups such as religious minorities, urban poor, sexual minorities, and survivors and families of victims of human rights abuses. They live and interact with these communities, observing and learning their daily lives and resilience, and later will analyze the groups' situations and challenges they face as well as make recommendations and plan of action to ensure the fulfillment and protection of rights for these communities. During the whole term, students also participated in *Kamisan*, a peace protest held every Thursday (*Kamis*) in front of the Presidential Palace by survivors, families of victims of human rights abuses, and human rights defenders.

Historical justice became a fundamental part of this program, as they introduced cases of past human rights abuses under the authoritarian regime that the state had not yet settled on to the participants. Included in the curriculum is the 1965 genocide, which to many of the young generation was considered distant and peculiar because of what they were taught differently in formal school. Even though the topic of the 1965 genocide is not explicitly held in this program, it was always discussed as case studies. The case was most frequently discussed within the topics of transitional justice, gross human rights violations, and gender-based violence.

Students were exposed to and involved in discussions on the genocide in class and during out-of-class activities. In-class activities include watching documentary films on the 1965 genocide, including Joshua Oppenheimer's award-winning films, *The Act of Killings* and *The Look of Silence* (Interview with Mulki, December 2022). Activities organized outside of class include visits to the elderly house of the 1965 survivors in Kramat, Central Jakarta. The house was dedicated by a parliament member who is a daughter of a former political prisoner and was officially opened by President Abdurrahman Wahid in 2000. Participants of SEHAMA visited the house to meet and have sharing sessions with the survivors of the 1965 genocide. TM, the person in charge of the house administration, who was a political prisoner himself, believes that such visits help the victims to feel accepted by the younger generation. This visit allowed them to tell the history of the nation's past, which the state authorities have permanently hindered. He hopes that through such visits, young people can learn about the truth, not forget what happened in the past, and learn so that past wrongs will not happen again in the future (Interview, June 2019).

Other than the visit, every Thursday, students also attended the peace protest *Kamisan* and interacted with some of the 1965 victims who were part of the protests. Bedjo, a former political prisoner who was one of the initiators of the *Kamisan*, assesses the presence and interaction built with young people, including with SEHAMA program participants, as a space for dialogue between generations. Together with his fellow survivors, Bedjo hopes that what was voiced by the victims and the families of the victims in *Kamisan* will become a valuable lesson that is impossible for young people to get at school (Interview, June 2019). *Kamisan* blurred the stigma attached to the victims of the 1965 genocide who, for years, had to suffer the consequences of being called communists. Such spaces like *Kamisan* allow them to tell history as it is, from what they experienced and understood regarding the events around 1965 to the present day. Some students continued to converse with him and invited him to various discussion activities both on and off campus.

Historical Memory Education: Emotions and Agency

The historical memory conveyed by the survivors of the 1965 genocide has an impact not only on new knowledge for students but also on the emergence of deep sympathy toward the victims and the injustices they experienced. Such feelings were shared by the four SEHAMA participant informants and the students we interviewed. This impacts their concerns for injustice, not only at the personal level but also in the context of society and the nation. In the words of Maulida,

> We were never told about these (past injustice) in our schools and campus before, and we knew almost nothing about the New Order regime, yet we felt the legacy such as fears of the ghost of communism and acceptance of state violence in our society." (Interview in Jakarta, January 2019)

The experience of injustice experienced by victims, even though it happened several decades ago, is no longer distant from them. The repression carried out against initiatives to gather and discuss related topics has intensified their concerns and criticism toward the government in power, which has continuously refused to confront the past wrongs. This gave them new enthusiasm and awareness to see injustice from a human rights perspective. Maulida, who was in the final stage of her study in international relations at one of the public universities in Bandung, West Java, admits that this realization helped her to complete her bachelor's research on human rights in international relations.

The experience, awareness, and network she gained while attending SEHAMA helped her determine her career after graduating from university. She and most of the alums continue their career pathways in areas related to human rights and democracy issues, including environment, minority group rights, and anti-corruption. Some others build their career as journalists, academics, and lawyers. Even for individuals whose work is not related to human rights, SEHAMA gave them the perspectives and experience that enable them to strive better in work and social life (Interview with Maulida, January 2018). For some alumni who choose political pathways to become politicians, participating in SEHAMA gives them an advantage in their qualifications to become political leaders. The graduates include a transitional justice agenda in their programs or activities. One of the cases of past abuses often being discussed and campaigned in their programs is the 1965 genocide. Due to the widespread and massive nature of the violence, in every area in the country, there are local cases and communities of victims that some of these graduates later work with.

SEHAMA works effectively in facilitating the transmission of the memory of past injustice and helps to shape new norms for its participants. They continue to work on demanding state accountability and, at the same time, keeping the memory of past injustice alive in society to build solidarity. The *Kamisan* is now being organized in other places, initiated by some SEHAMA alumni. Even though the impact is limited at the individual level, it promises a possible way of ensuring the human rights agenda is alive in Indonesia's democracy due to its roles and agency in society.

Such an impact cannot be found in learning historical memory in universities. As we have explained in the previous section, the limitations and challenges that arise in the learning process also impact the results of the process. Knowledge of the genocide in general, and the 1965 genocide in particular, is only a tiny amount of information in addition to the broader objectives in the courses given to students. This is inseparable from the obligation for lecturers to follow the provisions set by the National Accreditation Board for Higher Education (BAN-PT), which requires that each subject have learning outcomes that must be in line with the criteria for graduates from each study program. In this case, the requirements and targets for graduates have been determined in each study program, and each course must be designed to follow these criteria. Graduates of the study program must reflect specificity in their scientific discipline. As a result, each study program emphasizes mono-discipline in its curriculum.

Adopting historical memory is difficult for lecturers because this approach is multidisciplinary. In this way, the historical memory approach is carried out unstructured and only becomes a variation, especially as part of case examples of specific topics. However, in the last two years, the Ministry of Education and Culture has set eight indicators (*Indikator Kinerja Utama*, IKU) to evaluate the performance of higher institutions. One of the indicators includes the obligation to adopt case-based or project-based methods in teaching and learning in tertiary institutions. This method requires lecturers to facilitate students in analyzing certain cases or being involved in their projects during one semester of learning. This, of course, will be very accommodating for strengthening HME in courses taught at tertiary institutions. The challenge is that this rule still needs its derivatives in clear guidelines, especially at each university. Moreover, because this is new, many lecturers still have to learn to apply this method in their classes.

Critical History Education at Indonesian Universities

In contrast to educational programs such as SEHAMA which are conducted outside formal education institutions, learning about the 1965 genocide in universities is more limited and challenging, not only for lecturers but also for students. Several individual university lecturers took the initiative to introduce and critically discuss the history of the 1965 genocide in the classes they teach.

We found that genocides and other gross human rights violations, particularly the 1965 genocide, were not taught in-depth. The topics are deemed politically sensitive, and debates around the issue are mostly avoided in classes. We interviewed two academics from state universities, one with expertise in history while the other is in law. Both of them have research interests in the 1965 genocide. We also interviewed one of the students from the political science department at the state university in Jakarta who joined a study trip to learn about genocide in Cambodia in 2019.

Leftist ideas in tertiary education in general have been the target of censorship and cleansing since the 1960s, which was carried out through the banning of left-associated colleges and screening of lecturers, staff, and students in public universities (Wahid, 2018). Consequently, universities became insular to leftist perspectives and adhere almost monolithically to the state's narrative when issues of human rights and genocide were discussed. Courses that discuss said issues, such as political history, tend to focus more on how those events shape Indonesia's political structure and its elites, rather than their social dynamics and significance to the country's sociopolitical landscape. There has been very little in-depth discussion about genocide elsewhere in South East Asia, including on the Khmer Rouge. For example, when the topic of human rights came up in the course curriculum as seen in those who studied law, "international" issues such as the Holocaust were more often discussed, but cases in the region itself are seldom brought up. One particular exception is a course on Human Rights and Democracy in a political science department in Jakarta that discussed genocide in a comparative perspective. Students participated in a study visit to learn directly about the Cambodian genocide in Tuol Slang and the Extraordinary Chambers of the Court of Cambodia (ECCC). This is the first Indonesian university course to organize a study trip to learn about genocide and its legacy in Cambodia.

In most cases, lecturers must be creative in having discussions within their respective classes when it comes to the 1965 genocide. Historical memory is an approach introduced to students by these lecturers. The two lecturers interviewed in this study have expertise on genocide studies and 1965 affairs and often leveraged this expertise by using these cases to further discussion in class and by acknowledging elements in historical memory. They often circulated their writings on 1965 affairs or gave students assignments to read books or watch films that offer a more critical approach on the 1965 genocide.

For students, learning and researching genocides stimulates their interests and curiosity, especially since the topics are rarely discussed in most courses during their study (Khalid, personal communication, May 8, 2021). The study trip to Cambodia was a valuable experience to students who participated in the course. What they saw on the Tuol Sleng and the Killing Field opened their eyes on the tremendous horror of a genocide and how it dehumanizes people. The discussions they had with the museum's director and the ECCC's director as well as Cambodian students expanded their knowledge and capacity to compare with the Indonesian context. There was a sense of pride in them when returning to their campus and telling other students about their experience. At the occasions of discussions on campus related to human rights, they have the knowledge to share with others (Khalid, personal communication, May 8, 2021).

Khalid and some of his friends also had the opportunity to work on an internship given to him by one of his lecturers to digitize archives and documents related to the 1965 genocide. Many of these documents were testimonies from victims and survivors, including former political prisoners, and other essential documents he could not find in the public. Throughout this internship, Khalid gained new knowledge that resembled what he had learned from the genocide in Myanmar. He learned about the 1965 genocide in a course on democracy and human rights at his campus. However, he received more detailed information when he was doing this work.

The limitations in providing material about the 1965 genocide can be understood by looking at the number of risks the lecturers faced on and outside the campus. For example, one lecturer reported that they were being talked about behind their back and was suspected of spreading communism for teaching an alternative perspective on these cases in class (Leksana, personal communication, April 17, 2021). On the other hand, the other lecturer did not receive any complaints from the faculty or students (Wardana, personal communication, April 19, 2021). There was no sanction or penalty as long as they were discreet. Furthermore, these lecturers are productive and highly qualified, which makes them valuable assets for universities to increase their ranking. Consequently, their universities were cautious in handing out any sentence or repercussions to them.

However, discussions about genocide carry much more significant risks when brought to the public sphere than in academic classes. SAFENET, an Indonesian-based NGO for freedom of expression, recorded 47 cancellations of movie screenings and general discussions on the 1965 affairs from 2015 to 2017, 18 of which were managed by university students (SAFENET, 2021). These screenings and discussions were mainly shut down by the police and local vigilante groups, but university officials often were complicit in intimidating the organizers to stand down. Most of the events took place in Java, where top universities resided, indicating that academic freedom was under threat even in the most prestigious universities in the country.

The repressive condition did not wholly silence concerned academic staff and students. In May 2016, the Indonesian consortium for human rights lecturers (SEPAHAM, Serikat Pengajar HAM) issued an open letter complaining about the restrictive academic environment. It urged to stop repressive measures by the state's apparatus (SEPAHAM, 2016). The consortium consisted of lectures from the law, social sciences, and humanities from various universities, who actively advocated and promoted the discussion of human rights issues in Indonesia. One of their recent works was holding an online course on transitional justice in 2020 with a Bali-based NGO, Asia's Justice and Rights (AJAR), which was attended by 100 selected students from all over Indonesia (CHRM, 2020). Initiatives that aim to raise awareness of the importance of genocide studies in Indonesia also came in many forms, including a UNESCO-supported workshop and conference in October 2018. A book launch followed the events in March 2020, wherein schoolteachers, human rights lecturers, and students participated and learned about genocide (UNESCO, 2021).

Conclusion

In this paper, we examine several initiatives undertaken by civil society institutions and individuals in building a critical understanding of the 1965 genocide by using historical memory. In particular, we compared two separate initiatives: the informal SEHAMA school program organized by the KontraS NGO in Jakarta and the initiative of several individual lecturers at two state universities in Indonesia. These two initiatives emerged from the stagnation in efforts to officially settle the 1965 genocide in Indonesia and the state's denial of past wrongs. The regime has long carried out this denial of power by building a hegemonic historical narrative that emphasizes the event as a form of betrayal by the communist group against the integrity of the Republic of Indonesia.

The historical memory approach is a vital element in both of these initiatives. This approach emphasizes the collective memory of specific individuals or groups who experience a significant event that has an impact not only on them but also on society in general. This HME model builds interaction between generations, namely the generation of survivors and students, directly face-to-face and indirectly through stories and testimonies of victims. This kind of interaction model provides critical knowledge to students and evokes emotion and empathy, which eventually erodes the generational gap between the two. This criticism and empathy gradually developed as a modality for students to create agency and the ability to become actors of change in their communities.

SEHAMA provides a more intense and in-depth portion to its participants regarding the 1965 genocide, even though this program is designed to provide a comprehensive understanding of human rights. The historical memory of the 1965 genocide appears in many discussions, case studies, and even special meetings, which provide opportunities for participants to learn directly from survivors. Students also were tasked to write their project paper by conducting a participatory approach, including the victims of the 1965 genocide.

Meanwhile, the topic of genocide, and especially the 1965 genocide, is still a sensitive issue and is limited to discussions in university classes. The general perception of campus authorities and colleagues among the lecturers is still robust against communism and things with a leftist nuance. Because of this, historical memory is more widely discussed as a case example in delivering relevant topics. Just like SEHAMA, students are also asked to refer to or make assignments based on books and films containing victims' narratives. Some lecturers must bring out creativity with activities outside the classroom, such as study visits or internships digitizing archives. However, from this limited space, there are still students who are open-minded and even want to learn more from a human rights perspective and even register for off-campus programs such as SEHAMA.

With these limitations and obligations and technical procedures to limit their lectures to one discipline, historical memory needs more space to be developed in a more structured manner at universities. However, we recommend that these two initiatives are highly compatible and complementary. With the new Dikti provisions regarding the application of case-based and project-based learning methods, universities, through these individual lecturers, can collaborate with institutions outside campus, such as KontraS, to build and assist student learning processes by strengthening historical memory.

References

Abidin, N. F., & Salimi, M. (2021). Pursuing historical truth: The discourse of history teachers in teaching the history of 30 September Movement in Indonesia. *Education Research International* 2021. https://doi.org/10.1155/2021/2671682

Adam, A. W. (2007, March 15). Blunder Kejaksaan Agung dan Departemen Pendidikan Nasional. *Koran Tempo.* https://nasional.tempo.co/read/95550/blunder-kejaksaan-agung-dan-departemen-pendidikan-nasional

Bickford, L., & Sodaro, A. (2010). Remembering yesterday to protect tomorrow: The internationalization of a new commemorative paradigm. In Y. Gutman, A. D. Brown, & A. Sodaro (Eds.), *Memory and the future* (pp. 66–86). Palgrave Macmillan.

Corredor, J., Wills-Obregon, M. E., & Asensio-Brouard, M. (2018). Historical memory education for peace and justice: Definition of a field. *Journal of Peace Education, 15*(2), 169–190.

Farid, H., Simarmata, R., & Muddell, M. K. (2004). *The struggle for truth and justice: a survey of transitional justice initiatives throughout Indonesia.* International Center for Transitional Justice.

Głąb, K. M. (2018). History discourses and reconciliation process in post-Suharto Indonesia. *Sprawy Narodowościowe* 50, 1–14.

Leksana, G. (2009). Reconciliation through history education: Reconstructing the social memory of the 1965–66 violence in Indonesia. In B. Bräuchler (Ed.), *Reconciling Indonesia: Grassroots agency for peace* (pp. 197–213). Routledge.

Lembaga Ilmu Pengetahuan Indonesia. (2007, April 1). Istilah Gerakan 30 September Lebih Obyektif: Asvi Warman Adam, Sejarawan. http://lipi.go.id/berita/istilah-gerakan-30-september-lebih-obyektif-:-asvi-warman-adam-sejarawan/1850

Lopez, C., Carretero, M., & Rodriguez-Moneo, M. (2014). Telling a national narrative that is not your own. Does it enable critical historical consumption?" *Culture & Psychology, 20*(4), 547–571.

McCully, A. (2011). The contribution of history teaching to peace building. In G. Salomon & E. Cairns (Eds.), *Handbook on peace education* (pp. 213–222). Psychology Press.

Posada, R., & Wainryb, C. (2008). Moral development in a violent society: Colombian children's judgments in the context of survival and revenge. *Child Development, 79*(4), 882–898.

Pratama, S. (2022). Teachers' narratives about the possibility to teach controversial history of the 1965 affair in Indonesia. *British Journal of Sociology of Education, 43*(6), 1–18.

Purwanta, H. (2016). Discourses of the "1965's bloody coup" in Indonesian education historiography. *International Journal of Social Sciences & Educational Studies* 2(4), 59.

Ramírez-Barat, C., & Duthie, R. (2015). *Education and transitional justice: Opportunities and challenges for peacebuilding.* International Center for Transitional Justice.

Riyandanu, M. F. (2020). *Analisis wacana kritis teks Gerakan 30 September pada buku pelajaran sejarah Indonesia Kelas XII* [Unpublished doctoral dissertation]. Universitas Islam Negeri Maulana Malik Ibrahim.

Schultze-Kraft, M. (2022). *Education for sustaining peace through historical memory.* Springer.

Schwartz, S. J., Côté, J. E., & Arnett, J. J. (2005). Identity and agency in emerging adulthood: Two developmental routes in the individualization process. *Youth & Society, 37*(2), 201–229.

Southeast Asia Network for Freedom of Expression. (2021). *Daftar Pelanggaran Hak Berkumpul dan Berekspresi di Indonesia.* https://safenet.or.id/id/pelanggaranekspresi/

Suh, J. (2012). *The politics of transitional justice in post-Suharto Indonesia* [Unpublished doctoral dissertation]. The Ohio State University.

Tarabah, A., Badr, L. K., Usta, J., & Doyle, J. (2016). Exposure to violence and children's desensitization attitudes in Lebanon. *Journal of Interpersonal Violence, 31*(18), 3017–3038.

Wahid, A. (2018). Campus on Fire: Indonesian universities during the political turmoil of 1950s–1960s." *Archipel. Études interdisciplinaires sur le monde insulindien,* 95, 31–52.

Wahyuningroem, S. L. (2013). Seducing For Truth And Justice: Civil society initiatives for the 1965 mass violence in Indonesia. *Journal of Current Southeast Asian Affairs, 32*(3), 115–142.

Wahyuningroem, S. L. (2019). *Transitional justice from state to society, democratisation in Indonesia.* Routledge.

Wahyuningroem, S. L. (2022). Breaking the promise: Transitional justice between tactical concession and legacies of authoritarian regime in Indonesia. *International Journal of Transitional Justice,* 16(3), 406–421.

Teachers' Narratives about the Possibility to Teach Controversial History of the 1965 Affair in Indonesia

Stephen Pratama[1]

Introduction

The 1965 affair is categorized as one of the most controversial issues in Indonesian history. The controversy comes from the existence of contradictive accounts on this affair (Ahmad 2016). Its crucial point was the abduction and killing of Indonesian army generals by a group of soldiers called the September 30 Movement in the early hours of the 1st of October 1965 (Notosusanto and Poesponegoro 1984; Robinson 2018), in which there are competing versions of the perpetrator of the movement, while the official version in President Soeharto's New Order period (1966–1998) declared Indonesian Communist Party as the villain (Budiawan 2000). The incrimination of the communist party as the culprit caused every- thing connected with communism to be outlawed in Indonesia since 1966 (Robinson 2018).

The narrative that the communist party and its associated people were culpable and evil was to some extent marshalled by the army (Budiawan 2004; McGregor 2007; Roosa 2020). Under Soeharto's military-backed regime, the depiction of communists' evilness was spread through educational means. The Indonesian National History textbook issued by Soeharto's Ministry of Education was the authoritative source for school textbooks

[1] First published in *British Journal of Socialogy of Education* 2022, Vol 43, no. 6, 898–915. http://doi.org./10.1080 /01425692.2022.2070127 Reprinted courtesy of Taylor and Francis, https://www.tandfonline.com/

(Roosa 2020). The sixth volume of the book portrayed the September 30 Movement as a manifestation of the communist coup attempt (Notosusanto and Poesponegoro 1984). Another way in which the communist cruelty narrative spread was through the film The Treason of the September 30 Movement/Indonesian Communist Party, which was mandatory viewing for schoolchil- dren from 1984 to 1998 (Robinson 2018).

During Soeharto's reign, alternative accounts of the affair were restricted (Van Klinken 2001). Among them was Benedict Anderson and Ruth McVey's Cornell Paper (Syukur 2013), which narrated that junior army officers orchestrated the movement as a mutiny against an army high command (Robinson 2018). The fall of Soeharto's authoritarian regime in 1998 enabled alternative stories to flourish extensively. They extend across different accounts of who actually masterminded the September 30 Movement to stories of mass murders and detentions of innocent people identified to be members or supporters of the communist party or its related organizations, who were deemed culprits embroiled in the movement (Budiawan 2000, 2004). John Roosa's book Pretext for Mass Murder and Joshua Oppenheimer's docu- mentary films (The Act of Killing and The Look of Silence) about anticommunist bloodsheds were amongst the most novel alternative narratives (Adam 2018). Of equal note, journalists and some Non-Governmental Organizations (NGOs) played a role in constructing and spreading alternative narratives, especially stories of anticommunist violence (Robinson 2018).

As Hendrikx (2017) observed, the narrative of the 1965 affair in the history lesson curriculum and school textbooks in post-Soeharto Indonesia was not stationary. History textbooks of the 2004 curriculum contained contrasting accounts on who orchestrated the September 30 Movement. That curriculum was replaced by the 2006 curriculum in which the communist party was pictured as the villain. The government-issued textbook of the current curriculum (2013 curriculum) contains competing versions about the perpetrator while the story of anticommunist massacres remained unmentioned. Also, as Ahmad (2016) and Riyandanu (2020) elaborated, there was still an inclination to narrate the communist party as the culprit in the textbook, and the whole story was entitled September 30 Movement/ Indonesian Communist Party, a typical title that was used under Soeharto's regime to mark the culpability of all people connected with the party (Leksana 2009).

In post-Soeharto Indonesia, although it was still nascent, some teachers have attempted to inhibit the reproduction of the communist coup narrative as a single truth. They did it by incorporating the alternative versions in their teachings on the 1965 affair (Ahmad 2010; Hendrikx 2017; Robinson 2018). By doing so, they executed what is called teaching con- troversial history where students were provided with different comprehensive version(s) other than the story of communist coup (Ahmad 2016). However, not much has been studied about what enables teaching controversial history of the 1965 affair in Indonesia. Hence, this paper sets out to propose an explanation on it by drawing on history teachers' narratives.

On the possibility of teaching controversies

Research on teaching controversies is quite common outside Indonesia. A controversy is signaled by the existence of different or alternative viewpoints of it aside from the commonly accepted one and/or might be seen as objectionable by certain people (Ho et al. 2017). For instance, in the US, the depiction of privilege distribution across racial groups is one of the controversial issues since there are competing views of whether non-whites are socially disadvantaged (Shaver 2017; Vickery 2017).

Stories that we tell others or ourselves guide us to view social reality in a specific way and navigate action (Bochner and Riggs 2014). Previous studies present the role of teachers' stories of their life experiences and standpoints in orienting them to teach alternative accounts on social reality, such as different depictions of race or citizenship, to countervail the mainstream one (Epstein and Gist 2015; Rodríguez 2018, 2019; Salinas and Castro 2010; Vickery 2016). Vickery (2015, 2017) emphasized further that teachers do not assemble their stories out of a void. Personal stories that guide their teachings on controversies are connected to broader narratives (e.g., historical narratives) and surrounding socio-historical and political circumstances.

Teaching is not an atomized action so that it is intelligible by positioning teachers in relation to surrounding actors and existing structural constraints (Apple 2000). Researchers have pointed out that the ease or difficulties in the execution of teaching controversies can be affected by students, parents, school administrators (Misco 2016; Zembylas and Kambani 2012) or communities outside of a school (Hess 2008; Ho et al. 2017). School administrators can be resistant or supportive, with supportive administration creating more flexibility in teaching controversies (Shaver 2017). Meanwhile, students' adherence to a particular viewpoint hinders the teacher from discussing other perspectives (Cotton 2006; Nichols-Cocke 2014). Standardized testing and curriculum can also shape teachers' consideration about teaching controversies (Ho et al. 2017). As Misco (2012) exemplifies, the exclusion of controversies from national examination partly discouraged teachers from teaching them since it was inconsequential.

As presented in previous studies, to understand what enables teaching controversies, one can explore teachers' perspective of an issue they teach and how their circumstances influence their teachings. Nevertheless, there has been less emphasis on differentiations in teachers' viewpoint of a controversy and its changes throughout their life. Secondly, what remains less explored is whether the ease or challenge in teaching controversies is constant. Assisted by Margaret Somers' analytical framework, this paper regards such differentiations and dynamics to elucidate history teachers' agential capacity to engage with different narratives in presenting their views of the 1965 affair and navigating their teachings on it in certain contexts.

The narrative identity approach of Margaret Somers

Somers (1994) proposes a narrative identity approach to give a new nuance in the sociology of action and agency. She problematizes essentialist thoughts assuming that individuals will have the same experiences or generate the same action if their identity seemingly fits a single social category. For instance, Somers (1992) criticizes a line of thinking which links social action and social class as if there is a natural correlation between the two. Instead, it is narrativity and relationality that make up the condition of social being, consciousness, action, institutions and even society. With this analytical lens, history teachers' teachings on the 1965 affair can be understood by delineating their narrative preferences and relationships that condition their narrative choices and pedagogical action.

Narrativity comprises of interconnected parts (e.g., chronology of events or activities) that are selectively assembled by actors and are embedded in time and space. Actors employ multiple yet limited available narratives to construe social reality, navigate their action and constitute identity. The availability of narratives is contextual, meaning that in a different time and space, there can be different existing narratives that are not set in stone. Somers (1994) argues that actors can contest predominant narratives with alternative narratives. Narratives that will predominate is the result of contestation and also a question of power distribution.

Somers (1992, 1994) classifies four narrative levels that are used in this paper to characterize history teachers' narratives that orient their teachings. The first dimension is ontological narratives referring to personal stories (autobiographies) that define who we are and direct our action. Ontological narratives can be related to other dimensions or layers of narratives. The second dimension is public narratives that are attached to social arrangements (family, organization, nation) beyond a single individual and exist in intersubjective networks or institutions at local or macro level. The third dimension is conceptual narratives that are scholarly explanations, concepts and theories. The last dimension which can have a global currency is metanarratives that can be conceptualized as epic dramas of a certain time, for instance, communism versus capitalism.

Actors do not acquire or fabricate narratives in a vacuum. A myriad of social and political relations became a medium to incorporate narratives into self (Somers and Gibson 1994). Somers (1994) accentuates that self is constituted and reconstituted through relations of time, place and power that are in flux. Consequently, it is necessary to embed actors and their narratives within volatile relationships to make sense of their identity and conduct. She even replaced the term society with a notion of relational setting consisting of relationships among people, practices, narratives and institutions where each component is understandable in relation to others. Essentially, what is social is necessarily relational (Somers 2008). This relational framework is of use to illuminate relationships that influence teachers' narrative choices and teaching practices.

Research method

This research targeted history teachers who incorporated multiple versions in their teachings on the 1965 affair by deploying three strategies to reach them. First, approaching previous researchers, who had conducted similar studies, to connect the researcher with their interlocutors. Second, approaching people who have networks to certain history teachers, such as book authors and ex-history teachers who have concerned themselves with the case of the 1965 affair. Third, using a snowball sampling method (Bryman 2012) through which interviewed teachers connect the researcher to other history teachers.

This text departs from an assumption that all experiences take place in the field of narrative (Somers 1994). Narratives can illuminate how actors make sense of their world from a specific socio-cultural vantage point (Eastmond 2007). Instead of exploring teachers' stories of their entire life, this study delimited its scope to two parts of their ontological narratives: the shaping of individual views of the 1965 affair and experiences of teaching it. Accordingly, open-ended interview questions were set to capture: (1) engagement with different narratives to comprehend the affair; (2) the socio-historical and political context of narrative preferences; (3) characteristics of the teaching environment.

Table 1. Overview of History Teachers.

Pseudonyms	Gender	Age	School Type	Teaching Experience (years)
Andrew	Male	28	Private religious	5
Daliyah	Female	45	Public	16
David	Male	28	Public	5
Filbert	Male	28	Private religious	5
Francisia	Female	45	Private religious	21
Harry	Male	57	Private religious	18
Immanuel	Male	28	Private religious	2
Maria	Female	59	Public	34
Nanda	Female	48	Public	24
Sally	Female	28	Public religious	3
Troy	Male	26	Public	2.5

Eleven high school history teachers were sampled and individually interviewed from June to August 2019. Semi-structured interviews took place at restaurants, schools a hotel, a stall or a teacher's house; ranging from around 1 to 4 hours for each teacher. For teachers' confidentiality, pseudonyms are used (Table 1).

This study does not attempt to test whether the narratives that the teachers conveyed during interviews replicate objective reality. Following Eastmond (2007), narratives are treated as creative constructions or interpretations about the past instead of one-to-one perfect depictions of reality. Moreover, although their narratives might not be factual, they still reflect the truth of actors' view of themselves (Kvale and Brickman 2009). All narratives were digitally recorded and transcribed to be analyzed. Narrative analysis allows under- standing to dynamics of actors' practices and self-construction within context and capturing differentiations among actors within the same social standing (Mayness, Prince, and Laslett 2008). For the purpose of analysis, teachers' narratives were coded. This was done by assign- ing labels derived from the conceptual framework, themes covered in previous studies or the emerging new ones.

The formation of teachers' standpoints on the 1965 affair

Actors' characterization of themselves is a precondition for their action (Somers 1994). Thus, it is crucial to capture teachers' narratives of their viewpoints of the 1965 affair, i.e., ontological narratives, to understand their teachings on it. As will be shown, how they differently present their stances is inextricably tied to relationships between their past expe- riences, socio-historical and political environments where they are embedded and narratives that are not of their own making.

Opposing the communist coup narrative

The collapse of Soeharto's regime paved the way for liberalization. Some NGOs flourished and institutionally, it was easier to market and circulate books containing alternative accounts on the 1965 affair. Situated in this sociopolitical setting, Harry developed his opposition to the narrative of communist uprising. His membership in an NGO, whose concern was advocating victims of anticommunist violence, channeled access to networks of ex-political prisoners and their public narratives about wrongful imprisonment. Through his interactions with fellow NGO members, Harry also encountered other narratives of victims collected by them. He knitted those public narratives with conceptual narratives in John Roosa's and Geoffrey Robinson's books that he once read to be a story representing his view that it was elites of the communist party who perpetrated the September 30 Movement, not the whole communist party and its associated people. For him, teaching history was an attempt to enlighten students about the falsehood of the New Order narrative of communist coup. The following quote illustrates his attempt to enlighten students by circulating certain conceptual narratives and victims' public narratives to them.

> When teaching history, I screened videos of victims' testimony of how they were detained, which was produced by the NGO that I joined. I gave students copied parts of texts I read [. . .] I gave them additional notes about unmentioned stories in the curriculum.

Interaction with people who criticized the New Order regime and its anti-communism can also affect one's standing. Troy's ontological narrative depicted his opposition to the New Order's anticommunist view, a standpoint which was developed in his family and social circle in university. He assigned the story about the notoriety of Soeharto's military-dominated regime from the context of interactions with his father. That negative narrative of Soeharto and his regime was congruent with his friends' public narrative that he encountered during university.

> They opined that the narrative of the 1965 affair in many mainstream books is Soeharto's fairy tale. It is reproduced through our educational system and so forth. 'You better read these books in order to know about other perspectives', they said.

Meanwhile, his argument about what happened in 1965 was mainly influenced by the conceptual narrative in John Roosa's book that he managed to access through the same social circle during university. For him, there were three possible perpetrators: the leaders of the communist party, the junior army officers, or imperialist powers. However, as he emphasized, many alleged communists were accused as the villain and victimized. He drew on competing narratives of the scenario of the September 30 Movement and narratives of anticommunist purges to teach about the 1965 affair.

Despite having a different view of who orchestrated the September 30 Movement, Immanuel has a similar past trajectory with Troy's. In Immanuel's narrative, schooling experience and friendship circle partly formed his standpoint that the communist uprising narrative was problematic. His teacher at school did not transmit a negative image of communism to students while his membership in a peer group, which was hostile towards the New Order regime, developed his opposition against the regime and its remnant, the communist rebellion narrative. Further, he narrated that liberalization after Soeharto's era spurred the dissemination of alternative narratives of the 1965 affair in scholarly formats that could be accessed, for instance through university library and membership in a student community. Conceptual narratives in the Cornell Paper and John Roosa's book were amongst appropriated scholarly accounts that he intertwined to ground his view that the communist coup narrative is problematic since the murder of army generals manifested the mutiny of junior army officers against top army officers and not a coup attempt by the communists. His narrative of the 1965 affair guided him to problematize the story of com- munist coup when teaching history. Also, he specifically drew on Roosa's academic narrative to navigate his teachings on the mass murders of alleged communists who were accused of partaking in the September 30 Movement.

Heavy restrictions on attempts to spread counter narratives under Soeharto's regime did not entirely stop them from diffusing. They circulated through a micro and hidden network of social relations. Nanda's embeddedness in such a context facilitated her to access them and influenced her narrative choice that shaped her disagreement with the narrative of the culpability of all people associated with the communist party. Her uncles were troops who participated in the September 30 Movement and were imprisoned afterwards. After being released, they and fellow ex-prisoners regularly gathered at Nanda's house and spoke about their past. Employing her uncles' stories, Nanda narrated herself as a co-victim who disagreed with the communist coup narrative taught at school around three decades ago. Their public narratives depicted that only elites of the communist party orchestrated the movement, but laypeople like Nanda's uncles were deemed guilty and imprisoned without trial. Meanwhile, her social connections with other people provided access to conceptual narratives. While her sibling shared academic versions of the perpetrator, her view of mass killings originated from the conceptual narrative in John Roosa's book given by a fellow teacher. The conceptual narratives guided her to teach about alternative accounts on the perpetrator and about the mass killings of approximately two million people.

Different from the previous teachers whose narratives of the 1965 affair were mainly influenced by certain public and/or conceptual narratives of it, Maria primarily fabricated her narrative based on personal experiences decades ago. She portrayed herself as someone who doubted that the communist party was blameworthy and suspected that it was actually Soeharto who committed the coup. Around 1966, little Maria witnessed the anticommunist killings in her village. She saw a truckload of people to be murdered and was informed by her father about the execution. The murder of her innocent and helpless neighbors identified as communists caused her to doubt the story of communists as rebels. Meanwhile, Soeharto's perceived authoritarian measures made her hypothesize that it was Soeharto who attempted the coup in 1965 to seize power. Since her early career in the mid-1980s, Maria consistently performed her narrative by teaching her students the possibility of Soeharto as the villain and the story of anticommunist killings.

> When I taught my students about the 1965 event, I told them that the story is actually different from the one in their books. I've done this since the start of my teaching career! History is man-made. [. . .] It depends on who holds the power.

Nevertheless, teaching is not necessarily a constant action over time. The changing landscape of the history curriculum in the post-New Order era slightly altered her teachings. To recap, the short-lived textbooks of the 2004 curriculum contained contrasting academic versions of the 1965 affair. Those conceptual narratives navigated her to teach about various possible perpetrators besides activating a part of her ontological narrative that is the childhood memory of witnessing anticommunist purges when teaching about the affair.

Avoiding right and wrong perspectives

Actors can creatively arrange parts of their narratives in light of a certain theme (Somers 1994). They can give primacy over a certain theme, but can also incorporate contrasting themes. Francisia and Andrew were examples of teachers who integrated competing themes in their narratives of the 1965 affair. By doing so, they did not pass any judgement as to which version is the right one.

Francisia portrayed herself as an open-minded teacher who embraced contrasting accounts and did not pass a singular judgement to the communists. She activated her ontological narrative by encouraging students not to judge that the conceptual narrative in their learning materials was wrong due to the absence of the episode of anticommunist bloodbaths in it.

> My students asked, "Mam, does it mean that the history lesson we read is wrong?" I answered, "There's no need to point fingers or debate about who's wrong or right. You guys just need to know of the untold stories."

Her standpoint was cultivated through her social relationships to different actors. At home, Francisia often had discussions with her father who raised her to think of alternative interpretations of any historical event, including the 1965 affair that was unquestionably correlated with the communist coup under Soeharto's regime. During university, her lecturers introduced students to a variety of historical sources that predisposed her to be aware of complex interpretations. Finally, it was her participation in a short course organized by one NGO in the early 2000s that made her notice of an untold episode in the course of events in 1965. In that course, she was exposed to conceptual narratives of anticommunist violence. Stories of communist coup and anticommunist massacres guided her to imagine that the communists could be the villain or the victim, a stance that was manifested in her teachings. She associated her teachings with a broader context where narratives of anticommunist violence spread massively in the last 10 years. She taught about the episode of mass killings as an anticipation if students already had familiarity with it and wanted to explore further.

Just like Francisia, Andrew expressed himself as a person who embraced competing versions without defining which one is the most valid. This ontological narrative drove him to teach all accounts without directing students to a particular version. Since high school, he already doubted the story of communist rebellion. Then, social relationships during university enabled his acquisition of different narratives that made him aware of the existence of contrasting storylines. He joined student forum discussions where various narratives were employed to explain what happened in 1965. His friends also introduced Joshua Oppenheimer's films that enlightened him about anticommunist purges. On top of that, Andrew positioned himself within a context of the liberalization in the post-New Order era that correlated with the availability of alternative conceptual narratives. Freer publishing environment allowed the marketization of books on the 1965 affair, which, according to Andrew, added more narrative choices to zoom in on the affair from multiple angles. Alternative narratives from various versions of the perpetrator to stories of anticommunist bloodsheds were involved in his teachings as the school textbook did not contain those stories.

Self-transformation

Theoretically, self and identity are volatile (Somers 1994). In different time and space, there could exist different narratives to be employed by actors to constitute their identity, fathom social reality and guide their conduct. This subsection delves into teachers' self-transformation by exploring what conditions them to appropriate alternative narratives reversing their standpoint from a proponent of the communist coup narrative into becoming its opponent.

In the relational framework, the alteration of self is not an isolated phenomenon since it is connected to a shift of one's social embeddedness. In David's and Filbert's stories, there was a distinction between their social environments before and during university that correlated to a change in their narrative choices to interpret the 1965 affair.

History education in high school inculcated them with the communist coup narrative which shaped their view that in 1965 all communists were deplorable. Contrarily, during university, they were embedded in peer groups where there were public narratives that many alleged communists were not necessarily blameworthy. The public narratives fleshed out conceptual narratives in several books that they read, for example, John Roosa's book, and they modified David and Filbert's viewpoint of the affair. Their appropriation of conceptual narratives was conditioned by liberalization of publications and authorships in the post-Soeharto era. They accentuated that over time, historical findings that many alleged communists were not guilty mushroomed and were more accessible.

Since renouncing the view that all communists were blameworthy, David and Filbert drew on alternative narratives—i.e., public and conceptual narratives of different possible perpetrators and anticommunist bloodsheds—that were mostly acquired during university to envision the 1965 affair. Aside from one congruity, they differently saw the mastermind.

> David: It was the elites of the communist party [. . .] Their rebellion did not represent the party as an organization.

> Filbert: What I got from discussions and my readings let me to the conclusion that the 1965 affair was about Soeharto's creeping coup.

However, they shared a view that myriads of people identified as communists were accused as culprits and were executed. The change in their narrative preferences also influenced their teachings. They taught different versions of the villain alongside narratives of mass killings. This manifested a pedagogical action to counterpoise conceptual narratives in the school textbook that, according to them, still inclined to depict the communist party as the villain and did not show anticommunist bloodbaths.

Daliyah also once envisioned the communists in a negative light. Her story represents Emirbayer's (1997) argument that an actor does not enter interactional contexts with pregiven attributes. Alterations in her identity from an anticommunist to a representative of all victims were shaped through experiences in different contexts. While history education of Soeharto's regime initially influenced her to associate the communists with rebellion, the revelation of her family story initiated her transformation. Her mother and other family members informed her about the murder of her grandfather due to being accused as a communist. The public narrative about her grandfather made her question her negative view of communism and constituted her identity as a co-victim afterwards. Ever since, she changed her narrative choices to conceive the 1965 affair and joined a network of victims of anticommunist violence organized by an NGO formed after Soeharto's era. From that network, Daliyah assigned public narratives of anticommunist mass detention to imagine victims' suffering. Her implication in that network modified her identity to be a representative of all victims instead of merely a grandchild of a victim. She also acquired conceptual narratives from a book on the political backgrounds—cold war and national politics—of the 1965 affair and Joshua Oppenheimer's films. Overall, stories of the political aspects of the affair and anticommunist violence rendered her to narrate that the communist party was not necessarily blameworthy and many people associated with communism were victimized. At school, she stimulated students to criticize the story of communist coup and taught about anticommunist massacres. According to her, she performed her teachings on the behalf of all victims.

Among all informants, Sally was the only teacher who once loathed communism. This hostility was cultivated in her family and neighborhood where she was told to be careful with an ex-political prisoner associated with communism in the neighborhood. However, in a different time and interactional context, there could exist different narratives that might transform one's view. Sally's interactions with seniors in the beginning of her university studies made her encounter their public narratives of communism that challenged and slowly reversed her view that all communists were undeniably evil. Since then, she actively explored conceptual narratives of the 1965 affair in some books and assigned different public narratives of it from student discussion groups that she joined. Also, she wrote a thesis about a communist party's affiliated organization (Indonesian Women's Movement), met survivors of anticommunist violence and appropriated public narratives of how they were mistreated. She weaved different parts of the acquired conceptual and public narratives to construct her view that elites of the communist party masterminded the September 30 Movement, yet the whole communists were deemed reprehensible and many of them were tortured or exterminated without trial. The story of her transformation and stories of anticommunist violence oriented her to teach about the victims' suffering, which was non-existent in the curriculum, according to her. She also taught competing versions of the perpetrator.

The ups and downs in performing narratives

The last section demonstrated the context of the teachers' narrative choices to envision the 1965 affair and navigate their teachings on it. However, the extent to which they can easily teach in accordance with their narratives is conditioned by the social and political contexts of its execution (Ho et al. 2017). As will be delineated, their teaching experiences are related to other actors inside or outside of a school and their narratives of the 1965 affair and communism, as well as any practice that affects their teachings. This section also highlights that some teachers' teaching experiences fluctuate.

Partially covering identity

Discrepancy between a teacher's narratives about the 1965 affair and narratives of it or communism preferred by surrounding actors could be a source of challenge for teaching counter narratives of the affair. Nonetheless, a teacher can strategize to prevent perceived potential issues from happening. This subsection delineates strategies of Troy, Sally and Nanda so that they could still teach competing narratives without having to openly demonstrate their actual stances.

Echoing Somers' (1994) argument, Elliot (2005) contends that the narrative construction of identity is context-dependent. This indicates that actors can differently present themselves in different contexts. At school, Troy did not want to declare his stance as an opponent of the military-dominated New Order regime and its anti-communism since some students came from military families. If he showed his actual standpoint by bluntly condemning the New Order's version of the 1965 affair, the students might tell their parents and they could sue him for his teachings. Instead, he partially performed his ontological narrative by telling students about competing interpretations of the 1965 affair without sharply criticizing Soeharto's regime and its communist coup narrative.

> What I experienced was that my student gave an opinion based on what he heard at home. He comes from a military family [. . .] I didn't want to judge whether he was wrong or indoctrinated by the New Order narrative of communism. I only said, 'OK, but that's not the only version, there are alternatives.' [. . .] I had to choose appropriate words.

With that strategy, he could perform his teachings without any problem, and he also asserted that there was no measure to veto teaching alternative versions so that he could freely teach them.

Similar to Troy, Nanda and Sally did not teach straight in line with their ontological narratives of how they perceived the 1965 affair. Nanda concealed her status as a co-victim, who disagreed with the narrative of the culpability of all people associated with communism, as she was worried that if students told their parents about it and if some among them employed the narrative of communist rebellion and perceived her as a niece of rebels, they would condemn her. Instead, she chose against sharing the story of the wrongful imprisonment of her uncles and told students that competing versions are all equal. She also took into consideration the public narrative of communist uprising existing outside of her school. As explored by Hendrikx (2017), the public narrative of communist rebellion in 1965 remained powerful in the post-Soeharto public space. Considering that situation, Nanda reminded students to keep what she taught off-the-record since people who adhered to the public narrative of communist coup might negatively react to her teachings.

> I might be seen as a threat due to my teachings. [. . .] People still associated the 1965 affair with the communist rebellion. [. . .] I told students about the fact (of mass murder), but I empha- sized that it was off-the-record. 'It is only for this class.'

Nanda's story echoes the arguments of Hess (2008) and Ho et al. (2017) that community outside of schools can potentially hinder teaching controversies. Yet, such an issue was successfully prevented by Nanda's teaching strategy.

Different from Nanda, Sally's issue emanated from her teaching milieu comprising of fellow teachers who embraced negative narratives of communism. One dominant theme of the public narratives in her religious school was conflictual relationships between a religious group and the communists in the past. Those narratives oriented her fellow teachers to envision communism negatively. Situated in such a teaching environment, she chose not to fully and bluntly express her actual identity as a person who opposed the narrative of communist coup and threat. Thus, despite lack of control and direct intervention over her teachings by the school leaders, she carefully presented multiple versions without straightforwardly problematizing the communist coup narrative.

> I must be careful when disseminating competing versions to students because my school is very religious [. . .] I always tell my students, 'I am not completely impartial. You guys have learnt that history is very subjective since there are competing historical interpretations.'

Identified as a communist

> They said, 'Daliyah is a communist teacher.'

> My students responded, 'Oh sir Filbert, you are a communist.'

> My students spoke to religious leaders as they often spent their times together [. . .] Then, the religious leaders insinuated me [. . .] They said, 'Hmm, (Andrew is) a communist.'

Above quotes are parts of the three teachers' ontological narratives about their teaching experiences. The accusation as a communist stemmed from the discordance between narratives that guided their teachings on the 1965 affair and narratives about it and communism employed by those who labelled them as such. As a note, in Indonesia, among anticommunist groups, there was a dominant public narrative that anyone who disseminated alternative accounts on the 1965 affair sided with or was part of the communists (Hendrikx 2017; Miller 2018). Probably, the same narrative circulated among those who identified the teach- ers as a communist.

Daliyah's narrative as a representative of victims who highly questioned the communist coup narrative oriented her to teach its counter versions. At school, she was known for her persistence to screen Joshua Oppenheimer's The Look of Silence as a mainstay of her teachings on anticommunist purges. A stigma of a communist given by fellow teachers, who adhered to the anticommunist narrative, was a backlash to her teachings. However, narratives and other constitutive elements (e.g., people, practices) of relationships that shape one's experience are not set in stone (Somers 1994). According to Daliyah, some teachers had begun to change their negative narrative of communism to an opposite direction while the school principal who stigmatized her was replaced with a new one who was more supportive towards her teachings. The alteration in their narrative of communism was influenced by Oppenheimer's film that Daliyah continuously screened. According to her, they began to have an interest in the film or what she taught to students and embrace alternative versions. Therefore, she finally could teach alternative accounts without facing any adverse reaction.

Contrary to Daliyah, the label addressed to Filbert was posed by students. He was called a communist when performing his narrative by telling students that the party was not necessarily deplorable. The students assigned the narrative of communist uprising from their textbook and home to counter alternative narratives in Filbert's teachings. Then, Filbert responded them.

I responded, 'No. I am absolutely not a communist. I do not even agree with communism. When we talk about history, we should be aware that there are multi-interpretations.'

He enhanced a part of his ontological narrative which displayed his identity as a person who actually disagreed with communism despite opposing the communist coup narrative. Besides, instead of imposing his version of Soeharto's creeping coup on students to respond their challenge, Filbert reminded students of the existence of contrasting narratives that they could freely refer.

The public narrative of Andrew as a communist arose from social interactions between students and religious leaders at a private religious school. Students spoke to them that Andrew screened Joshua Oppenheimer's films about the anticommunist massacres. As Andrew hypothesized, he was seen as a communist due to teaching stories of communists as victims that were conflicting with the dominant public narrative of the communists' evilness existed among others at school. That public narrative of communism was sustained through a regular public viewing of the film about the communist treachery in 1965, a remnant of Soeharto's regime. Nonetheless, the public narrative of him as a communist eventually disappeared, so he no longer faced any challenges. It happened after he countered it with a powerful narrative of his ethnic background, which was perfectly suitable with the ethnic identity of fellow teachers.

> Ethnically, I am Batavian, and actually, it is impossible for a Batavian to be a communist [. . .] At my school, all teachers are Batavian as well, and historically, no Batavian embraced communism.

Ease of teaching

Unlike the teachers in the previous discussion, Immanuel, Harry, Maria and David narrated that they never encountered any difficulty or only faced little challenge, verging on insig- nificant. In the relational perspective, the ease in teaching controversial history is not only conditioned by the absence of institutional prohibition on such teachings but is also linked to the presence of surrounding actors and their narratives of the 1965 affair and communism.

Immanuel and Harry taught in two religious private schools with the same religious characteristic as in Sally and Andrew's schools. However, Immanuel and Harry experienced no difficulty to teach students that the communists were not necessarily culpable. Seemingly, there was no negative narrative of communism within their religious teaching environments, or if it existed, it was not publicly dominant and was not activated by others to resist their teachings. This situation was different from that in Sally and Andrew's schools where they were confronted with the predominant anticommunist narrative. Specifically, Immanuel elaborated that his school was managed by a religious organization that historically was inclusive towards alternative accounts on the course of events in 1965.

> I have not yet faced any obstacle at this religious school. The religious organization which manages my school acknowledges alternative versions of the course of events in 1965 [. . .] The same goes to religious leaders of this religious organization.

Moreover, among his fellow teachers, there was a public narrative of a doubt over the blameworthiness of the communist party which was somewhat consonant with Immanuel's narrative that the attack on army generals was orchestrated by junior officers. This school context allowed him to teach in accordance with his ontological narrative by problematizing the communist coup narrative.

The compatibility between the teacher's narratives and students' narrative choices to construe what happened in 1965 eases teachings on it. Maria's narrative that the communist party was not necessarily reprehensible was in tune with students' narrative that the September 30 Movement was a manifestation of the mutiny of junior army officers against the army high command. Besides, students apparently were receptive towards her childhood memory of witnessing anticommunist killings.

> Stephen: How was their response mam?

> Maria: Of course, cried! They cried. They cried when I was conveying it.

Also, she articulated about the absence of any prohibition from fellow teachers and even government officials on her teachings. Thus, Maria constructed a narrative of herself as a teacher who can freely and easily teach controversial history for about 22 years at her school. Nonetheless, during the authoritarian New Order era, she reminded students to keep the narrative about the possibility of Soeharto as the villain off-the-record as she might be accused of teaching an illegitimate narrative.

David recounted that a few students assigned the public narrative of the communists as a dangerous insurgent from social media and a religious extracurricular group. Regarding the religious extracurricular, David informed that it was under the influence of a religious group which routinely set-in motion the anticommunist narrative across settings. Inspired by the negative narrative of communism, the students insisted that the communist party committed a coup in 1965 when David informed competing accounts. He acknowledged that it was onerous to discuss with the students as they kept referring to the communist coup narrative. However, as he emphasized, there was no significant resistance to his teachings as those students were proportionally small and thus, the anticommunist narrative was possibly not dominant among overarching students. Furthermore, David underscored a freedom to teach alternative versions since there was no measure from the school leaders and government officials to prohibit such teachings and no complaint about his teachings from parents.

Struggling with the exit examination

At school, Francisia's pedagogical action of informing students about the variant narratives appeared to be legitimate since it was a move appreciated by her school principal. Among those narratives, the conceptual narrative in the Cornell Paper received public recognition from the students since, according to her, it was their main reference. As emphasized, compatibility between the teacher's and the students' narratives facilitates the teaching of alternative narratives of the 1965 affair. Conversely, during exit exam preparation, Francisia found it challenging to uphold her narrative identity as an open-minded teacher who refused to pass a singular judgement to the communist party.

Exit exam questions and the framework to develop them could vary between administrative zones. Schools were grouped according to these zones, and selected teachers from each zone collaboratively constructed exam questions for schools in their area. Francisia recounted that when she worked with teachers from other schools, they adhered to the exam framework that instructed them to employ the communist coup narrative to formulate the question on the 1965 affair. Francisia acquiesced because the other teachers' students might be unable to answer if she insisted to embed alternative narratives in the exam. Other informants had similar experiences, for instance, Harry and Immanuel who complied with other teachers' narrative of communist coup in their respective areas. Meanwhile, Andrew who had no experience in developing exit exam found a question requiring students to identify the communist party as a rebel, a typical question which was non-existent in some localities, for example in David's and Maria's zones.

While other teachers tended to let students select any narratives for the exam, Francisia prepared her students to stick to one version. For instance, Harry, Immanuel, Sally and Troy did not want the exam question to direct their teachings and thus, let students choose any narratives. Contrarily, Francisia performed a role as a teacher who predisposed students to employ the communist coup narrative, a teaching mode opposite of her ontological narrative as an open-minded teacher. It was not only influenced by the exam question that was built upon the communist coup narrative since the school principal wanted students to succeed in the exam. Additionally, in Francisia's observation, it might be challenging for students to align their narratives with the communist coup narrative. Unlike them, Andrew's students were accustomed to employ the conceptual narrative of communist coup in their textbook so it was unnecessary to attune them to manifest it for exam purposes. However, similar to Francisia, Andrew also encouraged students not to disregard the alternative narratives. In this light, teachers, as Apple (2000: 135) argues, are never simply passive puppets. They did not let the exam fully control their teachings.

Concluding discussion

Teachers' narratives depict their agential capacity to counterbalance or even contest the narrative of communist coup in 1965 in the history lesson curriculum and textbooks. They did it by including alternative versions in their teachings on history of the 1965 affair. These findings corroborate Wayne Au's (2009) criticism for a structural analysis which overly emphasizes the reproductive role of schools and neglects the agential role of individual actors in a more micro social setting. He underlines the role of individuals within schools to resist or mediate the reproduction of dominant societal norms. Besides, this paper discusses that teachers are not self-acting actors, are subject to changes and have similarities and differences, all of which are conditioned by certain narratives, the presence of others, and events in their circumstances.

The teachers engaged with different narrative levels in presenting their views of the 1965 affair and navigating their teachings on it. Their standpoints, which were shown in their ontological narratives, were influenced by the relationships between their experiences, surrounding socio-historical and political contexts and narratives of the 1965 affair. Despite having different narrative references leading to differentiations in their standpoints on the perpetrator, they shared narratives of violence against many people associated with communism. For most teachers, social relations with others provided access to alternative narratives that are not of their own making, i.e., public and/or conceptual narratives of the perpetrator and anticommunist violence. The alternative narratives also enabled some teachers to transform their identity. The teachers who once favored the communist coup narrative to understand the 1965 affair eventually became its opponents after acquiring alternative narratives through interactions with others in certain moments in life. Notably, access to alternative narratives was also conditioned by larger socio-political dynamics. Liberalization after Soeharto's era spurred the marketization and circulation of scholarly books containing narratives that countervail his regime's communist coup narrative, which structured the availability of more narrative choices to conceive the 1965 affair.

The teachers were free to teach alternative narratives since institutionally, it was not forbidden in the education field. However, teaching experiences varied contextually and were related to surrounding actors and their narratives of the 1965 affair and communism. The challenge faced by some teachers mainly stemmed from the incompatibility between their narratives of the 1965 affair and narratives of it and communism employed by others inside or outside of the school. However, some teachers' challenges did not last nor appear incessantly. For example, while Daliyah and Andrew were no longer regarded as communists, Francisia's difficulty to teach contrasting stories only occurred during exam preparation. Contrarily, some other teachers experienced an ease to teach in line with their narratives of the affair. It was because in their surroundings, the anticommunist narrative was seemingly absent or was not publicly dominant and activated to counter their teachings.

In sum, history teachers' narrative choices, surrounding people and their narratives, as well as perceived absence of prohibition on teaching alternative narratives conditioned the possibility to teach multiple narratives of the 1965 affair. The ease and challenge in teaching controversial history of the 1965 affair was mainly a question of degree of compatibility between narratives which navigate the teachers' teachings on it and narratives of it employed by surrounding actors. However, the role of power might also be pivotal. Presumably, some teachers possess high-octane symbolic power conferring strong legitimacy on their narrative choices, which eases their teachings on the 1965 affair, whereas others might lack adequate power making it relatively difficult for them to teach in line with their narratives. This calls for a further study to chart the structure of power distribution among history teachers and their surrounding actors in relation to the ease and challenge in teaching controversy.

Acknowledgements

This article builds on research materials in Stephen Pratama's (2020) master's thesis at Uppsala University. I thank Mette Ginnerskov-Dahlberg and Mikael Börjesson for their valuable comments on the thesis. Also, I thank Belicia Ranti Setiamarga, Fransisca Ria Susanti and the two anonymous reviewers for reviewing this article and Lavanya Mani for editing it. Finally, I thank all teachers who participated in my research project.

Disclosure statement

No potential conflict of interest was reported by the authors.

References

Adam, Asvi Warman. 2018. "Beberapa Catatan Tentang Historiografi Gerakan 30 September 1965." [Some Notes on the Historiography of September 30, 1965 Movement]." Archipel 95: 11–30. doi:10.4000/archipel.604.

Ahmad, Tsabit Azinar. 2010. "Implementasi Critical Pedagogy dalam Pembelajaran Sejarah Kontroversial di SMA Negeri Kota Semarang." [The Implementation of Critical Pedagogy in Teaching Controversial History in Public High Schools in Semarang City]. Master's thesis. Universitas Sebelas Maret.

Ahmad, Tsabit Azinar. 2016. Sejarah Kontroversial di Indonesia. Perspektif Pendidikan [Controversial History in Indonesia. An Educational Perspective]. Jakarta: Obor.

Apple, Michael. 2000. Official Knowledge. Democratic Education in a Conservative Age. 2nd ed. New York: Routledge.

Au, Wayne. 2009. Unequal by Design. High-Stakes Testing and the Standardization of Inequality. New York: Routledge.

Bochner, Arthur P., and Nicholas A. Riggs. 2014. "Practicing Narrative Inquiry." In The Oxford Handbook of Qualitative Research, edited by Patricia Leavy, 195–222. Oxford: Oxford University Press.

Bryman, Alan. 2012. Social Research Method. 4th ed. Oxford: Oxford University Press.

Budiawan. 2000. "When Memory Challenges History: Public Contestations of the past in Post-Suharto Indonesia." Southeast Asian Journal of Social Science 28 (2): 35–57. https://www.jstor.org/stable/24492957.

Budiawan. 2004. Mematahkan Pewarisan Ingatan: Wacana Anti-Komunis dan Politik Rekonsiliasi Pasca-Soeharto [Breaking the Immortalized Past: Anti-Communist Discourse and Reconciliatory Politics in Post-Suharto Indonesia]. Translated by ELSAM. Jakarta: ELSAM.

Cotton, D. R. E. 2006. "Implementing Curriculum Guidance on Environmental Education: The Importance of Teachers' Beliefs." Journal of Curriculum Studies 38 (1): 67–83. doi:10.1080/00220270500038644.

Eastmond, Marita. 2007. "Stories as Lived Experience: Narratives in Forced Migration Research." Journal of Refugee Studies 20 (2): 248–264. doi:10.1093/jrs/fem007.

Elliot, Jane. 2005. Using Narrative in Social Research: Qualitative and Quantitative Approaches. London: Sage.

Emirbayer, Mustafa. 1997. "Manifesto for a Relational Sociology." American Journal of Sociology 103 (2): 281–317. doi:10.1086/231209.

Epstein, Terrie, and Conra Gist. 2015. "Teaching Racial Literacy in Secondary Humanities Classrooms: challenging Adolescents' of Color Concepts of Race and Racism." Race Ethnicity and Education 18 (1): 40–60. doi:10.1080/13613324.2013.792800.

Hendrikx, Paula. 2017. "'1965'" in Indonesia Today. The Politics of Memory in post-Suharto Indonesia and the Perceptions of the 1965-66 past among High School Students in Yogyakarta in 2016." Master's thesis. Leiden University.

Hess, Diana. 2008. "Controversial Issues and Democratic Discourse." In Handbook of Research in Social Studies Education, edited by Linda S. Levstik and Cynthia A. Tyson, 124–136. New York: Routledge.

Ho, Li-Ching, Paula McAvoy, Diana Hess, and Brian Gibbs. 2017. "Teaching and Learning about Controversial Issues and Topics in the Social Studies: A Review of the Research." In The Wiley Handbook of Social Studies Research, edited by Meghan McGlinn Manfra and Cheryl Mason Bolick, 321–335. Malden, MA: John Wiley and Sons. http://ebookcentral .proquest.com/lib/uu/ detail.action?docID=4825480.

Kvale, Steinar, and Svend Brinkmann. 2009. Interviews. Learning the Craft of Qualitative Research Interviewing. 2nd ed. California: Sage.

Leksana, Grace. 2009. "Reconciliation through History Education: reconstructing the Social Memory of the 1965–66 Violence in Indonesia." In Reconciling Indonesia. Grassroots Agency for Peace, edited by Birgit Bräuchler, 175–191. London: Routledge.

Maynes, Mary Jo, Jenifer L. Pierce, and Barbara Laslett. 2008. Telling Stories. The Use of Personal Narratives in the Social Sciences and History. Itacha, NY: Cornell University Press.

McGregor, Katharine E. 2007. Ketika Sejarah Berseragam. Membongkar Ideologi Militer dalam Menyusun Sejarah Indonesia [History in Uniform: Military Ideology and the Construction of Indonesia]. Translated by Djohana Oka. Yogyakarta: Syarikat.

Miller, Stephen. 2018. "Zombie anti-Communism? Democratization and the Demons of Suharto-Era Politics in Contemporary Indonesia." In The Indonesian Genocide of 1965: Causes, Dynamics and Legacies, edited by Katharine McGregor, Jess Melvin, and Annie Pohlman, 287–310. Cham: Palgrave Macmillan.

Misco, Thomas. 2012. "The Importance of Context for Teaching Controversial Issues in International Settings." International Education 42 (1): 69–84. https://trace.tennessee.edu/ internationaleducation/vol42/iss1/5.

Misco, Thomas. 2016. "'We Are Only Looking for the Right Answers': The Challenges of Controversial Issue Instruction in South Korea." Asia Pacific Journal of Education 36 (3): 332–349. doi:10.1080/02188791.2014.940031.

Nichols-Cocke, Cathy. 2014. "Controversial Issues in United States History Classroom: Teachers' Perspectives." Doctoral Diss., Virginia Polytechnic Institute and State University.

Notosusanto, Nugroho, and Marwati Djoened. Poesponegoro. 1984. Sejarah Nasional Indonesia VI (Indonesian National History VI). Jakarta: Balai Pustaka.

Riyandanu, Muhamad Fajar. 2020. "Analisis Wacana Kritis Teks Gerakan 30 September Pada Buku Pelajaran Sejarah Indonesia Kelas XII" [Critical Discourse Analysis of a Text on September 30th Movement in the 12th Grade Indonesian History Textbook]. Bachelor's thesis. UIN Maulana Malik Ibrahim.

Robinson, Geoffrey. 2018. The Killing Season. A History of the Indonesian Massacre, 1965–1966. Princeton, NJ: Princeton University Press.

Rodríguez, Noreen Naseem. 2018. "From Margins to Center: Developing Cultural Citizenship Education through the Teaching of Asian American History." Theory & Research in Social Education 46 (4): 528–573. doi:10.1080/00933104.2018.1432432.

Rodríguez, Noreen Naseem. 2019. "Caught between Two Worlds": Asian American Elementary Teachers' Enactment of Asian American History." Educational Studies 55 (2): 214–240. doi:10.1080/00131946.2018.1467320.

Roosa, John. 2020. Buried Histories. The Anticommunist Massacres of 1965-1966 in Indonesia. Madison: The University of Wisconsin Press.

Salinas, Cinthia, and Antonio J. Castro. 2010. "Disrupting the Official Curriculum: Cultural Biography and the Curriculum Decision Making of Latino Preservice Teachers." Theory & Research in Social Education 38 (3): 428–463. doi: 10.1080/00933104.2010.10473433

Shaver, Erik James. 2017. "Controversy and Counternarrative in the Social Studies." Doctoral diss., Indiana University.

Somers, Margaret R. 1992. "Narrativity, Narrative Identity, and Social Action: Rethinking English Working-Class Formation." Social Science History 16 (4): 591–630. doi:10.2307/1171314.

Somers, Margaret R. 1994. "The Narrative Constitution of Identity: A Relational and Network Approach." Theory and Society 23 (5): 605–649. doi:10.1007/BF00992905.

Somers, Margaret R. 2008. Genealogies of Citizenship. Markets, Statelessness, and the Right to Have Rights. Cambridge: Cambridge University Press.

Somers, Margaret R., and Gloria D. Gibson. 1994. "Reclaiming the Epistemological 'Other': Narrative and the Social Constitution of Identity." In Social Theory and the Politics of Identity, edited by Craig Calhoun, 37–99. Cambridge, MA: Blackwell Publishers.

Syukur, Abdul. 2013. "Pengajaran Sejarah Indonesia Kurikulum 1964–2004: Sebuah Stabilitas yang Dinamis" [Teaching of Indonesian History in Curriculum 1965–2004: A Dynamic Stability]. Doctoral diss., Universitas Indonesia.

Van Klinken, Gerry. 2001. "The Battle for History After Suharto: Beyond Sacred Dates, Great Men, and Legal Milestones." Critical Asian Studies 33 (3): 323–350. doi:10.1080/14672710122604.

Vickery, Amanda E. 2015. "It Was Never Meant for us: Towards a Black Feminist Construct of Citizenship in Social Studies." The Journal of Social Studies Research 39 (3): 163–172. doi:10.1016/j. jssr.2014.12.002.

Vickery, Amanda E. 2016. "'I Know What You Are about to Enter': lived Experiences as the Curricular Foundation for Teaching Citizenship." Gender and Education 28 (6): 725–741. doi:10.1080/09540253.2016.1221890.

Vickery, Amanda E. 2017. "You Excluded us for so Long and Now You Want us to Be Patriotic?": African American Women Teachers Navigating the Quandary of Citizenship." Theory & Research in Social Education 45 (3): 318–348. doi:10.1080/00933104.2017.1282387.

Zembylas, Michalinos, and Froso Kambani. 2012. "The Teaching of Controversial Issues during Elementary-Level History Instruction: Greek-Cypriot Teachers' Perceptions and Emotions." Theory & Research in Social Education 40 (2): 107–133. doi:10.1080/00933104.2012 .670591.

Capturing the Reverberations of the 1965–66 Killings in the Balinese Landscape:

The Artistic Work of Leyla Stevens

Vannessa Hearman[1]

Introduction

In a darkened room, projected on a large screen is the image of a woman sitting on a tiled floor and singing what sounds like a soulful lament. Two other screens flanking the center screen show the gnarly, weathered trunks of an old banyan tree and its small green leaves. The woman, with her hair pulled back into a tight bun and wearing a black blouse and a batik sarong, sings a song in Balinese language. Viewers are given the impression that she, and they, are encircled and embraced by a large, shady, and old banyan tree. As part of the Perth Festival, Leyla Stevens's exhibition *Dua Dunia* or Two Worlds (alternatively also translated as dual worlds) at Fremantle's PS Art Space in Western Australia in February 2021 reflected on the layers of historical violence that had affected Bali, in particular the 1965–66 killings.[2] Stevens's artistic work, which relies on speculative "spectral cartography," places the natural environment and its more-than-human inhabitants at the center as markers of memory, including to reflect

---

[1] Vannessa Hearman is Senior Lecturer in History in the School of Media, Creative Arts and Social Inquiry at Curtin University (Perth, Western Australia). The author acknowledges Rachel Ciesla, Leyla Stevens, Mark Winward and Siddharth Chandra, as well as editors and anonymous referees, for their assistance in the preparation of this article. The author takes responsibility for any omissions and errors.

[2] Leyla Stevens, *Dua Dunia* exhibition, PS Art Space, Fremantle/Walyalup, Australia (Exhibition Dates February 13–27, 2021).

on the practices of witnessing and of marking absences.[3] By examining Stevens's works about Bali, this article analyzes how artistic practice acts as a means of storying sites of contested histories, such as the 1965–66 mass killings. These storying efforts, in turn, can perform reparative work by providing a topography to loss and absence in the landscape.

Landscape and the More-Than-Human World as Productive Sites of Inquiry

In this article, following Catherine Allerton, landscape is referred to as "a historical process of interaction between people and the environment in which both are shaped."[4] By giving importance to historical processes and human activity in shaping landscape, the same physical environment can thus give rise to several possible landscapes, including a spiritual one.[5] Such a landscape is one in which people "imagine spirit forces and energies" as emerging or being connected to places and to the attitudes that people hold to realms beyond the visible.[6] As Katharina Schramm has argued, the memory of violence is "not only embedded in peoples' bodies and minds but also inscribed onto space in all kinds of settings: memorials, religious shrines, border zones or the natural environment."[7]

In putting forward the concept of storying the landscape, I refer to the definition proposed by Louise Gwenneth Phillips and Tracey Bunda of storying as "the act of making and remaking meaning through stories."[8] The verbification (or anthimeria) of *story*, storying, reflects the idea that a story is "living and active rather than fixed, archived products."[9] In a practice that Thom van Dooren and Deborah Bird Rose, in their work on extinction, have referred to as "becoming-witness," they point out, "Storytelling is one of the great arts of witness, and in these difficult times telling lively stories is a deeply committed project, one of engaging with the multitudes of others in their noisy, fleshy living and dying."[10] Van Dooren and Rose are referring here to witnessing in relation to their work on extinction, observing, and writing about animals, plants and natural phenomena, such as lava and volcanoes. They argue that engaging in storytelling as an ethical practice demonstrates that stories are powerful contributors to a shared world, not least because it also entails making new connections, with the obligations and responsibilities that it brings.[11] In telling difficult histories through landscape, this article argues that artists can perform reparative visual work that provides both distance and

---

[3] Rachel Ciesla, "*Leyla Stevens: Dua Dunia* Exhibition," Perth Festival 2021, PS Art Space, Fremantle: Western Australia, https://www.rachelciesla.com/leyla-stevens-dua-dunia (site discontinued).

[4] Catherine Allerton, "Introduction: Spiritual Landscapes of Southeast Asia," *Anthropological Forum* 19, no. 3, (2009): 236.

[5] Allerton, "Introduction," 236.

[6] Allerton, "Introduction," 237.

[7] Katharina Schramm, "Introduction: Landscapes of Violence: Memory and Sacred Space," *History and Memory* 23, no. 1 (Spring/Summer 2011): 5.

[8] Louise Gwenneth Phillips and Tracey Bunda, *Research through, with and as Storying* (Abingdon, UK: Routledge, 2018), 7.

[9] Phillips and Bunda, *Research through, with and as Storying*, 7.

[10] Thom van Dooren and Deborah Bird Rose, "Lively Ethography: Storying Animist Worlds," *Environmental Humanities* 8, no. 1 (2016): 91.

[11] Van Dooren and Rose, "Lively Ethography," 89.

Figure 1: Banyan tree on the left screen and performer Cok Sawitri on the center screen
facing the viewer as part of the video work *Kidung*. Photograph by Robert Frith
(used with permission from Acorn Photo and Rachel Ciesla).

intimacy simultaneously, opening up possibilities for dialogue and different memories to
be articulated and expressed.

Bali 1965–66: Place and Memory

Bali has been an international center of artistic production, undergoing a radical
transformation in the 1930s, attracting the attention of Western artists and art collectors
who in turn influenced global understandings of Balinese art.[12] But in 1965-66, it
was also the location of some of the most violent suppression against members and
sympathizers of the Indonesian Communist Party (Partai Komunis Indonesia, PKI).
The anti-PKI operations in Bali, part of a national army takeover of power, provides
the context for Leyla Stevens's work. With the pretext of blaming the PKI for a coup
attempt in Jakarta, the army organized and assisted its local allies to suppress the party

---

[12] On the interactions between Balinese artistic production and global understandings of art produced in
Bali, see Adrian Vickers, "Balinese Art versus Global Art," *Jurnal Kajian Bali* 1, no. 2 (2011): 34–62.

and its mass organizations, including the leftist cultural organization Lekra (Lembaga Kebudayaan Rakyat, People's Cultural Institute). In Bali an estimated 80,000 people were killed; many of those were already in army or police custody and were then "cold-bloodedly executed, and then buried in unmarked mass graves."[13] Despite the organized and systematic nature of the anti-PKI operations, the massacres in Bali remain largely understood as comprising instances of spontaneous violence, if they are discussed at all.[14] The massacres have been treated as an anomaly in an apolitical, harmonious society, or as proof of Bali's exoticism.[15]

Anthropologist Kenneth George has referred to the effects of the 1965-66 repression on artists and writers of the left as "a terrible fury," with "prominent figures like painter Hendra Gunawan and novelist Pramoedya Ananta Toer spending decades in prison or under restrictions" during the Suharto New Order regime.[16] George described a lacuna after October 1965 where "political differences and cultural polemics that shaped two decades of post-independence Indonesian art fell mute with the collapse of the left."[17] In the years immediately following the 1965 events, artistic depictions of the mass violence were few and far between, but not only due to the New Order regime's restrictions on art deemed political. The silence perhaps also related to the arrival of a new phase in Indonesian art, with the end of the stultifying Sukarno era and the sidelining of the previously dominant social-realist school and the LEKRA artists.[18] The 1965 violence was only obliquely dealt with in the visual arts until the end of the New Order in May 1998.[19]

Bali underwent a rapid transformation into a site of mass international tourism following the rise of the New Order regime. John Roosa writes that, "From a site of mass graves," its transformation has been predicated on the premise that the Balinese are "a peaceful, artistic, prepolitical people who prioritize aesthetic beauty and social harmony above all else."[20] Notwithstanding the fact that the tourism industry employed many of those who were persecuted in 1965–66, the New Order's tourism marketing of Bali as an idyllic and unchanging society has helped the process of forgetting, in the view of one survivor and scholar, Degung Santikarma, and allowed the suppression of past traumas.[21] With the West welcoming the change of regime in Jakarta, countries such as Australia and the United States were complicit in this process of forgetting, with many

[13] John Roosa, *Buried Histories: The Anticommunist Massacres of 1965–1966 in Indonesia* (Madison: University of Wisconsin Press, 2020), 152. On the estimate of eighty thousand out of a population two million, see Geoffrey Robinson, The Killing Season: A History of the Indonesian Massacres, 1965–66 (Princeton: Princeton University Press, 2018), 8.

[14] Roosa, *Buried Histories*, 152.

[15] Geoffrey Robinson, *The Dark Side of Paradise: Political Violence in Bali* (Ithaca: Cornell University Press, 1995), 1.

[16] Kenneth M. George, "Some Things That Have Happened to *The Sun After September 1965*: Politics and the Interpretation of an Indonesian Painting," *Comparative Studies in Society and History* 39, no. 4 (1997): 603–34, https://doi.org/10.1017/S001041750002082X.

[17] George, "Some Things," 605.

[18] See George, "Some Things," 617.

[19] Wulan Dirgantoro, "From Silence to Speech: Witnessing and Trauma of the Anti-communist Mass Killings in Indonesian Contemporary Art," World Art 10, no. 2–3 (2020): 301–22.

[20] Roosa, *Buried Histories*, 182.

[21] Degung Santikarma, "Taman 65: Retak tapi Tidak Pecah," in *Melawan Lupa: Narasi-narasi Komunitas Taman 65 Bali*, ed. Agung Wardana and Roberto Hutabarat (Denpasar, Bali: Taman 65 Press, 2012), 85.

of their citizens coming as tourists to cement its reputation as a newly declared island paradise.

The fall of the New Order opened more opportunities for scholars, activists, and artists to investigate the mass violence and its effects on Balinese society.[22] However, there were few party cadres left when scholars began to study the violence in earnest, with the PKI being quite thoroughly purged in Bali and no single massacre having been studied in any detail.[23] While democratization has led to a degree of community interest in the mass violence leading to the production of films and books about the plight of survivors in Bali, the unwillingness of the Indonesian government to deal with past human rights abuses has meant that families affected still find it difficult to acknowledge their relationship to the purges.[24]

In regarding the Balinese cosmology as one of balance in polar principles between the "seen" and the "unseen" (*Sekala* and *Niskala*), there has not been as much attention to the question of agency and active choices being made by the Balinese in determining how to deal with the purges. As Roosa points out, "Understanding Balinese culture requires an attentiveness not just to the invisible world that the Balinese see but also to what they *pretend* not to see."[25] We should be attentive, in his view, to what he terms the "seen unseen," in which, he suggests, "the Balinese since 1965 have lived in full awareness of the mass graves lying all around the island," yet "many of them have become adept at pretending that those graves are not there."[26] Some of the reasons for this choice not to see can be found in the intimacy of the violence, how it was at times perpetrated by family members, relatives, and neighbors, creating complexities in dealing with the aftermath, particularly when perpetrators and survivors/victims are forced to live in close proximity to one another. To remember the violence is to enter a domain in which, as Leslie Dwyer and Degung Santikarma describe it, "families and communities remain fractured by memories of suspicion, betrayal and the intimate reproduction of state

---

[22] See Leslie Dwyer and Degung Santikarma, "Speaking from the Shadows," in *After Mass Crime: Rebuilding States and Communities*, ed. Béatrice Pouligny, Simon Chesterman, and Albrecht Schnabel (Tokyo: United Nations University Press, 2007): 190–214; Adrian Vickers, "Where Are the Bodies? A Transnational Examination of State Violence and Its Consequences," *The Public Historian* 32, no. 1 (2010), 45–58; Mary Ida Bagus, "West Bali: Experiences and Legacies of the 1965–66 Violence," in *The Contours of Mass Violence in Indonesia, 1965–68*, ed. Douglas Kammen and Katharine McGregor (Singapore: NUS Press, 2012), 208–33; I. Ngurah Suryawan, Ladang Hitam di Pulau Dewa: Pembantaian Massal di Bali 1965 (Yogyakarta: PusDeP, 2007); Robert Lemelson and Luh Ketut Suryani, "The Spirits, NGEB, and the Social Suppression of Memory: A Complex Clinical Case from Bali," *Culture, Medicine and Psychiatry* 30 (2006): 389–413; and Angela Hobart, "Retrieving the Tragic Dead in Bali," *Indonesia and the Malay World* 42, no. 124 (2014), 307–36, https://doi.org /10.1080/13639811.2014.933503.

[23] Roosa, *Buried Histories*, 181. In 2006, in my preliminary research for my doctoral dissertation, I also found few former political prisoners, particularly former PKI cadres, to be interviewed.

[24] Judith Goeritno, Kuntjara Wimba P., Lembaga Penelitian Korban Peristiwa 65-Bali (LPKP 65-Bali) and Jepun Klopak Enam, *Kawan Tiba Senja: Bali, Seputar 1965* (Denpasar, Bali: 2004), and *Melawan lupa: Narasi-narasi Komunitas Taman 65 Bali*, ed. Agung Wardana and Roberto Hutabarat, (Denpasar, Bali: Taman 65 Press, 2012) are examples of a film and a book produced from civil society activists and groups.

[25] Roosa, *Buried Histories*, 182. On sekala and niskala and their influence on peace and reconciliation, see for example, Annette Hornbacher, "Global Conflict in Cosmogenetic Perspective," in *Reconciling Indonesia: Grassroots Agency for Peace*, ed. Birgit Braeuchler (London: Routledge, 2009), 42.

[26] Roosa, *Buried Histories*, 182.

power."[27] Such a domain may often be more painful than one in which a survivor is asked to relive state violence.

The difficulties in dealing with the legacies of the 1965–66 violence in Bali can be seen in the challenges experienced by activists involved in the 1965 Park, or *Taman 65*. The park began in 2005 in Kesiman, Bali, as a garden memorial to remember the suffering of the victims of the violence. Civil society activist Agung Alit, brother of Degung Santikarma, set up the site in the family compound near Denpasar initially to memorialize their father who disappeared and other family members detained.[28] Attesting to the informality of its evolution, when asked, some activists could not remember the exact date of its founding, but recall having begun "hanging out" at the site approximately in 2005 or 2006.[29] An intergenerational chasm developed between those younger generation activists who were motivated by ideas of universal human rights and transitional justice and those who had survived the violence, who had, over the years, cultivated a new life for themselves.[30] In a reflection on some of the rifts that arose at Taman 65, Santikarma argues that the reliance on human rights discourse by younger activists was unable to deal with the local manifestations of the violence, nor to account for the instability of seemingly fixed categories such as "victim/survivor" and "perpetrator."[31] Such a discourse also established a proprietary and exclusionary hold by some over the "right" kinds of memories, those who are privileged in human rights accountability work.[32] In his view, spaces for sharing experiences (*ruang untuk berbagi pengalaman*) are more important than a predominantly rights-based discourse.[33] The efforts of Agung Alit and activists in Taman 65 represent what Vickers refers to as an attempt to reconcile the "physical and the felt landscape" in the "unresolved landscapes" of Java and Bali, where most of the killings had taken place in 1965–66 and "a reconciliation of individual felt knowledge with public lack of acknowledgment."[34]

A widely shared belief in communities in Bali and Java, Indonesia's most populous islands where the highest number of people were killed, is that those who have died violently become restless spirits who need to be appeased, with the land needing to be purified for normal life to resume.[35] Sites where bodies are buried or dumped are considered spiritually impure (in Balinese, *tenget*).[36] The idea of pollution has been used to justify the murder of communists, murder being interpreted by some local leaders

[27] Dwyer and Santikarma, "Speaking from the Shadows," 210.

[28] Vickers, "Where Are the Bodies?," 57.

[29] I. Ngurah Suryawan and Roro Sawita, personal communication, September 22, 2021.

[30] Leslie Dwyer, "Beyond Youth 'Inclusion,'" *Journal of Peacebuilding & Development* 10, no. 3 (2015): 16–29.

[31] Degung Santikarma, "Taman 65: Retak tapi Tidak Pecah," 77.

[32] Dwyer, "Beyond Youth 'Inclusion,'" 23.

[33] Santikarma, "Taman 65: Retak tapi Tidak Pecah," 77.

[34] Vickers, "Where Are the Bodies?" 57-58.

[35] Vickers, "Where Are the Bodies?" 57. On mass graves investigation work by former political prisoners, see Annie Pohlman, "No Place to Remember: Haunting and the Search for Mass Graves in Indonesia," in *Places of Traumatic Memory: A Global Context*, ed. Amy L. Hubbell, Natsuko Akagawa, Sol Rojas-Lizana, and Annie Pohlman (Cham, Switzerland: Springer), 61–82.

[36] Ida Bagus, "West Bali," 229.

and executioners as purifying the land by expunging a foreign ideology, communism.[37] Attempts to rebury victims of the violence in Java have met with opposition, also as a result of the remains of leftists being regarded as polluting the landscape, therefore memorials or markers to mass grave and killing sites tend to be low-key or nonexistent.[38] Some Muslim and Hindu leaders in Java and Bali manipulated religious symbols to cast the anti-PKI operations as a holy war against nonbelievers.[39]

How nature can be regarded as polluted is contingent on the perspectives of the protagonists. Mass graves in Bali used to dispose of the victims' remains are located, for example, in family wells, on sandy beaches, and in old cemeteries or cremation grounds—in many ways, quite ordinary, everyday places in which the living must continue to engage with the dead.[40] Despite the discourses on pollution, and while the remains of communists were deemed impure in some communities, Balinese anthropologist Ngurah Suryawan's experiences of conducting an ethnographic study in the early 2000s showed that visiting mass grave sites allowed opportunities for the researcher to talk to local residents about the 1965–66 violence.[41] His experience suggests that concerns about pollution and rejection of the victims were not universally shared across the island.

Dealing with the legacies of the violence in Bali has involved the performance of funerary rituals, such as cremations of symbolic and actual remains to purify the land and appease the spirits, as part of fulfilling family obligations, or as part of an ethics of care.[42] Outside of family relationships, Mary Ida Bagus shows that, in West Bali, some engage with spiritual landscapes by performing caring duties at sites of killing and burial, looking after graves of those who died unnatural deaths, and erecting shrines, all signs of local inhabitants caring for those who might not be mourned in family shrines (*palinggih*) as is usually practiced by Balinese Hindus.[43] The psychological impact of the killings has also led to some Balinese survivors experiencing changes in their perception of the physical landscape. In their study of the transcultural psychiatric expressions of

---

[37] Nelly van Doorn-Harder, "Purifying women, Purifying Indonesia: The National Commission for Women's Rights and the 1965–1968 Anti-Communist Violence," *Cross Currents* 69, no. 3 (2019): 301–18.

[38] On the attempted reburial of remains of victims of the anti-communist purges at Kaloran, Central Java, see Katharine McGregor, "Mass Graves and Memories of the 1965 Indonesian Killings," in *The Contours of Mass Violence in Indonesia, 1965–68*, ed. Douglas Kammen and Katharine McGregor (Singapore: NUS Press, 2012), 245. A small memorial at Plumbon, Central Java, recognized by UNESCO and the International Center for the Promotion of Human Rights (CIPDH-UNESCO) as part of the project #MemoriasSituadas, seems to be the only physical, public marker to the victims of the anti-communist purges in Indonesia, https://www .cipdh.gob.ar/memorias-situadas/en/lugar-de-memoria/fosa-de-plumbon/.

[39] See Robinson, *Dark Side of Paradise*, 300–1.

[40] Suryawan, *Ladang Hitam di Pulau Dewa*, 209–43; and Roosa, *Buried Histories*, 180.

[41] Suryawan, *Ladang Hitam di Pulau Dewa*, 209–43.

[42] Hobart, "Retrieving the Tragic Dead in Bali," 325 refers to the symbolic cremation held for the Balinese governor AA Sutedja who disappeared in 1966 as having taken place in 2006, while Vickers, "Where Are the Bodies?," 55 refers to it as having taken place in 2007. On the 2015 exhumation of a mass grave and cremation of remains found, see Jewel Topsfield and Amilia Rosa, "Communist Victims Exhumed in Bali to Stop Their Spirits Disturbing Villagers," October 31, 2015, https://www.smh.com.au/world/communist -victims-exhumed-in-bali-to-stop-their-spirits-disturbing-villagers-20151031-gknm72.html. On the practices of symbolic cremation permitted during the New Order, see M. Fauzi (ed.), *Pulangkan Mereka! Merangkai Ingatan Penghilangan Paksa di Indonesia* (Jakarta: Lembaga Studi dan Advokasi Masyarakat, 2012), 217.

[43] Ida Bagus, "West Bali," 229.

mental illness in Indonesia, Robert Lemelson and Ni Luh Suryani have found that one of their patients regards himself as being plagued by *wong samar*, literally "indistinct humans," a kind of spirit who make urgent demands on the living.[44] In this sense, as Kar-Yen Leong has argued, sites associated with the mass violence "can be brought together into . . . a moral landscape or geography" that can "offer a space for counter-narratives to the New Order regime's official version of history which demonized the PKI and its ideas."[45] Harnessing the power of these sites of violence can create a new moral landscape in which to entertain doubt, ambivalence, and questioning about the events of 1965–66 and their reverberations.

Democracy, Mass Tourism, and Art

Since the democratic era began in 1998, artists have predominantly tended to rely on testimony and pedagogy in commenting on the 1965-66 mass violence.[46] One such artist who relies on these approaches is the diasporic Indonesian artist Dadang Christanto, based in Queensland, Australia.[47] A humanistic artist, his earlier works also treated the 1965–66 violence in a more oblique fashion, but after 1998 when he and his family moved to Australia, he began to depict more explicitly and, confrontingly, the treatment of the human body in the violence, in which his father, Tan Ek Tjioe, disappeared.[48] Dadang does this through the images in his paintings, but also in a performance in which he draws his own blood, titled *Toothbrushing*. Many of his works focus on the human head, a reference to the fate of those who were decapitated in the killings and the spectacular displays of severed heads in public thoroughfares in Indonesia to strike fear into the hearts of suspected leftists. According to Katharine McGregor, Dadang's *Heads from the North*, a sculptural installation at the National Gallery of Australia (NGA) consisting of sixty-six bronze heads, constitutes the only transcultural memorial to the 1965 violence.[49] Part of the NGA's Sculpture Garden, the heads were installed in a pond of rushes in 2004 as a memorial to the victims.[50] The memorial as artwork is imprinted in a landscape that itself is not a stranger to the occurrence of genocide and marginalization, located as it were in Ngunnawal country.[51]

[44] Lemelson and Suryani, "Clinical Case Study."

[45] Kar-Yen Leong, "Invisible Threads Linking Phantasmal Landscapes in Java: Haunted Places and Memory in Post-Authoritarian Indonesia," Memory Studies, 16, no. 2 (2021): 18, https://doi.org/10.1177/1750698021995968.

[46] Dirgantoro, "From Silence to Speech," 302.

[47] Dirgantoro, "From Silence to Speech," 302.

[48] Caroline Turner and Glen St John Barclay, "Recovering Lives Through Art: Hidden Histories and Commemoration in the Works of Katsushige Nakahashi and Dadang Christanto," Life Writing 8, no. 1 (2011): 77–79, https://doi.org/10.1080/14484528.2011.542639.

[49] Katharine McGregor, "Heads from the North: Transcultural Memorialization of the 1965 Indonesian Killings at the National Gallery of Australia," in The Indonesian Genocide of 1965: Causes, Dynamics and Legacies, ed. Katharine McGregor, Jess Melvin, and Annie Pohlman (Cham, Switzerland: Palgrave Macmillan, 2018), 246.

[50] "Your Guide to Navigating the NGA's Sculpture Garden," https://visitcanberra.com.au/articles/48/your-guide-to-navigating-the-ngas-sculpture-garden. Accessed September 29, 2021.

[51] Daniella White, "ACT Needs to Expose its Untold Genocides and Injustices: Ngunnawal Elder," The Canberra Times, March 10, 2021, https://www.canberratimes.com.au/story/7161656/act-needs-to-expose-its-untold-genocides-and-injustices-elders/.

The work of Stevens, as an Australian-Balinese artist, can be situated in the context of artistic works by other Indonesian diasporic artists, such as Dadang and Tintin Wulia, who "bear testimony from a distance," but also bring a transcultural perspective to the social issues they tackle.[52] Diasporic artists are simultaneously insiders and outsiders. They are insiders by having access to certain knowledges in and of Indonesia but being located outside of Indonesia, despite regular visits, means that they can be simultaneously *trusted* as outsiders to a degree by some informants. In the words of curator Alia Swastika, "In [Stevens's] regular visits she comes to Bali feeling partly like she belongs, with a nostalgia for home, and at the same time with a consciousness that she is a foreigner, an outsider."[53] For former political prisoners in Indonesia who have been cast as pariahs, outsiders may seem to them to be able to accord them an openness and a more sympathetic view than those in their immediate vicinity who have been forced to imbibe, for decades, the New Order regime's demonization of the Left. However, a risk for diasporic actors is that they can be more easily disowned and dismissed, and their loyalty to Indonesia questioned, perceived that as outsiders they can stir up the past because they have another country to head to. Diasporic artists, in making art that may be sensitive to authorities in Indonesia, thus run the risk of being declared irrelevant, or banned from the country in the case of those who hold a foreign citizenship.

In the face of shrinking democratic space in Indonesia and the failure of the government to fulfill its human rights accountability pledge, the work of artists, such as Leyla Stevens, can provide valuable tools for social repair by highlighting the experiences of political violence in a way that decenter the state from the focus of attention. One of the ways in which she does this is by focusing on the landscape and the layers of memories at such places that have accrued from historical processes and human activity. Decentering the state in this context means valorizing not only the efforts of those who have spoken out and denounced the crimes of the state, but also the many who have sought to forget, or to remember the violence in their chosen ways, ways that have allowed the survivors to create new lives for themselves and to protect their descendants. Her chosen medium is the moving image, predominantly videos that are then created into installations. Stevens chooses to address the violence by locating it spatially, "to pick [the violence of 1965] up as a heavy stone and observe its trajectory as it is thrown across the unfolding of contemporary Bali."[54] In considering different ways of dealing with 1965, Stevens's work examines the possibilities of redress that lie in the landscape. Focusing on landscape and the more-than-human world opens up possibilities for ambiguity, questioning, and hesitancy and, in so doing, opportunities for listening and conversation.

The Balinese landscape and its consumption have been a pivotal (and contested) aspect of the island's marketization in global tourism. As well as critiquing corruption and concerns for everyday survival, Balinese artists, such as Made Bayak and Wayan

[52] Dirgantoro, "From Silence to Speech," 303.

[53] Alia Swastika, "Curator's Essay: Their Sea Is Always Hungry Exhibition," https://art.uts.edu.au/wp-content/uploads/UTS-TheirSea-R7-Web.pdf.

[54] Leyla Stevens, "Of Love and Decomposition: Counterpoints in the Production of Space in South Bali," *Asian Diasporic Visual Cultures and the Americas* 3 (2017): 205.

Cekeg, have highlighted the depredations of mass tourism on the island's environment.[55] Environmental and heritage protection, when provided, has even resulted in contestations over space and resources.[56] Stevens also responds to these concerns in her artistic practice by examining the relationship between environmental degradation, social marginalization, and Bali's political history, fashioning these into a critique of enforced and socially accepted forgetting on the island. Her works, including *Kidung/Lament* (2019) and *A Line in the Sea* (2019), focus on reflections of the lived experience of Bali, an island marketed as a mass tourism destination but one in which historical violence continues to animate and reverberate in the landscape.[57] In her video installation in the exhibition *Of Love and Decomposition* (2016), she draws on two historical reference points, the 1965–66 violence and the rise of an international surfing culture that attracted tourists to Bali less than ten years after the killings had subsided. In so doing, according to Swastika, Stevens has established in her artistic works the link between the massacres, which brought the Indonesian army into power, and Bali's predicament.[58] Swastika argues that its commodification as a tourist paradise, founded on appealing to Western investment, can be linked to the destruction of popular movements when the army rose to power. The landscape also changed with the government's legally sanctioned confiscation of land and assets owned by accused leftists.[59]

Singing the Landscape

Returning to a consideration of *Kidung*, this work is part of a larger body of work by Stevens dealing with Bali and the intersections of political history and landscape. Many of her works were completed by working together with Balinese camera operator Wayan Martino. *Kidung* was part of an earlier solo exhibition, *Their Sea Is Always Hungry* (2019), at the University of Technology Sydney, which also included other moving image works, *A Line in the Sea* (2019) and *Rites for the Missing* (2019).[60] *Kidung* formed the core of the *Dua Dunia* (dual worlds) exhibition in Fremantle. This three-channel video installation consists of two screens showing the texture of a banyan tree, its trunk, branches, and leaves, flanking a screen showing a woman singing a "ballad of witness and testimony" as Rachel Ciesla describes in her 2021 curator's notes to the exhibition.[61] Balinese performance artist Cok Sawitri sings a *kidung* as if beside the banyan tree. The lush greenery behind her helps in creating this effect. The observational style of the video leaves the performer to sing, seemingly alone. Her voice rises and falls, beseeching and heartrending. At one point, Sawitri pauses and lights a cigarette before continuing to sing.

[55] Edwin Jurriens, "Art, Image and Environment: Revisualizing Bali in the Plastiliticum," *Continuum* 33, no. 1, (2019): 119–36, https://doi.org/10.1080/10304312.2018.1547363; and Vickers, "Balinese Art," 52–53.

[56] Agung Wardana, "Neoliberalizing Cultural Landscapes: Bali's Agrarian Heritage," *Critical Asian Studies* 52, 2, (2020): 270–85, https://doi.org/10.1080/14672715.2020.1714459.

[57] Leyla Stevens, dir., Kidung/Lament, 3 channel video, 10:58 mins., 2019; *A Line in the Sea*, 3 channel video, 9:45 mins., 2019.

[58] Swastika, "Curator's Essay."

[59] Rofiqi Hasan, "Kodam IX Udayana Digugat Korban Tragedi 1965," *Tempo* (December 11, 2004), https://koran.tempo.co/read/nusa/28989/kodam-ix-udayana-digugat-korban-tragedi-1965.

[60] On the exhibition *Their Sea Is Always Hungry* and video components, see https://leylastevens.com/Their-Sea-is-Always-Hungry.

[61] Ciesla, *Leyla Stevens*.

Figure 2: Performer Cok Sawitri singing a lament in the video work *Kidung*. Photograph by Robert Frith (used with permission from Acorn Photos and Rachel Ciesla).

In an interview with curator Jessica Taylor, Stevens describes the singing of the *kidung* as a "lament to the banyan tree and the memory of the missing dead there."[62] While the word *kidung* means song in Indonesian, in this context, it also refers to a poetry recitation style in Bali that is used to transmit knowledge orally.[63] Stevens describes *kidung* to one journalist as a ceremonial style of chanting specific to Bali.[64] Sawitri's performance of the *kidung* in this work, therefore, is one in which she transmits knowledge orally of the local history of the site of the banyan tree, which stands as a witness to the atrocities committed at this site.

Kidung is based on a script from an earlier video work, *Our Sea Is Always Hungry* (2018), which was then translated into Balinese and performed by Sawitri.[65] A reading of this script shows that both videos deal with the 1965–66 violence at several levels.

[62] "Leyla Stevens: Diaspora Pavilion 2 Artist in Conversation," International Creators Forum, June 20, 2020, https://vimeo.com/439990073.

[63] I Nyoman Darma Putra, "Kidung Interaktif," *Indonesia and the Malay World* 37, no. 109 (2009): 249–76, https://doi.org/10.1080/13639810903269276.

[64] South East Centre for Contemporary Art, "Leyla Stevens Interview ABC South East NSW," YouTube, October 27, 2020, https://www.youtube.com/watch?v=_9o4JalNzFM.

[65] Leyla Stevens, dir., *Our Sea is Always Hungry*, single channel video, stereo sound, 13:16 mins., (2018). See https://leylastevens.com/Our-Sea-is-Always-Hungry.

They establish the violence not as a one-off aberration, but as part of a longer history of colonialism and natural disaster on the island. In *Our Sea Is Always Hungry*, in a voiceover, two youths trace the history of the Lesser Sunda islands from the sea moving inland (scene 1). Images show the viewer the Mount Agung volcano in Bali, which erupted in 1963, and the forests, rivers, and gardens as sites of violence, haunting, and mass graves (scenes 2 and 3).[66]

The scripted subjects speak tentatively and probingly of the violent legacies of Balinese history. In scene 3, we are taken into what appears to be calmer scenes of lush greenery, whereupon a man appears, his lower torso visible but his face remains hidden by a piece of dried banana leaf, like many of the bodies covered hastily in leaves at places of execution. We are taken into a spiritual landscape where the dead dwell. The voices accompanying this image begin to describe the activities of *tameng*, civilian militias acting as auxiliary forces to the army and police, who came with trucks to capture those on their death lists. The next image is of a man rapidly climbing a coconut tree, showing great agility as he scrambles up, his feet tied by a piece of sacking. The scene represents a man who hid atop a tree to avoid these militias. Witnessing the killings below, he became haunted by *wong samar* in years to come. He was disturbed, *ngeb*, by their frequent appearance to him and grew withdrawn.

By employing euphemisms and code-switching from Indonesian to Balinese in the script the artist shows, through the youths' conversation, the difficulties of finding the words and locating the appropriate expressions, tone, and tenor to describe horrific experiences. Most strikingly illustrated in scene 3, they discuss one of the speakers' experiences in this excerpt:

> Voice #1: Best to tell it in Balinese. *Lebih baik diceritakan dalam Bahasa Bali.*
>
> Voice #2: Yes, ok. *Nah, dadi*
>
> I heard of one man, a rice farmer who managed to escape before they came to get him. He had a strong premonition before the militia arrived and slipped away. He found a tall tree, climbed up and up and hid at the very top.
>
> *Rage dapet ningeh, petani ne bise melarikan diri sebelum alihe jak milisine. Ngelah firasat ie sebelum milisi ne teke. Tepuk ie jak punyan tegeh, manjat ie menek terus lan diem ditu di paling atas.*
>
> From there he looked down and saw those men who came, march the accused villagers into an empty field. And hack them to death with machetes.
>
> *Uling ditu bise ie nyingakin ne di beten lan nyigakin milisene ento ne teke, ngabe orangorang ne di daftar ento ke lapangan kosong. Be keto bunuhe mekejang nganggon parang.*[67]

The speakers then discuss the participation of some villagers in the killing of their neighbors and the consumption of the fermented drink *tuak* by groups of militia men after the killings. One of the speakers switches from Balinese to Indonesian. In the video

---

[66] Unpublished script, *Our Sea Is Always Hungry*, provided to the author.

[67] Unpublished script, *Our Sea Is Always Hungry*. Translations are taken from the script.

itself, the use of Balinese language by the actors is much more prevalent than in the written script.

In scene 4, they discuss how those killed were disposed in mass graves in Bali, out of which grew new hotels and "villas" to accommodate tourism's ever-growing footprint on the island, showing the relentless growth of tourism in the face of gruesome violence. As one speaker remarks, "Strange how this island keeps growing villas." These developments are illustrated by images of a bridge and a toll road. Here, Stevens refers to the way in which tourists and tourism infrastructure are venerated while the remains of Balinese killed in the 1965–66 violence have been mostly left in mass graves with their families and friends unable to grieve openly.[68]

In the lush greenery that dominates scenes 5 and 6, and by placing a figure in the scenery, the video explores the world of the *wong samar*, and tries to convey this concept to transnational audiences, that the *wong samar* appear to those who suffer from *ngeb*, the after-effects of witnessing a frightening event. They are not ghosts, souls (*arwah*), nor humans but follow the farmer from scene 3 throughout his everyday life as the "guests that he should be kind towards." In the final scene, the two youths return their attention to the sea where they began. They reflect on how the sea, where ashes are deposited after cremation, is a bridge to cross over to the next world. They end by acknowledging that the bones of the dead are somehow speaking to them.

> Voice #2: Still, sometimes I can hear them.
>
> *tetap saja, saya masih mendengar mereka*
>
> Those missing. I can hear their bones
>
> *yang hilang itu. Saya bisa dengar tulang-tulang mereka*
>
> Calling from those forgotten places under the ground
>
> *memanggil dari tempat-tempat yang dilupakan di bawah tanah*
>
> They are still here
>
> *Mereka masih disini*

In this closing line, the artist puts a poignant emphasis on Bali's spiritual landscapes and their vitality, kept potent by what remained of the dead in the wooded places, busy roads, and waterways of the island. In titling her exhibition at PS Art Space *Dua Dunia*, Stevens highlights the dualism, in multiple spaces of the human and the more-than-human, and in the ways of speaking about the violence.

In her process of creating her works on Bali, Stevens evidently draws on scholarly research, for example, on Dutch colonial rule in Bali, the tensions and interparty rivalries between the PKI and its political rivals in the lead up to the 1965–66 violence,

---

[68] On this hierarchy of grief, see Degung Santikarma, "Monument, Document and Mass Grave: The Politics of Representing Violence in Bali," in *Beginning to Remember: The Past in the Indonesian Present*, ed. Mary Zurbuchen (Singapore: Singapore University Press, 2005), 312–23.

the eruption of Mount Agung, and the psychological impact of the violence.[69] Stevens also undertook her own field research, including through observations, interviews, and reflecting on intergenerational memories within her own family as part of a doctoral dissertation completed at the University of Technology Sydney.[70] These memories included her father's about the banyan tree marking the site of violent deaths, and of her grandfather's liquor stall being visited by executioners after a night of killing who, as he recalled, were surrounded by an aura of power that came from the taking of others' lives. In breathing new life into these memories and experiences through music, moving images, and performance, Stevens evocatively augments their emotive hold on the viewer by showing scenes not unfamiliar of Bali; but by speaking or singing the landscape to life in unexpected ways, the viewer is challenged to think and feel differently about these scenes and, ultimately, to consider what lies beneath.

The disjuncture in *Our Sea Is Always Hungry*—the jumps in the two interlocutors' conversation as they take in a wide range of topics from murdering militias drinking *tuak* to new villas being built—is suggestive of the gaps in knowledge and the uncertainties. The way they recount and weigh up rumors, ask questions, and share memories between them suggests that this disjuncture could indicate the state of knowledge about the violence where there continues to be uncertainty in many quarters about these events.

The natural environment, in particular the banyan tree, is a central motif within *Kidung* and other works by Stevens, an ambiguous yet politically charged plant that is rich with symbolism. In several of her moving image works, the tree stands as a marker, simultaneously, to absence and presence. She characterizes the site where one tree is located, near her family home in Bali, "as a counterpoint to state endorsed histories."[71] It marks the presence of atrocities and human remains, a mass grave nearby dated from the killings, but also an absence, from other landscapes elsewhere, of those whose remains are interred beneath. The figure of the banyan tree itself is highly ambiguous. Its imposing bulk enables protection, concealment, but also crowding out. The tree is a highly political symbol in Indonesia, of national unity in the state philosophy of Pancasila and of Suharto's ruling party, Golkar (Golongan Karya, Functional Groups), which purportedly unifies all Indonesians without recourse to politics. However, as Eben Kirksey has pointedly argued, such a tree, not unlike Golkar itself during the Suharto era, also crowds out others with its overwhelming presence.[72] As a sentinel, the banyan tree in *Kidung* symbolizes the violence, enabling the viewer to empathize with others' experiences through integrating bodily sensations, not dissimilar to the experiences of viewing scenes of seemingly familiar Balinese landscapes that are then animated by voices suggesting the possibility of other interpretations. The beach where tourists usually sat enjoying a seafood barbecue by torchlight or the river where they had participated in white-water rafting, Stevens reminds the viewer, were witness to other, less benign scenes in the decades previous.

[69] See, for example, Robinson, *The Dark Side of Paradise*; and Robert Lemelson and Luh Ketut Suryani, "Clinical Case Study."

[70] "Artist Bio," Their Sea Is Always Hungry," accessed June 9, 2021, https://art.uts.edu.au/index.php/exhibitions/their-sea-is-always-hungry/ (site discontinued).

[71] Stevens, "Of Love and Decomposition," 206.

[72] Eben Kirksey, *Freedom in Entangled Worlds: West Papua and the Architecture of Global Power* (New York: Duke University Press, 2012), 55.

Emotions and (Transnational) Impact

Distinct to the video work *Our Sea Is Always Hungry*, which features a conversation in Balinese and Indonesian and subtitled in English, *Kidung* contains no subtitles for viewers. Thus, it relies on the emotive value of the performance by Cok Sawitri, which could limit the viewer's engagement and ability to imbibe more knowledge without the aid of curators' notes and reference materials outside of the exhibition. But as a "non-verbal, non-depictive medium," with "a physical presence whose vibrations can be felt," music can work at non-cognitive or subconscious levels.[73] Perhaps also testament to the emotive way that images and sound resonate across cultures, *Kidung* received the 2021 Blake Prize in Australia, awarded to art that encourages conversations on spirituality and religion.[74] Though the work is highly place-based, the judges saw it as also speaking to other historical events throughout the world, including "the tragic Aboriginal histories also embedded in the Australian landscape," referring to the violent colonization of the continent by the British starting from 1788.[75] *Kidung* was subsequently acquired by the Art Gallery of New South Wales in Sydney, a major collecting institution in Australia's most populous state. The recognition accorded to Stevens's work affirms Dženeta Karabegović's observation of diaspora artists as being able to "engage with local populations in ways that other external actors do not" and that as a result, such artists can "position themselves as potentially significant actors in their homeland but also establish a presence within the host lands."[76] As a major source of tourism to Bali, and with its government's support for the New Order, Australian audiences have a certain degree of familiarity with Indonesia yet are largely at sea when it comes to grappling with the post-independence history of Indonesia.

The impact of such work in Bali itself is yet to be seen. These works are made by Stevens with the involvement of Balinese artists and creatives and draw heavily on Balinese history, politics, and spirituality. In more recent works, Stevens has also dealt with the labors necessary to produce what is taken for granted as Balinese culture and its appropriation as cultural capital, including through controlling the presentation and viewing of Balinese women, by Western artists, collectors, and collecting institutions.[77] The nature of video work is ephemeral, in that it confronts the viewers with some questions, but potentially leaves no mark on the sites of the violence themselves. It can unsettle, but not in any permanent way. But perhaps this is precisely the point, to unsettle in subtle ways in which concealment, ambiguity, and self-expression all represent strengths. Santikarma has argued that elaborate monuments, graves, or ceremonies are not needed to remember violence; remembering could simply be about having the freedom to speak without fear and to live together "with what can never be forgotten,

---

[73] Tia deNora, *Music in Everyday Life* (Cambridge: Cambridge University Press, 2000), 159.

[74] Linda Morris, "Masterful and Powerful Record of Bali Massacre Wins Blake Prize," *Sydney Morning Herald*, February 14, 2021, https://www.smh.com.au/culture/art-and-design/masterful-and-powerful-record-of-bali-massacre-wins-blake-prize-20210213-p5726j.html.

[75] Morris, "Masterful and Powerful Record."

[76] Dženeta Karabegović, "*Što Te Nema*?: Transnational Cultural Production in the Diaspora in Response to the Srebrenica Genocide," *Nationalism and Ethnic Politics* 20, no. 4 (2014): 472, https://doi.org/10.1080/13537113.2014.969151.

[77] These include, for example, Leyla Stevens, dir., *Patiwangi* (2021); *Labours for Colour* (2021), https://leylastevens.com/Selected-Work.

with losses that can never be restored."[78] Seemingly ephemeral, fleeting, and intangible, forms of artistic practice can facilitate remembrance in a way that renders the violence and its victims in a more complex and subtle light and, in turn, to forge new audience communities and solidarities.

Conclusion

Through art, Leyla Stevens addresses the at times unacknowledged absences in the landscape, in communities, and in families after political violence and performs reparative work through storying to deal with the legacies of the violence. While historical processes and human activity have changed landscapes over time, Stevens encourages us to examine how the more-than-human—spirits, nature, and the environment—can play a role in memorialization as fewer and fewer direct survivors of the violence remain today. Through the subtle insertion of the 1965–66 killings into the fabric of the land, its history, and system of knowledge, Stevens suggests that these killings have formed a part of several layers of conflict and change experienced on the island. While her work is necessarily speculative, telling (hi)stories about the violence across Bali is about proposing a shared world, consisting of the natural landscape and its inhabitants, a world with a complex web of relationships and accountabilities and aim to engender a sense of "proximity, ethical entanglement, care and concern."[79] Artists' examination of how violence reverberates in the landscape holds the potential, in emotionally and politically charged situations, for dialogue to take place and different kinds of memories to be expressed and considered.

---

[78] Santikarma, "Monument, Document and Mass Grave," 322.
[79] Van Dooren and Rose, "Lively Ethography," 89.

Singing the Memories:

Songs about the 1965 Anti-communist Violence in Banyuwangi

Arif Subekti and Hervina Nurullita

Kepingin seru ketemu . . . , eman

Nong kembang hang biso ngungdhang atine

Kadhung urip nong endi sangkane

Dhung wis mati, nong endi paesane

I am dying to meet you . . . if only

On a flower that is allowed to call the heart

If you are still alive, where do you reside now?

If you are gone, where is your grave?

This song, "Tetese Iluh" (Teardrops), is written in Banyuwangi's local language (Using) by Triyono Adi, famously known as Yon DD. The song expresses a person's longing to find someone that he/she loves, though the longing never came into being. Listening to this song, popularized by one of Banyuwangi's famous local singers, Catur Arum, nobody would have guessed that it refers to one of the most gruesome events in Indonesia's history. The songwriter, Yon DD, explained that this song is about the anti-communist killings in 1965–1966 in Banyuwangi. Losses and longings were the dominant feelings of the Banyuwangi people at that time, as their loved ones were taken away, detained, and killed by the military operation within that year, in collaboration with anti-communist civilian groups. This violence against the communists and the Left occurred throughout Indonesia in the period of 1965–1966 and in 1968 in some areas in East Java. Approximately 500,000–1,000,000 people were killed during those periods, while others experienced gross human rights violations and continuous persecutions (Komisi Nasional Hak Asasi Manusia RI, 2012). The killings were part of a national extermination project against the Indonesian Communist Party (PKI) and other leftist activists who were accused of being the masterminds of the 30 September Movement that caused the death of six high rank and one middle rank military officers. This event became one of the most controversial events in Indonesia's historiography, not only because of the debate regarding who was behind the September 30th Movement, but also because narratives about the mass violence have been largely excluded in Indonesia's national history. The following New Order regime, which was led by Suharto in 1966, took a very different approach to national policies that are geared heavily toward capitalism and liberalism, rather than the previous socialist tendency of Sukarno (Robison, 1986; Farid, 2005). Moreover, the regime also executed memory projects that aim to remember the death of the army officers, but at the same time, stigmatizing the communists as evil and a threat to the nation.

"Tetese Iluh" is one of the local songs that became a part of Indonesia's collective memory of the 1965 violence, which are embedded in localities and became part of society's everyday life in the present. Apart from the creative process of its writer and the individual experiences of 1965, the creation of this song could not be separated from Indonesia's political background and the democratic turn in 1998. In the previous Suharto era (1966–1998), the public discussion on 1965 had been largely centered on the death of seven military officers in the 30 September Movement, while the anti-communist violence and killings were continuously repressed. There were no spaces for commemorations of victims of this violence. However, after *Reformasi* in 1998, this discourse of the 1965 violence has taken a massive turn. The anti-communist narrative that long persisted with Suharto's authoritarian government was contested with the appearance of victims' testimonies and the acceleration of human rights and transitional justice discourse. This was followed by several steps taken by the post-authoritarian government after Suharto, who had taken several steps to eliminate practices that supported the anti-communist narrative, for example, putting an end to the "national ritual" to air the film *The Treachery of the September 30th Movement/Indonesian Communist Party* on national television every October 1st, releasing the remaining 10 political prisoners, by allowing all exiles to return to Indonesia, and apologizing to the victims' families for the 1965–1966 violence.[1]

These dynamics in the post-authoritarian era illustrate the emerging tension between the state or formal narrative with the previously repressed counter-narrative. This tension productively developed into an emerging genre, which Zurbuchen (2005) described as *historical memory*, where individual and social processes continued to be intertwined with in representing the past in the present (p. 7). After more than 20 years of Reformasi,

---

[1] These steps occurred under the leadership of Presdient Habibie and Abdurrachman Wahid. Until 1998, there were still around 1,400 Indonesians living in political exile in European countries. Most of them were diplomats, students, or correspondents who worked in socialist countries such as Cuba, China, the Soviet Union, or other Eastern European countries when the 1965 violence occurred. They refused to acknowledge the 1965 violence as a coup attempt by the communists, so their passports were revoked and they were threatened they would be detained if they returned to Indonesia (Budiawan, 2004, p. 44).

Indonesians are still living with both of these narratives. This is reflected, for example, in the study of university students' theses on 1965 that shows an increasing number after 1998. However, while the number of theses that fall under the topic of human rights and reconciliation is growing, the quantity that resonates with anti-communist narratives are also raising (themes such as the role of Islamic groups in annihilating PKI) (Leksana & Kammen, 2021). This is what Eickhoff et al. (2017) regarded as a dualism: although Indonesians still believe in the formal narrative about communism, it does not necessarily mean that they do not sympathize with victims (458). In other words, rather than a single collective memory, the 1965 violence generated multiple collective memories that are complex and layered but also coexist and entangled.

In the studies of genocide and mass violence, music has been one focus of these complex memory practices. The role of music can range from supporting certain formal narratives of violence to criticizing and questioning the violence and its current memorialization. For example, Pitic's (2021) study about commemorative music on the Srebrenica genocide is not only influenced by the grand narrative of the genocide, but also maintains and reinforces the dominant story that represents an important segment of the politically advantageous official collective memory and history of the genocide (p. 467). In the context of the Rwandan genocide, Mwambari (2020) focuses on music as a citizen-driven creative means that not only spread the memories of genocide, but also criticize state-organized commemoration practices (p. 1322). In relation to the trauma of Indonesia's 1965 violence, Pitaloka and Dutta (2021) examine a women's choir whose loved ones were implicated in the 1965–1966 anti-communist persecution. The Dialita choir demonstrates how music is used to make sense of the past and at the same time overcome trauma and distress and conveys this difficult history to Indonesia's younger generations (Pitaloka & Dutta, 2021). The Dialita choir also shows women's collective resiliency, agency, and recovery. All of these cases, from Bosnia, Rwanda, to Indonesia, pointed to the role of music as cultural movements to remember mass violence.

However, placing acts of commemoration merely in their relation to the state glosses over the fact that these practices actually emerge within a distinct local dynamic. Through this article, we want to examine how music as mnemonic practices of mass violence is not only a response toward state repression of the violence, but also an act of remembering that is shaped by the local cultural setting. This setting is constructed by two factors: the cultural traditions that were historically molded by postcoloniality and second, the violence that not only caused losses of lives, but also transforms those cultural expressions. Our research area, Banyuwangi, is a case in point. Their distinct language and music reflect a unique character and, in some cases, were used as a label against the communists. One example is the song "Genjer-genjer," which was written by a local Banyuwanginese and was a national hit in the 1960s. In the 30 September Movement, the New Order government fabricated a narrative that this song was sung by the women activists of Gerwani (a women's organization closely related to PKI) while they were torturing the generals (Wieringa, 2002). Since then, "Genjer-genjer" was labeled a communists' song and was no longer considered one of Indonesia's pop hits in the 1960s. This stigmatization affected the production of songs in the later generations of Banyuwangi musicians, particularly those who choose 1965 as their theme.

Looking at this local dynamic of music related to 1965, we want to discuss critical questions regarding music as a form of collective memory; to what extent are these memories of violence sustainable and effective if it is produced locally? Who are these songs intended for? Why use metaphor and analogies instead of explicitly expressing the violence? By discussing these questions, we analyze critically the function of music as a mnemonic practice and to counter the perception that the connection of music with the past is a linear one. As we will show in this article, even songs that were inspired by 1965 contain layers of experiences, narratives, and silence. These songs do not merely commemorate the violence, but also illustrate the negotiations between the structural repression and private strategies of remembering. To answer those questions, we talked to four Banyuwangi musicians in the course of 2013 to 2022. Two of them were from the older generation of musicians and were once members of Lekra. Meanwhile, the younger generation of musicians do not have any connections with Lekra, but have produced songs related to the 1965 violence.[2]

Memories of 1965 Violence

Indonesia's anti-communist collective memory was intensively constructed under Suharto's New Order government. History writing was highly controlled by the military, where the white book of the 30 September Movement, written by military historian Notosusanto, became its main reference (Notosusanto & Saleh, 1968; Notosoesanto et al., 1993). This grand narrative focuses on the military heroism of exterminating the PKI, while the violence against them remains untold. If the violence appears, it is depicted as a communal clash between leftist and religious or nationalist groups and that the army attempted to control the situation (Notosusanto & Saleh, 1968, p. 77). The anti-communist memory project continued in 1973 with the opening of the Pancasila Sakti (Sacred Pancasila) Monument and museum complex in Jakarta, where it depicted the torture, killings, and the Crocodile Pit (Lubang Buaya) where the generals bodies were found. The monument complex became a site of commemoration of *Kesaktian Pancasila* Day on October 1, where Indonesians remember the death of the army officers, but not the victims of anti-communist persecutions. The Lubang Buaya monument became a site that only commemorates "the permissible aspects of the past," as Schreiner (2005) claims (p. 273). Another memory project emerged in 1984, through the production of the film *Penumpasan Pengkhianatan G30S/ PKI* (Combating the Betrayal of G30S/ PKI), directed by Arifin C. Noer. The film focuses on the night of abduction of the military officers and their torture and killings in Lubang Buaya.

These New Order memory projects show the practice of power in constituting collective memory. Anti-communism became what is called dominant memory, which refers to "the power and pervasiveness of historical representations, their connections with dominant institutions and the part they play in winning consent and building alliances in the process of formal politics" (Popular Memory Group, 1982). However, this dominant memory does not mean that other narratives are silenced or diminished. On the contrary, different narratives may emerge in what Foucault (1995) pointed to as popular memory, the capacity of ordinary people in preserving and recording their own history, particularly when they are inhibited from drawing up their historical accounts (p. 25). The memory of the 1965 violence reflects the tension between these memories. On one hand, the dominant memory is constantly reproduced by state-led memory projects,

---

[2] Part of this data was also used in the master's thesis of Nurullita (2015) and the article by Subekti (2015).

but on the other, memories of violence against the left remain alive in the grassroots and among survivors, although largely marginalized.

Even after the fall of Suharto and the democratic turn in Indonesia, attacks against survivor groups, along with fear and stigma against communists, persist. Furthermore, the effort for reconciliation faced a dire challenge when the Truth and Reconciliation Commission (TRC) Law was struck down by the Constitutional Court in 2006.[3] Nevertheless, public debates and discussions on the 1965 violence, such as the Indonesia People's Tribunal in The Hague in 2015 and the National Symposium on 1965 in Jakarta in 2016, have undoubtedly opened spaces against dominant memory.

However, the practices of remembering the 1965 violence are more complex than a mere state versus counter-narrative binary approach. Silenced and hidden narratives of violence have created their own language and distinct ways of representing the past, creating layered and interconnected memories. Although memories could not be articulated, they are attached in places, objects, or sites that remind the survivors of the violence against their loved ones (Santikarma, 2008, p. 207). Another example is fictional literatures in the early period of the New Order, which carried the theme of 1965 violence, such as the short stories in *Horison* magazine. Although the writers described the killings in the stories, they presented it as an act of justification to save the nation (Roosa et al., 2004). Stories of violence also emerge in forms of haunted places such as the study of Kar Yen Leong in Central Java (Leong, 2021). In the same province, specifically in Klaten, memories of the 1965 violence are anchored in sounds of kentongan or the slit drum, which was played to alert residents of the violence that took place in their area. This event, which occurred between the last week of October to early November 1965, is famously known as *kentong gobyok*. However, it generated different memories between the nationalist and leftist groups in Klaten. For the first, *kentong gobyok* refers to the event where more than 100 people, mostly nationalists of the Indonesia Nationalist Party (PNI-Sukarno's political party), were killed by the communists. For the latter, *kentong gobyok* is related to the detention and killings of thousands of communists and leftists in Klaten (see Hadi & Hera, 2020). Moreover, narratives of violence remain in family memories that persisted through different generations. In his study of intergenerational memory, Conroe (2012) shows how memories of the second generation of victims' families became the driving force behind the human rights advocacy and reconciliation for the victim community. All of these studies show that the memories of anti-communist violence never diminish, even under decades of state repression. Instead, they persisted and expressed through different forms under local social political dynamics. It is these dynamics that influence various local mnemonic practices, including local music, such as the case of Banyuwangi.

The Violence in Banyuwangi

The anti-communist killings have generated different analyses on how they were executed, which can be divided into three categories: horizontal conflict, the structural

---

[3] One of the controversial articles that was revoked in the constitutional court was article 27, which regulated amnesty for perpetrators as a prerequisite for compensation for victims. The constitutional court then decided that without article 27, the law itself would be non-functional. Therefore, the court decided to revoke the whole law. This was very different from the request of the litigation group, who only wanted to revoke three problematic articles (Saptaningrum et al., 2007).

order approach, and the dualistic thesis (Roosa, 2016). In the official account, which is followed by several scholars (Sulistyo, 2000; Sudjatmiko, 1992), the killings were conducted as a result of horizontal conflict between the communists and religious groups. The army had minor roles in the violence, or even if they did participate, it was to create peace and order within this conflict. However, this analysis fails to explain how collective tensions could escalate into nationwide mass killings during a certain period of time (Sulistyo, 2000; Sudjatmiko, 1992). In contrast to this horizontal conflict theory, other scholars (McGregor & Kammen, 2012; Robinson, 2018; Melvin, 2018) have argued that the violence was structurally coordinated by the military. The different timing of the violence relates more to an alliance between the authorities and local civilians to carry out the violence and not an indication that there was no pattern in the nationwide violence (Robinson, 2018).[4] Meanwhile, the dualistic thesis argues that there is no overarching pattern that can be drawn from the nationwide violence because in some areas the army took the lead but in others, it was the civilians who moved more aggressively. However, the latest findings from Aceh (Melvin, 2018) and East Java (Luthfi, 2018; Leksana, 2021) have provided proof of the structural order in executing the violence.

Within these different approaches, East Java is usually presented as the example of horizontal conflict because of the intense clashes between the communists and religious groups, particularly the Islamic organization Nahdlatul Ulama (NU) and its youth wing, Ansor. The friction between these two groups has long-standing historical roots since colonial times (Sulistyo, 2000), which crystalized during the agrarian reform in the 1960s.[5] The 1965 violence became the culmination of this tension, turning East Java into one of the provinces with high numbers of deaths in addition to Central Java and Bali. Although the purge against communists in East Java was executed by various civilians' groups, such as Ansor, students' organizations, and nationalists' groups, these acts were coordinated under East Java's military command (Leksana, 2020). Different areas in East Java seemed to move more aggressively and faster against the communists, such as in Situbondo and Banyuwangi ("Report from East Java," 1986).[6] Mass violence was usually instigated after mass gatherings in public spaces in various cities in East Java, such as in Surabaya on October 16, 1965 ("Report from East Java," 1986) and Malang on October 14, 1965 (D. Setiawan, 2014). These meetings were a consolidation of mass mobilization and power aimed at targeting the Left. Moreover, these meetings were acknowledged and supported by Major General Soeharto as the military commander of the Operational Command for the Restoration of Security and Order (Kopkamtib) (McGregor & Kammen, 2012).

Although the total numbers of victims in East Java is hard to calculate, through a quantitative demographic analysis, Chandra (2017) managed to generate a total

[4] The mass violence against the Left, although it occurred nationwide, did not commence at the same time. For example, the violence in Aceh started very early in October 1965, while in East Java and Bali, the violence only began in late October or November 1965.

[5] The Basic Agrarian Law no. 5 was passed in 1960 to change the previous law that was established by the colonial government in 1870. The law aims to provide land for the people, particularly those who are landless. However, the implementation was complex and slow. This led to tension between the peasants and leftist organizations, such as BTI (Indonesian Peasant's Union that was affiliated with PKI) and the landlords who, in East Java, consist mostly of religious leaders (*kyai*) (see Mortimer, 1972).

[6] According to Robinson (2018), this difference does not indicate that the acts were not coordinated, but it suggests a different cohesive alliance between the military and civilians to carry out the violence. In areas where the military and civilians were unified against the Left, the violence started earlier than in other areas that were not (Robinson, 2018, pp. 15–17).

population loss of 175,169 people in East Java alone. He connected the aggregate achievement of the PKI in the 1957 election, the concentration and contestation of the PKI and NU-Masyumi along with their affiliated organizations in the area, and the expansion of *aliran* (*santri-abangan*). In Banyuwangi, PKI dominated the elections in 1957 (Chandra, 2017, p. 1070). Despite PKI's achievement in this area, the violence against them was massive. Using army documents, Luthfi's (2018) article on Banyuwangi shows various acts of violence, from death by civilians and the army, the replacement of 42 village leaders by the military, and harassment against members of Gerwani. To identify targets of violence, the army organized the formation of *Badan Koordinasi Komando Siaga* (BKKS) in every village. The records also reported the death of 6,008 PKI members in Banyuwangi until August 20, 1966, 1,040 people assigned for compulsory reporting (*wajib lapor*), 115 remained in detention, and 49 people escaped (Luthfi, 2018). In one of the "red areas" considered a PKI base of Banyuwangi occurred the famously known Cemetuk incident in Karangasem, where 60 Ansor youths were killed by the locals.[7] The New Order government commemorated this event with a monument called Pancasila Jasa in 1995.[8] Interestingly, despite this violence, Banyuwangi experienced an increase in its population of 105,914 people. This is interpreted by Chandra (2017) that Banyuwangi was seen as a safe haven for refugees during the violent events due to several factors, such as the high numbers of votes for PKI in Banyuwangi (as mentioned before) and the geographical remoteness of its southern districts.

Banyuwangi and Osing Popular Culture

Migration to Banyuwangi did not only occur because of the 1965 violence. Since the colonial era, Banyuwangi has been a destination for migrants, commenced by the colonial government themselves to repopulate the north end of Java Island. War, famine, and plague have contributed highly to the decrease and imbalance of the population in Java. From the VOC era to the British occupation, the colonial government had launched different strategies to initiate migration to Banyuwangi, although not all of them succeeded. For example, the government attracted people from Bawean and Madura to work on plantations, providing incentives for them, and even opening prostitution centers (Margana, 2007). Besides these strategies, the opening of the railway that connects Kalisat-Banyuwangi with other places in Java in 1903 had facilitated massive migrations to Banyuwangi. The railway also intensified the transformation of forest areas into plantations and rice fields. Until the early 20th century, Banyuwangi had the highest record of migrations compared to other regencies in Java (Beatty, 2004). This was proven by the first census in 1930, which noted that 47.2% of Banyuwangi residents were born outside of the area (Volkstelling, 1930, pp. 46, 94).

[7] There are different versions of this incident. In Cribb (1990, pp. 154–156), the incident happened when an anti-communist group from Ansor and PNI youths were ambushed by the communist group in Cemetuk. Well-known as a communist base, villagers in Cemetuk attacked the anti-communist group, who defended themselves with weapons. Fifty-one bodies were found on the street and in three wells. Meanwhile, the Report from East Java recorded that the Ansor group burned houses and attacked the villages. But then, a group of Gerwani disguised themselves as Fatayat NU (NU's women organization) and invited the Ansor youths into a house where they were attacked and killed by the communist group. A total of 64 victims were recorded in the report ("Report from East Java," 1986, pp. 137–138). In all of these versions, the army is portrayed to be the force that put an end of the confrontation and restore peace in the area.

[8] State-initiated monuments about 1965 resonate with the Pancasila monument in Jakarta that commemorates the death of army officers and depicts the communists as the threat of the nation (see McGregor, 2007).

Migrations have turned Banyuwangi into a lively multicultural environment. Living along with the migrants is the so-called Osing people, which are believed to be the remaining people of the Blambangan kingdom in Banyuwangi that was defeated after the struggle of King Wilis and Rempeg in 1761–1768 and 1771–1773 (see Margana, 2007). The struggle was the result of three different forces that compete for Banyuwangi—the Mataram kingdom in Central Java with their agenda of Islamization, the Menwi kingdom of Bali who wanted to turn Banyuwangi into their last resort against Islamization, and the VOC (Margana, 2007). But in the end, their defeat marked the end of the Blambangan kingdom and the beginning of the Dutch VOC occupation in Banyuwangi. This history of the last kingdom in Java to be conquered developed Osing into a distinct identity of the Banyuwangi people, with their unique language and culture. The Osing language has been identified as a distinct dialect since 1870s by the famous colonial linguist Van der Tuuk (Arps, 2009). The language, combined with the heroic history of the Blambangan kingdom, constitute a strong identity of the local people as Osing or as Banyuwangi, which differentiate them from Javanese and Balinese. This identity is expressed in Banyuwangi popular culture and appears in many public forms: slogans, brands, places, café names, the Osing Toursim Village, and street names such as Larus street—from *Lare Using* (Arps, 2009).[9]

Osing popular culture also emerged in the form of local music. The traditional music and dance of Gandrung became the icon of the area. Along with other traditional cultures of Banyuwangi, Gandrung carries religious values and symbols related to agricultural life of the locals (Sutarto, 2006). This music was popularized in the 1950s–1960s. In that period, Gandrung became a local performance that was maintained by Lekra (an artists' organization closely affiliated with PKI) and performed during PKI's political campaign. This led to the large number of Gandrung musicians and dancers who became affiliated with Lekra (Raharjo, 2016). Moreover, in conversation with Slamet Menur, one former Lekra artist described in detail how music played an important role within Banyuwangi society. Songs were used as a tool of resistance, as Slamet illustrates through the song "Padha Nonton." Banyuwangi songs commonly use metaphor, for example, flower is a symbol for a girl. These metaphors are used because the people of Banyuwangi wanted to convey messages of resistance that the Dutch could not understand. In this conversation, Slamet again emphasizes the character of Banyuwangi people, who are harsh resistors against the Dutch, which differentiates them from the Central Javanese, who collaborated with the colonials.[10]

Throughout the 1950s–60s, Lekra continued to produce songs that portray the everyday life of the locals. During the Asian African conference in 1955 in Bandung, Slamet, with the music group Srimuda (which is the abbreviation of Seni Rakyat Indonesia Muda/Young Indonesian People's Art) in Banyuwangi performed the song and dance of "Genjer-genjer," and the song "Rantag," which convey a message of unity between countries against colonialism. The dance of "Genjer-genjer" was created by Slamet in 1962.[11] Ahmad Arif, Endro Wilis, Mahfud Hariyanto, and Basir Noerdian were listed as the song writers and composers for Lekra Bayuwangi. They not only produced

---

[9] *Lare* means young people, which is different from the term young people in Javanese: *arek*. Other examples of the use of this term is in the names of places, for example Osing Cattery & Petshop, Osing bouquet, Osingdeles (souvenir shop), and Van de Osing café.

[10] Interview with Slamet Menur, Banyuwangi, October 23, 2022.

[11] Interview with Slamet Menur, Banyuwangi, October 23, 2022.

songs and performed at prestigious events, but also went to villages and taught art in *sanggar* (community-based art studios).

One of the most popular songs produced by a Banyuwangi musician was "Genjer-genjer," composed by Mohammad Arif, a musician, music teacher, and an official in the Banyuwangi branch of Lekra. The song is about a plant that usually grows in a particular area and is sold in the market to be consumed in daily meals. The song was first heard by a group of Lekra and PKI politicians and writers who were going to the Afro-Asian Writers Bureau conference in Bali in mid-1963. At their stop in Banyuwangi, they were treated with an angklung performance, which included Arif's "Genjer-genjer." Njoto, one of PKI's central committee members, was charmed by the song and considered it as a mix between traditionality and proletarian progressivity.[12] According to Slamet Menur, Arif was inspired by his wife's cooking of genjer leaves when he began to pay more attention to this particular plant.[13] From there, "Genjer-genjer" entered the popular music industry when two famous Indonesian pop singers, Bing Slamet and Lilis Surjani, recorded the song, and later on when it was aired on national radio and television.

The popularity of Banyuwangi local culture transformed completely along with the 1965 violence. Most of Banyuwangi's local artists who were involved in Lekra were detained and even killed during the anti-communist persecution.[14] The death of Banyuwangi's local artists affected deeply the once lively local music and performance scene. Not only did it sharply decrease performances and creative production, but "Gandrung" and "Genjer-genjer" were also stigmatized, following the 1965 violence. "Gandrung" was considered as the "Lekra" dance, and "Genjer-genjer" was given a very different meaning along with New Order anti-communist propaganda. The government circulated a narrative that Gerwani members danced to "Genjer-genjer" song while torturing the kidnapped officers in the 30 September Movement (Wieringa, 2002). This was obviously fabricated because the autopsy reports of the bodies did not find any traces of torture, gunshots were the main cause of death (Anderson, 1987). Unfortunately, to this today, "Genjer-Genjer" has lost its symbol of the progressive proletariat that M. Arief initially conveyed through the song (Zulkifli et al., 2014, pp. 118–119).

Years after the violence, the music life in Banyuwangi became dormant and its roots among the people were destroyed. But in the mid-1970s, a few Banyuwangi musicians tried to revive the musical life in the area by recording a new genre of Banyuwangi music, which was influenced by Islamic music. This was deliberately chosen to avoid the accusation of Banyuwangi as a "red" or communist area. Another group of musicians then developed another genre by combining Melayu music and Indonesia's famous *dangdut*. This was later on known as *kendang kempul* music of Banyuwangi, also because the instrument used to play this music was the kettledrum and *kempul* (a type of hanging gong in Indonesian gamelan). This era in Banyuwangi marked a shift in its music genres that were once rooted in the social political lives of the people into the religion-influenced style. This is not only to revive the music tradition in Banyuwangi, but also to counter the stigmatization of Banyuwangi as leftists.[15]

---

[12] From the account of Hersri Setiawan, one of Lekra's former activists in Arps (2011).

[13] Interview with Slamet Menur, Banyuwangi, October 23, 2022.

[14] For example, a Gandrung dancer explains that his teacher disappeared in the 1965 violence. Interview with Temu in Kemiren, March 28, 2014. Slamet Menur himself was also detained during his escape to Surabaya.

[15] Interview with Suhalik, April 1, 2013.

Reviving Osing, Remembering the Violence

Although the 1965 violence has affected the decline of Banyuwangi's cultural activities and music production, generations of musicians after M. Arif struggled to continue their work. Besides the emergence of "Kendang Kempulan" music in Banyuwangi, another genre appeared through the use of pentatonic scales. Several musicians, such as Andang C. Y., Nasikin, B. S. Nurdian, M. F. Hariyanto, and Endro Wilis, try to use the local Osing language in this music. Andang Chatib Yusuf, famously known as Andang C. Y., was born on September 19, 1934. He was a teacher, a friend of Mohammad Arif, and an activist for Lekra. He mostly wrote songs about love, religion, and politics and often used metaphors in his lyrics.[16] His first song was titled "Prawan Sunthi," circa 1966 or 1967, which was followed by another song, "Kembang Pethetan" (Dearest flower), composed around the 1970s.

"Kembang Pethetan"

Pethetan, yo kembang pethetan	Dearest, dearest flower
Sun tandu ring pucu pertamanan	I plant you in the corner of my garden
Esuk sore, sing kurang siraman	Day and night, never miss to water you
Sun jogo, sun rumat temenanan	I watch, I nurture you dearly
Pethetan, yo kembang pethetan	Dearest, dearest flower
Kembang mekar, gawe ati kedanan	When the flower bloom, I am drunk in love
Kadung sun sawang, tambah sun sawang	The more I look, the more I watch
Ati susah, dadio girang	This troubled heart becomes happy
Isun sing ngiro, lan isun sing nyono	I never thought nor wonder
Gagang tuklek, kembange sing ono	As the stem broke, the flower is perished
O . . . angin, kang liwat ring kono	Dear blowing wind
Melu takon, kang metik tangane sopo	I am asking you, whose hands have plucked them away?
Pethetan, yo kembang pethetan	Dearest, dearest flower
Kembang ilang, isun kang kelangan	My flower's gone away, I feel lost too
Masio mung kembang, piro regane kembang	It might be just a flower; it may not cost much
Tapi kang ilang, kembange kembang	But know that what's lost is the best kind of flowers

---

[16] Interview with Andang C. Y., March 29, 2014.

After the release of both songs, Andang was detained for 15 days in Koramil (the district military office). His songs were accused of containing communist symbolization. In Prawan Sunthi, the phrase "Suruh wanci kinangan" was misinterpreted as "the betel nut that turned red after it was chewed." Red, here, was identified as communism. Meanwhile, in "Kembang Pethetan," the line "sun tandur ring buju petamanan" was interpreted as the symbol of a hammer and sickle on a flag. Both of these songs were stigmatized as PKI songs, also because of Andang's background in Lekra (I. Setiawan, 2010). However, according to Andang, "Prawan Sunthi" is only a song about a girl entering adulthood and being ready to be married, while "Kembang Pethetan" is a love song. Rumors circulated that "Kembang Pethetan" was a song for his wife, who was taken away and married a member of the army after the 1965 operation.[17] This became Andang's inspiration for "Kembang Pethetan." He died on November 1, 2017.

"Prawan Sunthi"

Prawan Sunthi metu subuh ya ndika teng pundi	Dear girl, where are you going at dawn
Kang di suwun wanci kinangan suruh kuning	What you carry above your head is yellow betel and its bowl
Indhita ne beras sak elas ulihe nggagas	what you carry on your waist is rice grain, after scavenging its remain
Tayongane nggayuh lintang gancango padhang	The hand wave are reaching for the stars, hurry, sing
Ati-atinen nong dalan akeh eri lan akeh juglangan	Be careful on this road with thorns and holes
Esema na lare angon kang dhemen gridhoan	Smile to the shepherd who likes to play
Adhuh-adhuh prawan sunthi napa ndika jaluk	Oh, girl, what are you searching
Ngembung iluh usapana cindhe sutra	Covered in tears, wipe them with silk shawl
Keringete lare angon kang kula tadhahi	The shepherd's sweat that I collect
Adhuh nyawa gandholana ragan kula	My dear soul, hold my body close
Diudani dipanasi prawan sunthi kang kula gandholi	Under the rain and sun, the girl that I will hold
Bang-bang wetan srengene metu donyane padhang	On the eastern horizon of the sun, the world shines bright

---

[17] This was also confirmed by musician Yon D. D., who is the cousin of Andang, during our interview.

The next generation of artists that we mention at the beginning of this paper, Yon DD or Triyono Adi is one of those musicians who also speaks about losses caused by the 1965 violence. What differs between them and Andang's generation of Andang is their decision to not follow pentatonic rules, but to comply more with the market demands of popular Banyuwangi music. This is one of the critiques of Andang by the young generations of Banyuwanginese musician. Born inApril 24, 1963, Yon started his career as an artist by joining a theater group with the stage name Yono Samega. But his work as a musician only began when he was a technician in a *dangdut* group around the 1970s. From there, he became interested in song writing, which motivated him to learn from Andi Suroso, the leader of the orchestra Melayu Mutiara. In 1995, Yon DD began to write songs for a competition organized by the Blambangan Art Council. He won the second place in that competition and since then, Yon has become a very productive song writer.

The song mentioned at the beginning of this article, "Tetese Iluh," was created in 2000 by Yon DD and Banyuwangi's famous singer Catur Arum. This melancholic song is still a hit in Banyuwangi and is accessible on YouTube.

"Tetese Iluh"

Sedino-dino mung nangis gawene	Every single day, all I do is cry
sing leren-leren, sampek alum matane	can't stop it, my eyes are puffy from constant crying
Yo mesesegen, ilang suwarane	Sobbing, crying in silence
Kesuwen nangis, sampek nono iluhe	Been crying for too long, it dries my tears
Kepingin seru ketemu.., eman	I am dying to meet you . . . if only
Nong kembang hang biso ngungdhang atine	On a flower that is allowed to call the heart
Kadhung urip nong endi sangkane	If you are still alive, where do you reside now?
Dhung wis mati, nong endi paesane	If you are gone, where is your grave?
Arep sun kirim kembang,	I want to send you flowers
Hang wangi gandhane	Those with wonderful scent
Arep sun kirim gendhing,	I want to send you a song
Nawi tah biso nentremaken atine	That can calm the heart

Yon created this song from his father's stories, who was a village head in the area since 1963. During the creative process of composing, both he and Catur Arum investigated the experiences of surrounding villagers during 1965. Both have a mission with this song—that such an event should never happen again.

> To write that song, I observed some areas in my surrounding neighborhood in Banyuwangi, and I observed those who were left behind. Whether the children, who were left by their fathers, or their mothers because of the turmoil. That's

why I wrote that song. By coincidence, my father was the village secretary here, starting in 1963. So my father told me, although not so many, there were few people who were protected so they were not captured. My brother was a PNI (Partai Nationalis Indonesia/Indonesian Nationalist Party) in Banyuwangi. His name was Jalaludin, so there are quite . . . quite a lot who protect, to save people who were accused—let's just say so. Both my father and uncle have died. But this story was told directly by them to me. The same with Catur. He also observed his neighbours. Because coincidentally, in Catur's area, in Tembungan, Tembungan village is . . . according to people, is the basis. For example, in Catur's area, lived Pak Arif, who composed Genjer-genjer. He was from that village. Tembungan. So there were a lot of incidents in Tembungan village. . . . After I visited those people, we created the song "Tetese Iluh." So the background of "Tetese Iluh" is the history of 48 and 65. Why I composed it with Catur, so that these things will not happen again. That is why there are very hidden metaphors. It's from the incident of the children that were left behind.[18]

Yon's inspiration for "Tetese Iluh" came from his family's experience, specifically in providing protection for those who were accused. The song evolved when Yon and Catur talked to families of victims and explored their experiences. Yon and Arum's effort to commemorate the 1965 violence through their song is another example of how cultural means have become the vanguard in preserving the memory of violence. Within the dominance of the anti-communist narrative, these forms of cultural expression show the *silent* preservation of memories of violence. The case of Banyuwangi music about 1965 shows the capacity of music beyond its artistic or entertainment elements, but the capacity to articulate personal and collective memory (van Dijck, 2006) and the expression of identity (Barendregt, 2002). In this case, the anti-communist violence also constituted a large part of the identity of the Banyuwangi people.

But this premise also raises a question: if the songs about the 1965 violence show the identity and memory of the Banyuwangi people, how far can it resonate in the ears of the wider public? If the songs use deep metaphors, then how can the listeners know and remember the violence in 1965? In other words, if the meaning is very implicit, then how can the preventive message that the writer intended succeed in creating public awareness? To answer this question, we try to zoom into the semantic choices in the song. One element is the choice to use metaphoric words, describing the feelings of those who were left behind.

Those who were left behind was very young. They didn't understand. They only know their fathers or mothers through pictures. But they don't really know what happened to them. I asked, but they didn't know where, their existence. That's why I wrote the lyrics "adu ngurip nong ndi sanggane, dung wis mati, nong ndi paesanne." Back then, when I was writing, I wrote "dung wis mati, nong ndi kuburane." That was the initial lyric. But I . . . as if they were dead. If "nong ndi kuburane," it means that it was certain, oh the grave is there. But not even the grave, the tombstone itself did not exist. So I use the phrase "nong ndi paesanne."[19]

---

[18] Interview with Yon D. D., September 15, 2021.
[19] Interview with Yon DD, September 15, 2021.

Kuburan in Javanese means grave, while *paesan* means a tombstone. *Paesan* here has a symbolic meaning of a mark of the dead, and this is what Yon emphasizes. The tombstone that did not exist represents the confusion, the fuzziness, and the vague memory of the people who disappeared in 1965. Yon explains that their semantic choices foregrounded symbolic words to describe the feelings, rather than vulgar descriptions of violent acts.

Another element is a kind of self-censorship of the lyrics. Here, the writers avoid certain terms that do not fit with the metaphoric nuance of the song.

> In our first recording, in Jakarta before the music starts, there was my voice. Before the music, before the intro, Catur and I wanted . . . not a poem, but just me saying "*sewu sangangatus sewidak limo*" (1965 in Javanese). Then the music. . . . But, after we discuss it, it does not seem to fit. So we erased that sentence. But in a show before COVID-19, around two months before that, I did a show with Catur. Tribute to Yon DD-Catur Arum in El Royal. Catur Arum sang "Tetese Iluh," and he mentioned the year. It's on YouTube. Catur Arum's YouTube.[20]

It is highly possible that erasing 1965 from the lyrics involved multiple considerations, which include political reasons. Using the year in the song would not only reduce the symbolic nature of the lyrics, but might also put the song writers in danger, given the stigma of Banyuwangi as a base of communists. Writing lyrics in metaphor seems to be the middle ground to convey a message about 1965 without being accused of reviving communism.

The consequence of this choice of composing is that the message may not be received in full by the listeners. Yon DD certainly realized this limitation:

> Of course for the listeners, the message that I want could not be understood. But the song was only received as a song with smooth music and lyrics. The notes sound great. But the whole story in the song could not be understood by the listeners. Most of the listeners that I asked, why do you like this song, they answered, "Because the lyrics are very soft." The notes sound great. . . . They are easy to remember. Most of the listeners thought that the song was about love. Even a university professor had the same impression.[21]

Yon explained that *effectivity* was not their aim. The song was a form of artist's expression of an event that occurred in their surroundings and were part of their personal lives. Conveying the feeling of loss was a deliberate option of a common language that can create proximity with the listeners. But it is also likely that Yon learned from his predecessors' music, for example Arif's "Genjer-genjer" and Andang's "Kembang Pethetan," which were both stigmatized as PKI music and affected the composers' lives. The option not to speak about the violence is the musician's negotiation to portray the violence, on one hand, but on the other, to avoid the consequences that entail by exposing it.[22] In other words,

---

[20] Interview with Yon DD, September 15, 2021.

[21] Interview with Yon DD, September 15, 2021.

[22] How memories of violence are preserved in music also depends on the background of the composers. For example, the song "Mbok Irat" by Endro Wilis, a former member of the army who was assigned to Sanggau during the 30 September Movement, depicted the burned houses and bodies in the streets of Banyuwangi, his hometown. His ability to write in a straightforward way seems to be influenced by his profession in the army—an officer close to the state (Nugraha, 2021).

the songs about 1965 that were produced by the current generation not only contain the memory of mass killings, but also the memory of stigmatization that came afterward against local Banyuwanginese musicians (and of the regency in general). Opting not to speak of violence is also similar with what Steedly (2013) encountered in her research of the women of Karo, Sumatera, who were forced to migrate because of the Revolution (1945–1950). This decision to avoid expressions of violence is seen by Steedly (2013) as a result of a negotiation between the inclusion of localities in the national narrative of war and heroism, and the violence directed by the state against its own subjects. In other words, to create a memory of a past event such as the revolution, it has to be done in such a way that will not endanger the local's position in the national narrative of the revolution. Therefore, Steedly also notes that although songs about the past generate certain feelings that connect a person to the situation, it is not clear where it will lead: whether to crisis, acceptance, or nostalgia.

Conclusion

As one of the areas that was hit hard during the anti-communist operation of 1965–66, Banyuwangi became an interesting case study to analyze how this event is remembered by society. Their cultural identity is highly related to the historical experience of Banyuwangi since the 18th century that affected migrations and confrontations. Osing became an identity that is preserved in Banyuwangi's popular culture, including their music. This locality was also the dominant aspect that characterized music and other art performances in the 1950s and 1960s, before the 1965 violence destroyed and constrained the Left in most cultural activities in Banyuwangi.

During the New Order and the Reformasi, there were numerous attempts to revive the cultural activities in Banyuwangi. Younger generations of musicians began to insert the violence of 1965 into their songs. These songs can be perceived as an effort to preserve the memories of violence, which are rarely discussed in the public sphere or commemorated. In other words, these songs are countering the state hegemony of 1965 history. However, as we have shown, music with 1965 themes presents complex dynamics of remembering, rather than a simplified tension between the hegemonic narrative versus counter narrative. The case study of Banyuwangi shows that under the continuous persecution against communists, blunt representations of violence may risk the career and life of the musicians. For example, when Catur Arum released the adapted version of "Genjer-genjer," his album was removed from distribution. Rather than a counter-memory, this music is a process of negotiation between the locality and the anti-communist narrative. Therefore, how music is used to preserve memories should be analyzed in its embedded contexts, particularly the local identity, violence, and the continuous persecution that follows.

References

Afrikartika, A. (2009, October 1). Kontroversi Lagu Genjer-genjer versi Catur Arum: Luncurkan 3000 keping, Langsung Distop. *Radar Banyuwangi*, 1, 7.

Anderson, B. (1987). How did the generals die? *Indonesia, 43*, 109–134.

Arps, B. (2009). Osing kids and the banners of Blambangan: Ethnolinguistic identity and the regional past as ambient themes in an East Javanese town. *Wacana, 11*(1), 1–38.

Arps, B. (2011, October 14). *The Lettuce song and its trajectory: The vagaries of a pop song in three eras.* Paper for Seminar Voice of the Archipelago, FKI VII, ISI Surakarta. Unpublished.

Barendregt, B. (2002). The sound of "longing for home." Redefining a sense of community through Minang popular music. *BKI, 158*(3), 411–450. https://doi.org/10.1163/22134379 -90003771

Beatty, A. (2004). *Varieties of Javanese religion. An anthropological account.* Cambridge University Press.

Budiawan. (2004). *Mematahkan pewarisan ingatan: Wacana anti-komunis dan politik rekonsiliasi pasca-Suharto.* ELSAM.

Chandra, S. (2017). New findings on the Indonesian killings of 1965–66. *Journal of Asian Studies, 76*(4), 1059–1086.

Conroe, A. M. (2012). *Generating history: Violence and the risks of remembering for families of former political prisoners in post-New Order Indonesia* [Unpublished doctoral dissertation]. University of Michigan.

Cribb, R. (1990). *The Indonesian killings of 1965-1966: Studies from Java and Bali.* Centre of Southeast Asian Studies, Monash University.

Eickhoff, M., Klinken, G. van, & Robinson, G. (2017). 1965 Today: Living with the Indonesian Massacres. *Journal of Genocide Research, 19*(4), 449–464.

Farid, H. (2005). Indonesia's original sin: Mass killings and capitalist expansion, 1965–66. *Inter-Asia Cultural Studies, 6*(1), 3–16.

Foucault, M. (1975). Film and popular memory. *Radical Philosophy, 11,* 24.

Hadi, K., & Hera, F. X. D. B. B. (2020). Peristiwa Kentong Gobyok: Di Antara Mengingat Sekaligus Melupakan Kekerasan 1965 di Klaten, Jawa Tengah. *Bandar Maulana: Jurnal Sejarah Dan Budaya, 25*(1), 1–13.

Komisi Nasional Hak Asasi Manusia RI. (2012). *Ringkasan Eksekutif Laporan Penyelidiakan Pelanggaran Hak Asasi Manusia Berat.* Komnas HAM RI.

Leksana, G. (2020). Collaboration in mass violence: The case of the Indonesian anti-Leftist Mass killings in 1965–66 in East Java. *Journal of Genocide Research, 23*(1), 58–80. https://doi.org/ 10.1080/14623528.2020.1778612

Leksana, G., & Kammen, D. (2021). Indonesian student theses on "1965": An overview. *Indonesia, 111,* 45–55.

Leong, K.-Y. (2021). Invisible threads linking phantasmal landscapes in Java: Haunted places and memory in post-authoritarian Indonesia. *Memory Studies, 1750698021995968.* https://doi .org/10.1177/1750698021995968

Luthfi, A. (2018). Kekerasan Kemanusiaan dan Perampasan Tanah Pasca- 1965 di Banyuwangi, Jawa Timur. *Archipel, 95,* 53–68.

Margana, S. (2007). *Java's last frontier: The struggle for hegemony of Blambangan, c. 1763–1813* [Unpublished doctoral dissertation]. Leiden University.

McGregor, K. (2007). *History in uniform: Military ideology and the construction of Indonesia's past.* Asian Studies Association of Australia; KITLV Press.

McGregor, K., & Kammen, D. (2012). *The contours of mass violence in Indonesia, 1965–1968.* University of Hawai'i Press.

Melvin, J. (2018). *The army and the Indonesian genocide: Mechanics of mass murder.* Routledge.

Mortimer, R. (1972). *The Indonesian communist party and land reform, 1959–1965.* Centre of Southeast Asian Studies Monash University.

Mwambari, D. (2020). Music and the politics of the past: Kizito Mihigo and music in the commemoration of the genocide against the Tutsi in Rwanda. *Memory Studies, 13*(6), 1321–1336. https://doi.org/10.1177/1750698018823233

Notosusanto, N., & Saleh, I. (1968). *The coup attempt of the September 30 Movement in Indonesia.* Pembimbing Masa.

Notosoesanto, N., Saleh, I., & Umar, M. (1993). *Tragedi Nasional percobaan KUP G 30 S/PKI di Indonesia* (4th Ed., cet. 1). Intermasa.

Nugraha, K. W. S. (2021). *Bersenandung di Tengah Badai: Musik dalam Dinamika Kekerasan Antikomunis.* Jurnal Sejarah.

Nurullita, H. (2015). *Perjuangan Mencari Identitas: Perkembangan Damarwulan, Gandrungan dan Musik Lokal Banyuwangi 1930an–2008* [Unpublished Master's thesis]. Universitas Gajah Mada.

Pitaloka, D., & Dutta, M. J. (2021). Performing songs as healing the trauma of the 1965 anti-communist killings in Indonesia. In M. S. Micale & H. Pols (Eds.), *Traumatic pasts in Asia: History, psychiatry, and trauma from the 1930s to the present* (pp. 226–244). Berghahn books.

Pitic, B. (2021). Musical commemorations and grand narratives: The case of the oratorio "Srebrenički Inferno" in post-genocide Bosnia. *Memory Studies, 14*(2), 466–482. https://doi.org/10.1177/1750698019843968

Popular Memory Group. (1982). Popular memory: Theory, politics, method. In R. Johnson, G. McLennan, B. Schwarz, & D. Sutton (Eds.), *Making histories: Studies in history-writing and politics* (pp. 205–252). Hutchinson & Centre for Contemporary Cultural Studies University of Birmingham.

Raharjo, B. (2016). Dinamika Gandrung di Banyuwangi 1950-2013. *Humanis, 15*(2).

Report from East Java. (1986). (B. Anderson, Trans.). *Indonesia, 41*, 134–149.

Robinson, G. (2018). *The killing season: A history of the Indonesian massacres, 1965–66.* Princeton University Press.

Robison, R. (2009). *Indonesia: The rise of capital.* Equinox Publishing.

Roosa, J. (2016). The state knowledge about an open secret: Indonesia's Mass Disappearances of 1965–1966. *Journal of Asian Studies, 75*(2), 1–17.

Roosa, J., Ratih, A., & Farid, H. (2004). Pengantar: Sejarah Lisan dan Ingatan Sosial. In J. Roosa, A. Ratih, & H. Farid (Eds.), *Tahun yang Tak Pernah Berakhir: Memahami Pengalaman Korban 65: Esai-esai Sejarah Lisan* (pp. 1–23). ISSI, ELSAM & TRK.

Santikarma, D. (2008). Menulis Sejarah dan Membaca Kuasa: Politik Pasca-1965 di Bali. In H. Schulte Nordholt, B. Poerwanto, & R. Saptari (Eds.), *Perspektif baru penulisan sejarah Indonesia* (pp. 201–215). KITLV, Yayasan Obor Indonesia, Pustaka Larasan.

Saptaningrum, I., Wagiman, W., Eddyono, S. W., & Abidin, Z. (2007). *Menjadikan Hak Asasi Manusia sebagai Hak Konstitusional: Pandangan Kritis atas Putusan Mahkamah Konstitusi terhadap Judicial Review UU KKR dan Implikasinya bagi Penyelesaian Pelanggaran HAM Masa Lalu* (No. 01; Briefing Paper). ELSAM.

Schreiner, K. (2005). Lubang Buaya: Histories of trauma and sites of memory. In M. S. Zurbuchen (Ed.), *Beginning to remember: The past in Indonesian present* (pp. 261–277). Singapore University Press.

Setiawan, D. (2014). *The Cold War in the city of heroes: U.S.-Indonesian relations and anti-communist operations in Surabaya, 1963–1965* [Unpublished doctoral dissertation]. University of California Los Angeles.

Setiawan, I. (2010). Merah Berpendar di Brang Wetan: Tegangan Politik 65 dan Implikasinya Terhadap Industri Musik Banyuwangen. *Imaji, 8*(1), 116–135.

Steedly, M. (2013). *Rifle reports: A story of Indonesian independence*. University of California Press.

Subekti, A. (2015). Mendendangkan Ingatan: Sejarah dan Memori Orang Banyuwangi (tahun 1925 dan 1965). In R. Ridhoi, N. B. Wijanarko, H. F. Hidayati, R. D. Prabowo, & Meralesi (Eds.), *Prosiding 3rd Graduate Seminar of History 2015 Perkembangan Mutakhir Historiografi Indonesia: Orientasi Tema dan Perspektif* (pp. 327–343). Departemen Sejarah, FIB UGM.

Sudjatmiko, I. G. (1992). *The destruction of the Indonesian Communist Party (PKI): A comparative analysis of East Java and Bali* [Unpublished doctoral dissertation]. Harvard University.

Sulistyo, H. (2000). *Palu Arit di Ladang Tebu: Sejarah Pembantaian Massal yang Terlupakan (Jombang-Kediri 1965–1966)*. Kepustakaan Populer Gramedia.

Sutarto, A. (2006, August 10). Sekilas Tentang Masyarakat Using. *Pembekalan Jelajah Budaya*, Yogyakarta.

van Dijck, J. (2006). Record and hold: Popular music between personal and collective memory. *Critical Studies in Media Communication, 23*(5), 357–374. https://doi.org/10.1080/07393180601046121

Volkstelling. (1930). *Deel VIII Overzicht Voor Nederlandsch Indie*. Departement van Economische Zaken.

Wieringa, S. (2002). *Sexual politics in Indonesia*. Palgrave Macmillan.

Zulkifli, A., Setiadi, P., & Yunus, S. (Eds.). (2014). Mati Suri Pencipta "Genjer-genjer." In *Seri Buku Tempo: Lekra dan Geger 1965* (pp. 116–122). KPG.

Zurbuchen, M. S. (2005). *Beginning to remember: The past in the Indonesian present*. Singapore University Press.

In Permanent Evolution:

An Epilogue

Baskara T. Wardaya

When contrasting memory and history, Pierre Nora's remark on memory is undoubtedly worth noting. While history is an organized past, he said, memory "remains in permanent evolution, open to the dialectic of remembering and forgetting, . . . vulnerable to manipulation and appropriation, susceptible to being long dormant and periodically revived."[1] By stating such a remark Nora reminds us that memory is not something fixed or merely about the past. Instead, memory fluctuates and is closely tied to the dynamics of the present. Other than being open to the "dialectic of remembering and forgetting," Nora believes that memory is always "in permanent evolution." In our context, this notion of memory is very applicable to the discourse on the memories of the anti-communist violence that swept Indonesia in 1965–66 and afterward.

At least two important aspects regarding the 1965–66 violence immediately come to mind: the violent events themselves and the memories of the events. As we see in this volume—and strongly echoing Nora's remark—Vannessa Hearman, and Arif Subekti and Hervina Nurullita, show us how memories of the 1965–66 mass violence continue to fluctuate "in permanent evolution" in the minds of many. They also show us how these memories are open to the present dialectic of remembering and forgetting. Likewise, they show us that while vulnerable to manipulation and appropriation, memories of the 1965–66 mass violence are susceptible to periods of dormancy and revival.

Through discussing Leyla Stevens's *Dua Dunia* art exhibition, Hearman demonstrates how memories of the 1965–66 mass violence in Bali, which for a long time were "dormant," are now being revived. Through reviving the memories, it is hoped that

[1] Pierre Nora, "Between Memory and History: Les Lieux de Mémoire," in "Memory and Counter-Memory," ed. Natalie Zemon Davis and Randolph Starn, special issue, *Representations* no. 26 (Spring, 1989): 7–24.

"different kinds of memories" of the violence will be expressed and considered more openly. Meanwhile, discussing the case of the Osing community in Banyuwangi, Subekti and Nurullita describe how the community's younger musicians have to negotiate to keep and pass the memories of the 1965–66 violence in the face of the government's repressive measures. Based on their observations they argue that music can function beyond entertaining. Other than entertaining, they further argue, music can also serve to remember and preserve the memories of the 1965–66 violence while conveying the message of peace and reconciliation.

After all, the 1965–66 violence had a huge impact on those who were affected. As demonstrated by Siddharth Chandra and Teng Zhang, Robert W. Hefner, and Mark Winward and Siddharth Chandra, who studied the impact of the violence in East Java and the South-Central area of Java, the violence did not only result in the death of hundreds of thousands of people but also in the local migration of countless residents who had to flee areas affected by the violence. Exploring the role of the political rivals of the Indonesian Communist Party (PKI) in committing atrocities and the spatial aspects of the PKI's resistance and response to the atrocities, Chandra and Zhang found a striking pattern. They found that there was a strong relation between members of the PKI's repulsion/resistance and the politically motivated religious mobilization in the escalation of the violence in East Java—a pattern that is also observed by Hefner in his multiyear research. Similarly, through their preliminary analysis of the village-level demographic dynamics in the Gunung Kidul regency, Winward and Chandra show us clear patterns of one-time population change caused by the 1965–66 mass violence in that South-Central part of Java.

Despite the magnitude and impact of the violence, for decades the Indonesian government discouraged any narrative that challenged the "it's all PKI's fault" version of the mainstream narrative on the 1965–66 violence. Yet, as shown by Stephen Pratama and Sri Lestari Wahyuningroem and Dyah Ayu Kartika in their studies, despite the pressures, many members of Indonesia's civil society refused to simply surrender. Instead, they produced initiatives to counter the government's dominant narrative. The initiatives, as Wahyuningroem and Kartika illustrate, came both through civil society organizations as well as formal educational institutions. In an interesting discussion, Pratama shares with us that among those who initiated the counter-narratives are teachers who had succeeded in transforming their own "selves" from being supporters of the government's narrative to its critics.

What Kar-Yen Leong presents is particularly thought-provoking. Building on the studies done by scholars of post-conflict societies and the effect of mass violence on the executors and bystanders, he observes the impact of the 1965–66 mass killings on those who were involved as perpetrators and witnesses. In particular, by using Igreja's concept of "embodied justice" and "moral bodies" (Igreja 2019), he shows us the affect of the killings on them long after their involvement.[2] He also shows us that by imposing silence among the populace, President Suharto's "criminogenic" structure of government "normalized" the killings, only to be continued by the succeeding governments. To

---

[2] Victor Igreja, "Negotiating Relationships in Transition: War, Famine and Embodied Accountability in Mozambique," *Comparative Studies in Society and History* 61, no. 4 (2019): 774–804. See also Igreja (2019), Hannah Arendt (2006), Lyn Parker (2003), Scott Straus (2017), Jess Melvin (2018), and Mery Kolimon (2015)

counter such a trend, Leong rightly calls us to pay closer attention to the affectivity and emotion aspects of the 1965–66 killings.

Recently a ray of hope in dealing with the issues of the 1965–66 violence appeared on the horizon in Indonesia. In August 2022, the Indonesian government formed an ad hoc team to deal with cases of past human rights abuses. Based on the team's findings, in January 2023 the president of Indonesia officially expressed his acknowledgment and regret on the cases of gross human rights abuses that had taken place in the country's past.

Yet, despite its magnitude and impact, the 1965–66 anti-communist mass violence was only mentioned as one of the twelve cases being acknowledged and regretted. Moreover, there was no certainty on how the acknowledgment and regret will be implemented on more practical policies, especially regarding the 1965–66 violence issues.[3] In the face of such uncertainty, further research and discussion on the 1965–66 violence topics—as suggested by the articles in this volume—are much needed and encouraged. Returning to Nora's remark, despite the government's acknowledgment and regret, the memory of the 1965–66 violence will never be fully settled. Just like other memories of past events, memories of the 1965–66 violence will continue to be "in permanent evolution." Consequently, the memories will require each generation to work on its own memories of one of the darkest chapters of Indonesia's postcolonial history.

[3] For further discussion on this, see Sri Lestari Widyaningroem, "Accountability Missing in Action," *Inside Indonesia*, February 7, 2023, https://www.insideindonesia.org/accountability-missing-in-action.

Stuart Robson (Trans.) with a commentary by Hadi Sidomulyo. *Threads of the Unfolding Web: The Old Javanese Tantu Panggêlaran*. Singapore: ISEAS, Yusof Ishak Institute, 2021.

Peter Carey

This remarkable book contains the first English translation of the Old Javanese *Tantu Panggelaran* (henceforth *TP*), a text that seems to have been compiled from oral sources circulating in East Java in the 15th century. No dates or author are mentioned in the *lontar* (palm-leaf) texts used here except for one colophon referring to AD 1635 (page 4). Unlike the much better known *Deśawarnana* (Description of the districts) alias *Nagarkrtāgama* (1365) of Mpu Prapañca, depicting the royal progress of the celebrated Majapahit ruler Hayam Wuruk (r. 1350–89), or the other *kakawin* (*kawi*) narrative poems set in the context of the 12th–15th-century East Javanese courts, the *TP*'s focus is Java's still untamed countryside. The mountains and *mandala* (abodes of religious communities belonging to the tradition of the *resi* or sages) of Central and East Java are its particular concern. Instead of Majapahit, the text looks back over two centuries to the kingdom of Kediri (1042–ca. 1222) as the backdrop for its allegorical tale of the history of Śaiwism and the spread of Bhairava Śaiwite hermitages in Java.

The *TP* starts at the very beginning, describing the original peopling of Java and the fixing of the island's labile foundations, which caused it continually to move up and down. This unfortunate circumstance was remedied by the actions of the gods. On the instructions of the supreme deity, Bhatāra Guru, they brought the top half of ancient India's sacred mountain, Mt. Mahāmeru, from "Jambudipa" (India) over to "Yawadipa" (Java) to weigh down the two ends of "Java." Here, significantly, these are just the two ends of the Javanese-speaking (*kejawen*) areas starting in Central Java in the vicinity of the Dieng Plateau, where the stump of Mt. Mahameru came to rest in the form of Mt. Kelāśa,[1] and extending to the very tip of Java's eastern salient, in particular the Hyang Massif between Probolinggo and Lumajang. *TP*'s Java is thus not the whole island. This is understandable because at the time and well into the early nineteenth century, "Java" was the *kejawen*. West Java, namely the Priangan (*parahyangan* "abode of the spirits") highlands and the Sundanese-speaking kingdom of Pajajaran, roughly contemporary with Majapahit, were both foreign entities in the Javanese view.[2] Indeed, when the Java War (1825–30) leader, Prince Diponegoro (1785–1855), left Semarang on the first stage of his journey into exile in Sulawesi (Celebes) on April 5, 1830, he wrote in his autobiographical chronicle that he was "leaving Java."[3]

But such astral journeys involving cloud-topped masses of rock and earth were not without their hazards even for the Hindu-Javanese deities: as the great bulk of Mahameru's top half was being transported further east from Dieng, the holy mountain

---

[1] Hadi Sidomulyo considers the present-day location of Mt. Kelāśa, looking first at Mt. Prahu, before rejecting this in favor of Mt. Rojojembangan, some twenty kilometees west of the Dieng Plateau, see pages 95–100.

[2] See Peter Carey, "Imagining Indonesia—An Historical Perspective, 1785–1942," in *Indonesia Sebagai Ruang Imajinasi*, Seri Studi Kebudayaan II, ed. Ary Budiyanto (Malang: Prodi Antropologi, FIB Universitas Brawijaya, 2018), 1–8.

[3] Carey, "Imagining Indonesia," 2.

began to crumble, falling to earth and giving birth to a series of peaks in the great chain of volcanoes from Mt. Lawu to Mt. Bromo, where Mahameru's remnants finally come to rest propped upright against Bromo's spacious caldera. Interestingly, this tale of the formation of Java's mountainous spine remained embedded in popular memory in East Java in the trope that the island's volcanoes were the "shadow" of the Himalayas.[4]

With the fixing of Java's foundations and the appearance of the first inhabitants of Java, the *TP* describes how more gods and holy sages were summoned to aid in the development of civilization. The practical expression of this process involved Śiwa as the Lord Iśwara acting as *gurudeśa* (teacher of village headmen). He was instructed by the supreme deity to establish the various branches of learning, including language and ethics, while the divine architect, Wiśwakarma, was responsible for the art of carpentry, Lord Mahādewa for that of goldsmith, and the skills of the painter were introduced by Mpu Ciptangkara, an incarnation of the sage Bhagawān Ciptagupta. In the meantime, Lord Brahmā, whose namesake east Javanese massif served as his forge, became the metal smith, Mpu Sujiwana, entrusted with the task of forging tools and weapons in the crater of Mt. Brahmā (Bromo). Lastly, Bhatāra Wisnu took on the role of world ruler, descending to earth in his seventh incarnation with his heavenly consort, the goddess Śrī, who is credited with the introduction of agriculture as well as the arts of spinning and weaving. In this way, the *TP* explains, the first civilized communities were established on Java (83–84).

TP's style, as befits its subject matter, is, in Stuart Robson's words, "simple, down-to-earth, even earthy . . . certainly not the product of the Hindu-Javanese court literary tradition" (4). And Robson honors that earthiness in his translation. He succeeds in drawing the reader along with his clear but stylish English, with only the occasional jarring turn of phrase such as his use of the quaintly colloquial "old chap" for the Old Javanese term *"bapa"* (Pigeaud 118 quoted in Appendix 3, 284) when Mpu Tapa-wangkeng, under the name of Ki Sameget-baganjing, is informing the King of Daha (Kediri) why the sun is not setting (58).

Robson's choice of title, *Threads of the Unfolding Web*, is a brilliant rendering of the Sanskrit loanword *tantu* "a thread, cord, string, line, wire, warp (of a web) . . . succession, line of descendants." Paired with the Old Javanese noun *panggelaran* (the action of extending, expanding, and rolling out), these underscore the process, vividly described in the *TP*, whereby religious establishments (*mandala*) were extended with new foundations being rolled out and deployed in new lines of succession (5). This ancient network of ascetic communities, as Hadi Sidomulyo explains in his Part 2 Commentary, "maintained an unbroken dialogue throughout the Hindu-Javanese period, impervious to the shifting of royal courts and accompanying political turmoil" (83). They also acted as the conduit of knowledge of the wisdom and lore of the Hindu-Javanese past into the post-1500 Islamic era through literary traditions that flourished in the mountain retreats of Central Java until quite recent times. One thinks here of the corpus of Merapi-Merbabu

---

[4] This was told to me by my late wife, Noes (Raden Ayu Koesmarlinah Retnojinolin, 1940–2000), who grew up in Paré-Kediri in the shadow of Mt. Kelud, and who seemingly knew about the trope from her Mangkunegaran relatives.

manuscripts discovered in the mid-19th century, many of which can be consulted in the Berlin Staatsbibliothek (Berlin State Library).[5]

Robson bases his translation of Old Javanese text on the *lontar* (palm leaf) manuscript (Text A) used by Pigeaud for his 1924 thesis, which the Dutch scholar corrected from a second closely cognate *lontar* (Text B). Both manuscripts were apparently loaned to Pigeaud by his archeologist colleague Pieter Vincent van Stein Callenfels (1883–1938), with whom he shared a house while they prepared their respective Leiden theses in 1921–24 (3n1). Unfortunately, neither of these *lontar* have ever been found either in the extensive Leiden collections nor yet in the equally rich National Library (Perpustakaan Nasional) holdings in Jakarta. So, Robson has not been able to check the originals. But he has made the best of establishing a textual concordance by using the variant readings listed by Pigeaud from three other, rather less reliable, texts, hailing from the Van der Tuuk collection and the main University Library (Leiden Cod. Or. 2212). He has also included Pigeaud's Old Javanese text as a seventy-page Appendix 3, along with three other helpful additions. These include his reduction of Pigeaud's original seven-part division of the text into just three more manageable sections, listed along with the range of topics contained in each (6–9); his "Notes on names and titles occurring in the text" (Appendix I), and a Lexicographical List of items mentioned in the notes that do not appear in Zoetmulder's *Old Javanese-English Dictionary* (1982) (303–4). Students of Old Javanese language will find much of value in these pages.

In his preface, Hadi Sidomulyo stresses that "although primarily directed at the scientific community, the [present] book has from the outset been conceived as a popular edition, designed to draw the interest of the general reader." Certainly, Sidomulyo's painstaking recreation of the text's topographical data in his extensive Part 2 Commentary—an aspect almost completely ignored in Pigeaud's 1924 thesis—will be read with fascinated interest by afficionados of Java's Hindu-Javanese past, but a popular bestseller it is not. And thank goodness! The mind boggles at the thought of Robson and Hadi Sidomulyo dumbing down the *Tantu Panggelaran* and producing a rewritten "novelistic" version such as has recently been attempted by Agus Wahyudi in his retelling of the twelve-volume *Serat Centhini* (*Suluk Tambangraras*) (1814).[6] Trumpetted as an attempt "to make it easier for readers . . . to enjoy the noble works of Javanese poets,"[7] Wahyudi's overwrought text makes a travesty of the Javanese original, which constitutes a veritable encyclopedia of Javanese manners and is one of the glories of modern Javanese literature.

By contrast, Robson and Hadi Sidomulyo take no hostages. Their scholarship is generally sure-footed. Sidomulyo's commentary, in particular, is a model of how such topographical plotting on Dutch ordnance survey maps should be done. He seems to

---

[5] See Th.G.Th. Pigeaud, *Javanese and Balinese Manuscripts and Some Codices Written in Related Idioms Spoken in Bali and Java*, Verzeichnis der Orientalischen Handschriften in Deutschland, vol. 31 (Wiesbaden: Steiner, 1975); and Titik Pudjiastuti and Thoralf Hansen, eds., *Catalogue of Indonesian Manuscripts. Collection Staatsbibliothek zu Berlin Preußischer Kulturbesitz. Bali, Java, Kalimantan. Lombok, Madura, Sulawesi, Sumatra, Sumbawa* (Jakarta: Museum Nasional, 2016).

[6] Agus Wahyudi, ed., *Serat Centhini 1: Kisah Pelarian Putra-putri Sunan Giri Menjelajah Nusa Jawa* (Yogyakarta: Cakrawala, 2015).

[7] Wahyudi, *Serat Centhini*, 7.

have walked every inch of the relevant sections of the mountainous terrain of East Java and also has a good command of the topography of Central Java and the Dieng Plateau, an area particularly associated with the cults of Śiwa and Ganeśa (85). In fact, his topographical skills in this domain were already on display in 2007 when he published his *Napak Tilas Perjalanan Mpu Prapañca* (In the footsteps of Mpu Prapañca's journey), which painstakingly traced back the route taken by King Hayam Wuruk in his 1359 progress through his east Javanese realm in Prapañca's *Deśawarnana* (Description of the districts).[8] At the same time, he knows how to use cognate texts like the Old Sundanese *Bujangga Manik* poem dealing with the journeys of the West Java pilgrim Bujangga Manik through East Java around the year 1500 (Figure 16), as well as the late fifteenth-century Middle Javanese *Kidung Pañji Margasmara*, to extend and corroborate the topographical details provided in the *TP*.[9] Most crucially, he is able to draw on the archeological and written records of the *Oudheidkundige Dienst* (Dutch colonial archeological survey), and his own knowledge derived from numerous field visits to local museums and archeological sites to enhance his commentary. Readers will find his regency-by-regency tabulation of the archeological record for the Tengger Highlands and the Hyang Plateau in Appendix 2 (pp. 212–22) especially helpful.

For the present reviewer, there are some pleasant surprises. It is reassuring to know, for example, that one of Java's earliest settlements at Mendang-Kamulan in the district of Wirosari, Grobogan, referred to by T. S. Raffles in his *History of Java*,[10] really did exist (85–91); as did King Jayaktyeng's (Jayakatyang's) mid-thirteenth-century *kraton* (court) at Gegelang (Gelang-gelang) (93n62), which Lucien Adam long since pinpointed in his "Historical Notes on the Residency of Madiun" (1938) as a location just to the east of the Madiun-Ponorogo highway between the villages of Daha and Glonggong.[11]

There is also an interesting connection between the mythic world described in the *TP* and the modern era. This occurs in the tale of the widow Rāga-runting, an incarnation of the goddess Śrī, who spent her days spinning thread in the shade of a *tanjung* (Mimusops elengi) tree at her Medang (Mendang)-tanjung residence near Boyolali (152–54). Disturbed by the presence of a greedy merchant, Parijñana, she sweeps him away to the east with her broom sending him flying over a hundred miles, as far as Mt Bañcak near the southeastern foot of Mt Lawu. This foothill would later become a *pundhèn* (revered holy site) when it became the grave of Ratu Maduretno (ca. 1782–1809) on November 16, 1809. A daughter of the Second Sultan of Yogyakarta, and beloved wife of her hero

[8] Hadi Sidomulyo, *Napak Tilas Perjalanan Mpu Prapañca* (Jakarta: Wedatama Widya Sastra, 2007).

[9] One of the episodes in the *Panji Margasmara* text, for example, includes a lengthy description of a journey along the western and southwestern flanks of Mt. Semeru from Singosari to the *mandala* of Kukub, during the abortive attempt of the *Adipati* (ruler) of Singosari (Singhasāri) to secure the marriage of his daughter, Ken Candrasari, to a local suitor, Jaran Warida, in a ceremony scheduled to be presided over by the *dewaguru* (head of the *mandala* community) of Kukub, see pp. 131–32, Figure 26.

[10] T. S. Raffles, *The History of Java* (London: John Murray, 1817), 2:53.

[11] Lucien Adam, "Geschiedkundige Aanteeekeningen omtrent de Residentie Madioen: Bergheiligdommen op Lawoe en Wilis; Restanten van Kalangs; Hindoe-Javaansch Tijdperk," *Djåwå* 18, no. 1-2 (1938): 107. See further, Christopher Reinhart, ed., *Antara Lawu dan Wilis: Arkeologi, Sejarah dan Legenda Madiun Raya Berdasarkan Catatan Lucien Adam (Residen Madiun 1934–1938)* (Jakarta: Kepustakaan Populer Gramedia, 2021), 77–85. For a recent Indonesian-language survey of the archaeological evidence relating to Gegelang (Gelang-gelang) and the district—Bhumi—of Wurawan in which it was supposedly situated, see Bambang Sulistyanto, ed., *Bhumi Wirawan* (Yogyakarta: Kemendikbud, Badan Penelitian dan Pengembangan Pusat Penelitian Arkeologi Nasional, Balai Arkeologi DIY, 2018).

husband, Raden Ronggo Prawirodirjo III (ca. 1779–1810), the senior administrator (*bupati wedana*) of Madiun (in office 1796–1810), she is described in a recent biography asking her spiritual mentor, the Pacitan-born Kiai Kaliyah, the name of the tree whose pungent scent she could smell wafting down to her Maospati residence. On receiving the reply that this was the *tanjung* tree, which grew on the summit of Mt. Bancak, she instructed that when her time came this tree should be planted at her grave.[12] And to this day visitors to Maduretno's *pundhèn* walk under the shade of a pair of ancient *tanjung* trees to reach the entrance to her colonnaded mausoleum.[13] In this fashion, timeless Java guards its ancient myths.

Tidak ada gading tanpa retak (there is no ivory without a blemish) as the Indonesian saying goes. In the event that there is a second edition, the authors might consider making some improvements by ensuring that all Śaka dates from the post-AD 78 Hindu lunar calendar have their AD equivalents—at the moment it is rather hit-and-miss (see pp. 118 and 123). At the same time, care should be taken in the bibliography, footnotes, and in-text citations to ensure that Dutch authors with prefixes are listed by their surname (Clercq, F. S. A. de; Hamer, C. de; Meulen, W. J. van der; and Tuuk, H. N. van der) and not the prefix itself (see pp. 296, 297, 298, and 302). Still on the bibliography, this needs to be made more comprehensive by including a separate section for the numerous Dutch Indies Topographical Service ordnance survey maps, which Hadi Sidomulyo has used to such good effect in his commentary. At the moment none are listed. The authors might also consider making it easier for readers by having the maps and plates listed separately as "Maps" and "Plates" rather than as currently under one consolidated rubric as "Figures." Whatever they decide, they should include a list of these illustrations after the list of abbreviations on page vi. Finally, more attention should be paid to the index to ensure that all page references are correct and needless double or triple entries are avoided, as with "Bancak/Bañcak, Mt" on page 306 and "Kalipadang" and "Padang (river)/Padang" on pages 311 and 316, which all seem to refer to the same toponym. But these quibbles in no way detract from Robson and Sidomulyo's overall achievement. They have succeeded brilliantly in bringing the *TP* text alive and anchoring it firmly in the archaeological, literary, and topographical record of fifteenth-century Java. In so doing, they have opened up a whole new perspective on the island's Hindu-Javanese past.

> Then felt I like some watcher of the skies
>
> When a new planet swims into his ken;
>
> Or like stout Cortez when with eagle eyes
>
> He stared at the Pacific—and all his men
>
> Look'd at each other with a wild surmise—
>
> Silent, upon a peak in Darien.[14]

---

[12] Akhlis Syamsal Qomar, *Banteng Terakhir Kesultanan Yogyakarta; Riwayat Raden Ronggo Prawirodirjo III, sekitar 1779–1810* (Jakarta: Kepustakaan Populer Gramedia, 2022), 113–14.

[13] Peter Carey, "Raja Yang Peduli Leluhur dan Sejarah Yogyakarta-Madiun," in *Hamengku Buwono IX; Pengorbanan Sang Pembela Republik*, ed. Seno Joko Suyono, Dodi Hidayat, and Agustina Widiarsi (Jakarta: Tempo, 2015), 175.

[14] John Keats, "On First Looking into Chapman's Homer," in *The Poems of John Keats*, ed. Ernest de Sélincourt (New York: Dodd, Mead & Company, 1905), 36.

John F. McCarthy, Andrew McWilliam, and Gerben Nooteboom (Eds.). *The Paradox of Agrarian Change. Food Security and the Politics of Social Protection in Indonesia.* Singapore: NUS Press, 2023.

Pujo Semedi

First of all, I would like to convey my appreciation to the editors and all authors for the publication. This book is constructive work that aims not only to gain an understanding of what is going on among farming and fishing communities but to take a step further to develop "possibilities for moving to a better system to provide vulnerable households with a 'rightful share' of the benefits being distributed." As the title indicates, this book discusses the paradox that took place in Indonesian agrarian communities as they move from poverty to prosperous life. Now, farmers live in well-built, nice houses, have motorbikes, and are capable of sending their children to school. In the midst of this prosperity, nutritional insecurity among farmers remains high.

To identify how the paradox operates in the farmers' and rural inhabitants' livelihood, John F. McCarthy, Andrew McWilliam, and Gerben Nooteboom propose three factors: (1) proximate actors and contextual triggers that are temporally and spatially close to the livelihood outcomes and agrarian changes pattern and that appear to facilitate them directly," (2) structural mechanisms that operate diffusely and shape the context, and (3) relational processes, "the informal and formal power relations that shape people's actions and lead to relations of debt and dependency." The three processes are assumed to operate in independent connection, one to another, which eventually lead to livelihood trajectories.

These three factors were observed through eight ethnographic cases among farming, fishing, and plantation communities in various parts of Indonesia, which ended in findings of eight scenarios of agrarian change: smallholder development, enclave, sideways, precarious developmental, fishing boom, resource degradation, boom crop agrarian differentiation, and subsistence-oriented. The findings indicate that the agrarian paradox and changes in Indonesia do not occur through similar paths and lead to the same future for farmers. This is one of the strong points of John McCarthy, McWilliam, and Nooteboom's work: sensitivity to the variety of agrarian change pathways. Another strong point can be found in the authors' conclusion, that to solve the agrarian change paradox in Indonesia there is a need to formulate "other redistributive policy settings and strategies . . . which shift the structural driven of inequality and invest in the productive capacity of people to empower their future".

I have a few notes for this book. First, is related to nutritional insecurity. Various studies show that life expectancy in Indonesia in the past was much lower than it is today. Among some other factors, it was related to poor nutritional status among Indonesians, that a slight infection could easily send people to their death. Now Indonesian life expectancy is higher, indicating that the prevalence and intensity of nutrition insecurity are no longer as severe as in the past. It is probable, that a better indicator for the paradox of agrarian change is not in the farmers' nutritional status, but in the nature of their prosperity.

With a lot of assets farmers now look prosperous but at the same time they are deeply indebted. Almost all the modern utilities owned by farmers were obtained through credit. The crops they cultivate nowadays require a high capital input. Advertisements for consumer goods that symbolize a prosperous life come from all directions. Farmers are pushed, lured, and trapped to join an unforgiving debt relationship with semi-formal and formal banks that know no delay in repayments. A TKO relation, thus Javanese farmers said: *tan kena ora*, a sure, undeferred obligation. When the time to pay comes, it has to be settled no matter what. Very probably the farmer's prosperity is a pseudo rather than a real one. It is based on perpetual debt, and very likely closer scrutiny will reveal that their balance sheet is negative, or at least they are bound to work for the banks forever.

Second, technically the deployment of "proximate actors and contextual triggers," "structural mechanisms," and "relational processes" in a set of independent connections to identify livelihood trajectory is capable to produce thousands of agrarian change scenarios. Each community is basically a particular ethnographic case with its own proximate actors and contextual triggers. Therefore, following the method above, each community would lead to a specific scenario, and this number would increase when some communities host more than one form of structural mechanism and relational process. The thing is, highly varied agrarian change scenarios would consequently make the recommendation to formulate "redistributive policy settings and strategies to deal with inequality and to invest in the productive capacity of people to empower their future" really hard to implement. If we take that to some extent ethnographic work has a parallel with algebra, i.e., to identify basic relations that operate behind various observable cases, it seems theorization in this book still needs further improvement.

Third, I perceive this edited volume as a critique of liberalism, but the voice of this book is still very much liberalistic. Farmers in the book are presented mainly as capital subjects and their future empowerment should be reached by investing in their productive capacity. Farmers, just like any of us, do not measure prosperity in terms of food, clothes, housing, and amenities but also in the fulfillment of their self-existence. In West Kalimantan, Dayak farmers perceive palm oil as a problem because its plantation-style cultivation is against their ethic of independence. Palm oil corrodes the ethic because it forces villagers to engage in the cultivation—otherwise, there is no place for him in society but as a proletariat or burden to other people. In the past, those who for one or another reason despised agriculture could nurture their social existence as fishers or hunters. Neighbors acknowledged their existence and appreciated their skill of bringing game and fish home to feed their families. With the arrival of the palm oil regime, everyone was forced to work in palm oil even though not everyone has an interest in the work or can stand to work in the palm oil fields. Many farmers are frustrated, they get intoxicated every day to forget the unhappiness of being forced to take work that they do not like. I wonder, what kind of "redistributive policy setting dan strategies" are capable of amending this situation. Once again, *terima kasih Mas John* and the authors for the excellent contribution to the agrarian study in Indonesia.

Sandeep Ray. *Celluloid Colony: Locating History and Ethnography in Early Dutch Colonial Films of Indonesia*. Singapore: NUS Press, 2021.

Josh Stenberg

Celluloid Colony is an important and salutary book, both for the way it uses film to analyze late colonial Indonesian society and for its intervention in the debates surrounding the role of film in historiography. Ray's object of study is the corpus of films made on location in the Dutch East Indies at the behest of institutes, agencies, and corporations intent on building support back home for the colonial enterprise. Viewed mostly in the Netherlands, they were preserved more or less fortuitously in the Colonial Institute archives and then long ignored before being brought to light from the late 1980s by a new generation of researchers and artists who discovered them in the Filmmuseum (now the EYE Filmmuseum), where they had been transferred in 1975. Slated for partial digitization as part of a larger initiative in 2006, this archive now makes for fascinating viewing, much of it accessible online. But, as Ray persuasively argues, it also represents a trove of important primary sources for ethnographic information and social history that allow us unique access to several areas of late colonial history.

A historian at the Singapore University of Technology and Design, Ray worked in Dutch archives over many years (this monograph evolved from his 2015 National University of Singapore doctoral dissertation), viewing not only the finished films but also consulting surviving offcuts and production information. Ray has spent the interval well, for the monograph shows no tell-tale traces of the dissertation genre and is accessible, assured, and compact. The hard yards have paid off: his most fundamental contribution consists in providing an initial chronology and typology for the considerable corpus of Dutch East Indies cinema and laying out the commercial, administrative, political, and religious concerns that created them. His period ranges from the earliest films made in 1912 until 1930 and covers Colonial Institute, corporate, and religious films in the three substantive middle chapters. This is a signal achievement, for the gap it begins to fill is vast, there being no comparable work about Indonesia on film in this period.

In the first two chapters, Ray situates his study as an answer to the question of how and why historians in general can and should make use of filmic sources and why historians of colonialism in particular should set about it. The framing and argumentation for doing history with documentary film is swift and jargon-free and the point made so persuasively that I found myself finding little but knee-jerk conservatism or text worship to oppose it (although diplomatic Ray's tone is never impatient). There is no reason to think that using documentary film to do history is a naive endeavor any more than the use of colonial documents is, and film's intended and incidental evidence can provide compelling information on the experience and mindset of those living in the colonial period. These literal glimpses can in turn corroborate, adjust, or challenge claims made based on textual materials alone. In some cases film also records practices that can be used to validate or even assist in reviving tradition, and moments of "inadvertent ethnography" (62) show us sides of Indonesian lives that would otherwise be permanently inaccessible to us. The colonial films served many masters—from movies intended to show scientific progress to those soliciting funds for

Catholic missions to Flores—and they can serve the historian now, too, hopefully for very different purposes.

Documentary films seem especially useful and urgent in the case of Indonesia, due to the lacunae in early cinematic history produced by the survival of little or any colonial-era fiction films and what Ray takes to be disinterest among the historians of modern Indonesian film in overtly colonial work. But acknowledging the salience of these materials by no means signifies that they represent comfortable viewing, and it is likely precisely the awkwardness of the films for us—from this historical vantage point, these films are not by the "right" people, on the "right" subjects, or for the "right" purposes—that happened to preserve them. Historians' dismissive and (as Ray convincingly argues) embarrassed attitude toward the phenomenon of archival film has reached its natural term, and now these documentary films must be taken as seriously as the newspaper archives that have elucidated so many aspects of sociocultural history in the colonial period (and of which Ray also makes good use).

Particularly interesting is Ray's exposition of a change in aesthetic over time, going from the beautified vision of the colony in the earlier period to a greater focus on documenting economic development and modernization, both with their different projects complicit in creating "the charade of a peaceful colony" (3) that led much of the Dutch population to conclude that their imperial endeavor was humane and ethical. Some of Ray's most striking findings are how much humiliation and violence could be incorporated into what were evidently intended to be positive representations of, for instance, migrant labor for the Sumatra plantations. Viewers in 1920 were, it seems, expected to watch very small children picking through tea plants, or a Dutch official move to strike a recently disembarked Chinese laborer, without shock or disapproval.

Ray is generous and clear about the predecessors in film and academia who paved the way for his approach. Among these is the filmmaker Vincent Monnikendam, whose 1995 splicing of documentary footage into *Mother Dao, the Turtlelike* is treated very gently—it would also have been legitimate to query the film's exoticizing, de-historicizing, and mystifying as an orientalist project, considering its modern recordings of spiritual Indonesian verse transposed over colonial ethnographic footage. Clear-eyed about the technical difficulties of filming in Indonesia at this period, Ray pays tribute to the sheer quixotic nature of attempting to film and develop on-site with the technology of this era, and he also gives us some insight into the filmmakers' biographies and ambitions. Besides his primary sources, Ray draws extensively on Dutch colonial and English-language academic sources, although one might wish that Indonesian academia or the colonial Malay press had made a more prominent appearance. (One notes again in passing how regrettable it is that academics from the region must travel to the West rather than within the region for many types of primary sources.) Perhaps a future study will tell us something about women's involvement in these projects, for they appear only on screen in this account.

The author's reticence to dwell on the entanglements of filmmakers with the colonial project, on whose errand one way or another they made their recordings, is part of an approach that is resolutely dispassionate, matter-of-fact, and purposeful in its presentation. Presentation is studied, ethically engaged, and factually reliable, never turning—faced with an especially knotty archive—to solace in easy recrimination or in the shadier byways of theory. This restraint engenders opportunities for future research: expanding the comparison with other colonial projects and understanding colonial filmic legacy in enduring images of Indonesia; deeper analysis of its relationship to the (alas, almost entirely lost) colonial-era films by Chinese-Indonesians; role of these films in a revision of Dutch film history. The archive is now opened, surveyed, and introduced rather than exhausted; many future projects will be indebted to Ray for chronology and typology as well as analysis, now that the archive is so much more available, often only keystrokes away.

Speaking of chronology, one might wish for a little more robust framing of the time range. Ray is certainly correct to say that the colony was changing in 1930, but the end point seems a little arbitrary, and we read relatively little on the legacy of colonial filmmaking products and networks beyond that date. More connections or contrasts with the filmic projects of the Japanese imperial occupation in Southeast Asia, or some sense of the relation of this corpus to the post-independence industry in either Indonesia or the Netherlands would have been welcome. One is left with a guess that there was seldom overlap between the technical and creative crews of these films and of the burgeoning (mostly Chinese and Indo) narrative cinema, which if it is the case would also be a powerful illustration of the racial segregations of the colony. And the nitpicker in me found some linguistic fodder, such as the rough treatment of French, with "sans profit" rendered as "sand proft" and "Abbé de Choisy" as "Abbe de Choise." None of these queries or grumbles detracts from the book's great merits.

Celluloid Colony (its euphonic title certain to embed it in the Indonesianist mind) is a balanced and insightful approach to a category of material that has been unreasonably if understandably neglected. The book's clarity and brevity make it a good text for documentary film or archive courses, or in tandem with other materials for teaching the Indonesian road to independence. Use in the classroom is facilitated by the fact that many of the materials analyzed by Ray are now available on the YouTube channels of Eye Filmmuseum and the Netherlands Institute of Sound and Vision (Nederlands Instituut voor Beeld & Geluid). Ray admirably completes the important task, as Karen Strassler has done for photography or Matthew Isaac Cohen for theater, of providing an analytical survey of how one genre sheds light on the not-so-far-distant late colonial past.

Sylvia Tidey. *Ethics or the Right Thing? Corruption and Care in the Age of Good Governance.* **Chicago: HAU Books, 2022.**

Corruption has long been a captivating subject for social scientists who study post-Reformasi Indonesia. Scholars of contemporary Indonesian politics and governance have been both intrigued and repulsed by the efforts of the Indonesian state and international agencies to revive the country from the aftermath of Suharto's corrupt regime. Despite Indonesia's endeavor to transition to a liberal democracy, many believe that it still suffers from persistent patronage politics and clientelism. In the immediate post-Reformasi years, the efforts to combat corruption appeared heroic. The endeavor to establish democracy under the banner of "good governance" was supported by "the international development and financial community" (3), and this has greatly influenced the perception of corruption as a problem rooted in the traditions of rational choice and economic liberalism, advocating for a lean state approach to address it.

Ethics or the Right Thing? Corruption and Care in the Age of Good Governance was primarily written during a period when anti-corruption discourses were being institutionalized in Indonesia. The establishment of the Corruption Eradication Commission (I. Komisi Pemberantasan Korupsi, KPK), along with auditing bodies and anti-corruption courts served as evidence of this trend (3). At the time of Sylvia Tidey's fieldwork in Kupang, a city located in Indonesia's southernmost province of East Nusa Tenggara, anti-corruption efforts were deemed crucial for facilitating the country's transition to "a desired state of liberal democracy" (4). It is thus not surprising that this book marks another profound turn in the study of governance, politics, and ethics in Indonesia. Instead of exploring how civil servants in Kupang City have come to accept a global consensus regarding corruption, democracy, and the concept of good governance, Tidey reevaluates the relationship between these three elements by posing the opposite question: "what if anti-corruption efforts actually make governance worse? If we look beyond hegemonic understandings of corruption and conceptions of the governmental good, what shapes can good governance take and how does corruption figure within it?"

Anyone who has visited East Nusa Tenggara can attest to the province's abundance of cultural and natural attractions, which have made it a significant draw for tourists. From exploring the Komodo National Park to creating your own tenun ikat in Sikka Village, East Nusa Tenggara offers an array of irresistible experiences in exchange for the province's local income. However, as Tidey notes, "the province of East Nusa Tenggara is among Indonesia's poorest" (6). The irony of living below the national poverty line despite having ample cultural and natural resources is best exemplified in the jokes about the acronym by which the province is known, NTT. Instead of Nusa Tenggara Timur, NTT stands for Nanti Tuhan Tolong (God will help later), Nasib Tak Tentu (uncertain fate), or Nusa Tetap Tertinggal (the island left behind) (6). People in Manggarai, one of East Nusa Tenggara's regencies where I conducted some of my research, use the same joke when discussing the roles of development projects in their communities. This highlights the contrast between the struggles people face to improve their lives and the abundant resources present in their neighborhoods.

The geographic location of East Nusa Tenggara signifies sociopolitical and structural attributes that give rise to a sense of remoteness, distance, and inaccessibility. These spatial discourses, based on East Nusa Tenggara's geography, underpin the logic of many intervention programs in the region. See, for example, Jesse H. Grayman's findings on the use of a "geographic vocabulary of fields (*medan*, *lapangan*) and topography (*topografi*)" by the village facilitators for the World Bank–funded program PNPM Generasi[1] during routine supervision in the Manggarai highlands to address problems of scale and governance. These sociopolitical and structural features of East Nusa Tenggara's geography persist in development intervention practices and also continue to shape scholarly work on Eastern Indonesia.

Gerry van Klinken and Edward Aspinal acknowledge the factors that contributed to the construction of the "remoteness" of East Nusa Tenggara.[2] Firstly, infrastructural development is concentrated on the central island of Java, leaving East Nusa Tenggara with underdeveloped transportation. Secondly, only a few local politicians have the means to participate in the money politics of the heartlands. Finally, the differences in languages, religions, and lifestyles between people in Java and those in eastern Indonesia legitimize the notion of "Eastern people." Van Klinken and Aspinal argue that these factors influence how the term "distance" is understood geographically, institutionally, and in terms of class and culture in this region. Similarly, Tidey's research demonstrates the importance of studying provincial towns to understand decentralized Indonesia today. Her ethnography also provides a more nuanced understanding of the effects of anti-corruption efforts in Indonesia.

Tidey's ethnography brings us to the city that Transparency International ranked as the "most corrupt" in 2008 (21), where we are encouraged to explore the moral-ethical assemblages that shape the social-moral worlds in which people live and operate in an unreflective and unreflexive manner. As Tidey demonstrates, these assemblages bring together institutional, public discursive, and embodied moralities to form these particular worlds (20). Drawing on the work of Sarah Muir and Akhil Gupta, Tidey shows how corruption complaints reflect people's disappointment and dissatisfaction with a program that promised to improve governance but actually undermines their expectations of what is fair, just, and good in the way resources are shared (8). Tidey claims that allegations of corruption signify more than just a failure of political change; they also indicate "a transgression of care; a dereliction of the caring responsibility of the state to ensure possibilities for its people to forge worthwhile lives" (8). Tidey's research demonstrates that good governance does not necessarily lead to a good life; in fact, it may even make life worse.

Tidey's fascinating account of Indonesian politics and governance is both rich and complex, defying easy summary. Her analysis of corruption extends beyond the prevalent economic liberalism's preference for lean government and instead emphasizes the "relational intertwining of care and kin in Kupang" (64) as an alternative possibility

[1] An offshoot of the National Community Empowerment Program (Program Nasional Pemberdayaan Masyarakat, or PNPM). PNPM Generasi (Generasi Sehat dan Cerdas; Healthy and Smart Generation) focuses on providing maternal and child services.

[2] Gerry van Klinken and Edward Aspinall, "The Making of Middle Indonesia: Middle Classes in Kupang Town, 1930s-1980s," in *Verhandelingen van het Koninklijk Instituut voor Taal-, Land-en Volkenkunde/Power and place in Southeast Asia*, edited by Rosemarijn Hoefte and David Kloos (Leiden: Brill, 2014), 6–10.

for visions of a governmental good. Although Tidey reminds us that an ethics of care and exchange, which is based on the caring responsibilities among family members, may also give rise to "suspicions of distance, estrangement, and not belonging" (65).

Readers interested in Indonesian politics and governance will find Tidey's analysis compelling and thought-provoking. For example, Tidey's observations on the definition of corruption during and post-*reformasi* are particularly insightful. She shows that the specific additions of *collusion* and *nepotism* in the unholy trinity of *korupsi, kolusi,* and *nepotisme* (KKN) imply that corruption in Indonesia has particularly problematic relational connotations. However, it was not this relational character of corruption in itself that violated popular visions of governmental good. According to Tidey, the national economy ought to be organized based on the principles of the family (69). Therefore, when the public interest, the common good, and the sense of fairness in economic distribution are disregarded, this can be viewed as a transgression of care, which both the state and the people need to address collaboratively to work toward the common good.

In post-reformasi Kupang, the question of care remained central to everyday life (p. 70). As social relationships in Kupang are often interchangeable with kin relationships, Tidey effectively shows the association between corruption and care in the context of dire economic precarity (72). According to Tidey, the Indonesian nation-state and the people of Kupang are engaged in a long-standing logic and practice of gift exchange. The government offers civil service positions and enables Kupangese to achieve the locally valued personhood that is embedded in caring responsibility. In short, as Tidey's ethnography among civil servants in Kupang suggests, the definition of corruption in post-*reformasi* Indonesia goes beyond a breach of public-private boundaries, as the Weberian definition of corruption suggests. Thus, the alternative governmental good that Tidey proposes is one rooted in relationality, gift-giving, and an ethics of care. Tidey's outstanding ethnography paves the way for a more nuanced and complex understanding by focusing on situated moral complexity rather than the narrow-minded or rule-based prescriptive morality of "good governance."